ARIOSTO'S
ORLANDO FURIOSO

ARIOSTO'S

ORLANDO FURIOSO

Selections from the Translation of
Sir John Harington

Edited by
Rudolf Gottfried

Principibus placuisse viris non ultima laus est
HORACE

INDIANA UNIVERSITY PRESS
Bloomington

Contents

5

Introduction

THE career of Sir John Harington illustrates a human paradox that he was himself well fitted to appreciate. The translation for which he is chiefly remembered, long and arduous as he must have found the task before he finished it, originated in a light-hearted *jeu d'esprit;* on the other hand, the serious part which he hoped to play in public affairs was always to lie beyond his grasp. He was Queen Elizabeth's godson; and as a young man of good family, with A.B. and M.A. degrees from Cambridge, he probably began to frequent the Court as early as 1581, when he was studying at Lincoln's Inn. Although he soon had a wife and a growing family in Somersetshire, he seems to have spent long periods in London and Westminster, at least until 1596; in that year the Queen dismissed him for publishing *The Metamorphosis of Ajax,* a Rabelaisian pamphlet on water closets which, ironically enough, he had written in order to secure official favor. He suffered a further disgrace after the Earl of Essex knighted him on the ill-fated Irish expedition of 1599. Still seeking the preferment which never came, Harington sent a flattering New Year's gift to James of Scotland a few months before the death of Elizabeth; but neither this nor a treatise he had written in behalf of the Scottish succession served to advance his fortunes under the new monarch. He must have been desperate by the time he proposed, in 1605, that he should be appointed Archbishop of Dublin and Lord High Chancellor of Ireland, citing examples to prove that it is "not new or strange" for "a knight, a layman, and

9

one much conversant in light studies and poetry to be made a bishop," and asserting that "a poet hath one step unto a prophet." Clearly, the important people at Court regarded him as a light-weight, a charming, witty man whose naïve exuberance was fitted for literary entertainment rather than for serious affairs.[1]

It was as a literary entertainer, characteristically, that Harington initiated his most ambitious work. According to a tradition which has the earmarks of truth, he began his version of the *Orlando Furioso* by translating the "wanton" tale of Jocundo from Canto XXVIII; this he circulated in manuscript among the ladies of the Court. When it reached the attention of the Queen, she affected to be shocked by some passages, possibly those attacking the virtue of women, and reprimanded her godson for endangering the morals of her maids of honor; as a fitting punishment she sentenced him to stay away from Court until he had translated the whole of Ariosto's poem, approximately sixty-five times as long as the Jocundo story by itself. This verdict, which probably owed more to her sense of humor and enjoyment of Ariosto than to any moral indignation, can hardly be of later date than the mid-1580's since Harington had already completed his huge assignment by 1591.

The edition of the *Orlando* which he published in that year is a small folio containing not only his translation of the poem, running to nearly 33,000 lines, but a dedication to the Queen, his well-known essay called "A Brief Apology for Poetry," "A Brief and Summary Allegory" of the poem, "The Life of Ariosto," and a textual commentary both in the margins and at the end of each canto. With the forty-six engravings which summarize the story canto by canto, the volume has a monumental completeness which is unusual even in the sixteenth century; if the translator includes portraits of himself and his dog Bungay on the title page, as well as many personal

1. For the biography of Harington see Norman E. McClure's Introduction in his edition of Harington's *Letters and Epigrams* (Philadelphia, 1930) and Elizabeth S. Donno's Introduction in her edition of Harington's *New Discourse of a Stale Subject Called the Metamorphosis of Ajax* (New York, 1962); for both biography and a full study of Harington's *Orlando Furioso* see Townsend Rich, *Harington and Ariosto* (New Haven, 1940).

allusions in the commentary, he also reveals his familiarity with a large body of scholarship and literary criticism, not, for example, overlooking the attempt of the Italian Fornari to defend Ariosto's seriousness by allegorizing his narrative. This is a work which he has spared no effort to enrich, and the same loving care leads him to make numerous small corrections in the text of the book when he republishes it in 1607. To be sure, continually exploiting the comic aspects of his material as he does, Harington always has something of the literary wag about him; but a careful reading of his *Orlando* would never justify the conclusion that he was merely a literary dilettante.

The value of the translation itself has sometimes been questioned; in fact, there seems to have been no question in Ben Jonson's mind when he told a friend "that John Harington's Ariosto under all translations was the worst." The freedom with which his contemporaries usually rendered foreign works into English must have offended Jonson, and Harington's *Orlando* is surely very free. He seldom gives us exactly what Ariosto wrote; he often contracts, so that his version falls almost 6,000 lines short of the Italian; and on the other hand, he expands his material now and then, occasionally adding moral truisms of the kind that Elizabethan readers enjoyed. To note the liberties he has taken is not, however, to condemn them. His practice was in line with the prevailing view of translation, and a case might still be made for allowing considerable freedom to any translator who has the energy to reproduce so long a narrative poem in the verse form of the original. But Harington can be justified on more specific grounds. The *Orlando* is not a work with the dense verbal and intellectual texture of *The Divine Comedy,* and a looseness which would be criminal in rendering Dante does little harm to Ariosto. At the same time Harington has caught the spirit of the *Orlando* better than any other English translator has ever done. Occasionally, it is true, he slips into doggerel, and he often sacrifices the superficial refinements of his source; but in his own rough and ready way he also succeeds in giving us the primary effects which lie at the heart of the Italian poem.

For an understanding of these primary effects it will perhaps be useful to take a backward glance at Ariosto's career and literary antecedents.

Like Harington, he was attached to a court, in this case the ducal court of Ferrara, the north Italian city which the Este family had ruled for nearly three hundred years when the *Orlando Furioso* was written; but unlike Harington, Ariosto found it only too easy to secure employment in the affairs of his masters. His father had been a public servant, and in 1503, when Ludovico was twenty-nine, it was natural that he should enter the service of Cardinal Ippolito d'Este. During the next decade he was frequently sent as Ippolito's personal emissary to the hostile Papal Curia (on one occasion Ariosto escaped the anger of Julius II by leaving Rome in disguise); but in 1517, when he demurred at going to Hungary in the middle of the winter, he was abruptly dismissed from the Cardinal's service. A year later he entered that of the Cardinal's brother, Duke Alfonso I of Ferrara. Almost at once his family became embroiled with the Duke in a protracted legal battle over property which they eventually lost; and in 1522, as a further reward for his fidelity, Alfonso appointed Ariosto military governor of the Garfagnana, a wild district high in the Apennines, where the poet spent three years chasing cattle thieves and risking his life among barbarians. He expressed the frustrations of this experience in his vigorous satires as well as in more than 150 letters which survive from the period. When he returned to Ferrara in 1525, he seems to have retired from Court to the modest house which he built for himself in one of the city's back streets, where it can still be visited today. There, during the time that remained before his death in 1533, he seems to have lived happily with Alessandra Benucci, the woman whom he had wooed so long and ultimately married.[2]

In spite of the hard and often vexatious duties he performed for

2. For Ariosto's life see Michele Catalano, *Vita di Ludovico Ariosto* (Geneva, 1930-1931); for the Italian text of the *Orlando,* the edition of Santorre Debenedetti (Bari, 1928); for an accurate translation into English prose, that of Allan Gilbert (New York, 1954); for background and criticism, Ernest W. Edwards, *The Orlando Furioso and Its Predecessor* (Cambridge, 1924) and Benedetto Croce, *Ludovico Ariosto* (Bari, 1946).

the Estensi, Ariosto remained a prolific artist throughout his life. As a young man he made a name for himself at Court with his comedies and lyric poetry. Later, during his years of public service, he managed to write not only his satires but the *Orlando* itself; and in 1516, while he was still in the employ of Ippolito d'Este, he published the first version of his masterpiece, a poem of forty cantos which was inevitably dedicated to the Cardinal, who had borne the expense of printing. When a second edition appeared in 1521, it contained thousands of small revisions, if no extensive emendations; in the years immediately following, as the *Orlando* began to find a wider audience, this version was reprinted seventeen times. Meanwhile, after retiring to his own house in Ferrara, Ariosto began to recast large segments of the narrative and to add whole episodes, even writing and then discarding some hundreds of stanzas which have survived; the result of these important changes was the third and definitive version, a poem of forty-six cantos which he published in 1532; and before the end of the sixteenth century this text was reprinted in some 180 more editions of the Italian, as well as some forty in translation.

It would be wrong, therefore, to assume that Ariosto's career as a public servant defeated or seriously inhibited his career as a poet; but it would also be wrong, I think, to infer from this that his career as a public servant had no effect on the kind of poetry he wrote. His satires are a direct, pungent attack on the conditions of court life in Ferrara; in the *Orlando,* written under the same conditions, his reaction takes a form less obvious but more comprehensive and more valuable as art. A work which is dedicated to one of the Estensi and contains the most lavish eulogies on every prominent member of the family, going back to the ninth century, can hardly afford to attack the specific trials which some of them have inflicted on the author; in fact, Ariosto was sufficiently indiscreet when he chose *"pro bono malum"* (for good, evil) and *"dilexisti malitiam super benignitatem"* (you have esteemed malice above kindness) as the cryptic mottoes of his poem. But rather, in the transition from reality to art, his bitter disillusionment with the Estensi has been expanded and purified into an ironic disillusionment with the whole of life, a recognition that human folly and depravity are inseparably mingled with human fidelity and tolerance, and a commitment, as poet, to accept and somehow to harmonize all of the disparate elements in the world he describes. Ariosto's situation at the Court of Ferrara seems then to have indirectly determined, or at least abetted, the central point of view from which he looks at his material; and with this important factor in his development we must couple the literary tradition which provided a vehicle for his ironic art.

The subject of the *Orlando* goes back to the historical figures of Charlemagne and Roland (that is, Orlando), who lived in the eighth century and who, as uncle and nephew, became the protagonists of the *Chanson de Roland,* an heroic epic written three hundred years later; but this Carolingian matter had been completely transmuted before it reached Ariosto. Early in the twelfth century Geoffrey of Monmouth brought to light the stories which had grown up around King Arthur, and by the end of the century the French poet Chrétien de Troyes had already begun to convert the Arthurian material into a series of chivalric romances, emphasizing the aristocratic code of love, honor, and ultimately religion. The vogue for chivalric literature soon led many Mediaeval poets to rework other and unrelated stories as tales of knightly adventure; in this way the Carolingian cycle too became a knot of chivalric narratives. Eventually the romances passed from an aristocratic to a popular audience, and a class of traveling singers, known as *cantastorie,* brought them into northern Italy, where there was a strong preference for the tales which had gathered around the figure of Charlemagne. Here, at the end of the fifteenth century, the debased tradition of the Mediaeval romance was briefly raised to the level of literature again. In his *Morgante Maggiore* the Florentine bourgeois Luigi Pulci turned the familiar Carolingian material into a fantastic burlesque. At the aristocratic court of Ferrara, on the other hand, Matteo Boiardo restored Charlemagne and his knights to some of their original dignity.

Boiardo's *Orlando Innamorato* is a huge unfinished poem of

more than 35,000 lines, a fragment which is not altogether successful as art. The style is monotonous and the organization awkward;
the poet's real talents appear in short episodes and lyrical descrip-
tions rather than in prolonged narration; and he fails to adopt a
consistent attitude to his characters, mingling some rather earthy
humor with an aristocratic respect for Mediaeval chivalry. Never-
theless, the *Orlando Innamorato* is literally the first installment of
the story which Ariosto completed, a generation later, in the *Orlando Furioso;* and it allows us to see what he owed to the romance
tradition which reached him in good part through Boiardo.

To begin with, Ariosto's *ottava,* or eight-line stanza, had been the
traditional verse form of the Italian romances for two centuries, and
its value as a medium for rapid narrative was well-established. The
canto unit was also traditional, originally representing the amount
a *cantastorie* could sing or recite in a single evening. What was
more important, the whole vast amorphous subject matter of the
romances was available to the poet, centered in such well-known
figures as Renaldo and Orlando, but providing infinite opportunities
for the invention of character and incident around these fixed
points; since Boiardo, for example, had already intruded Arthurian
material into the Carolingian framework of his poem, there was
nothing to keep Ariosto from transporting Merlin's tomb to France;
and the use of magical elements, married as they were to the long-
accepted themes of love and war, gave the poet a freedom of action
which he has never enjoyed since the sixteenth century. With this
variety of materials went a narrative method which was both loose
and complex, allowing him to alternate the many strands of his story
at will, with more or less art, as if he were weaving an intricate de-
sign in tapestry. But if the romances provided an astonishing lati-
tude in both subject matter and organization, they gave the poet
what was perhaps even more important, the freedom to develop his
own point of view or attitude to the strange, complex, and often
ambiguous things he wrote about: a freedom which might serve as
either an opportunity or a pitfall. When faced with the nobility and
the absurdity of Mediaeval chivalry, Boiardo, as we have seen, failed

to clarify his point of view, and he leaves us with an uneasy sense that he has never brought his poem into psychological focus. For Ariosto, on the other hand, taking up where the *Orlando Inna-morato* left off, this very lack of focus became an opportunity to in-fuse the story with his own consistent and well-considered view of life. Like a cuckoo of genius he laid his egg in Boiardo's disordered nest.

Ariosto's view of life, the element which determines all the pri-mary effects in the *Orlando Furioso,* may be described as one of ironic disillusionment. But the word *ironic* itself requires explana-tion. For our purposes it does not mean *sarcastic* or *merely comic;* and while irony in its original sense was a kind of honest dissimula-tion, revealing truth by seeming to assert untruth, in the hands of poets it has always had a more creative function than dissimulation would suggest. With its tendency to associate things which are unlike or opposite to one another, irony can readily become a har-monizing force, holding the discordant parts of our complex world together in solution. Thus Ariosto's smiling disenchantment works a new enchantment by pervading and unifying the whole gamut of human experience, from farce to what, considered by itself, would be sheer tragedy or horror. If his numerous characters are not so clearly individualized as those of a realistic novelist, it is large-ly because he sees all of them as terms in the great human paradox; if, at the same time, he constructs their adventures with even more freedom and elaborate ingenuity than can be found in the tradi-tional romances, he does so in order to create as many ironic dis-parities as possible. It might almost be said that nine-tenths of Arios-to's art is fostered by this single view of things.

The irony which underlies the whole of the *Orlando* is not, of course, to be described in two or three pages, but at least its range or scope can be suggested by citing a few examples of its various forms: cases of what might be called, for want of better terms, the comic, the pathetic, and the violent forms of Ariosto's irony.

The first of these, the common or garden type of irony, finds a rather obvious illustration in the fiasco which overtakes Sacrapant in

Canto I. The Saracen knight is discovered in the woods, complaining to himself of his hopeless love for Angelica; he delivers several stanzas of amorous clichés, spending his grief on that stalest flower of Renaissance poetry, the virgin rose, which is bound, of course, to be plucked and desecrated, and thus symbolizes the fate which he fears that his mistress has suffered at the hands of some more successful lover. At this point Angelica herself, who has overheard his words, appears to him; and since she needs his help, she shows him more than her usual favor, even assuring him that she is still a virgin. The information, which Sacrapant believes, has an immediate effect on him; his grief is turned to joy, and in his mind he contemplates with sensual relish the very image which a moment earlier had filled him with despair:

> I'll gather now the fresh and fragrant rose,
> Whose beauty may with standing still be spent;
> One cannot do a thing, as I suppose,
> That better can a woman's mind content.

But just as he is about to work his manly will on Angelica, he sees another knight riding forward to attack him; he arms himself and mounts again; in the combat which follows, his horse is slain under him; and his assailant gallops off, leaving Sacrapant stunned on the ground. Then, to increase his ignominy, he learns from a passing messenger that he has been unhorsed by a woman. In the end, all he and Angelica can do is to mount her beast together and ride on as unromantically as if they were married.

This episode is a series of ironic peripeteias, designed to needle the conventional postures of the Renaissance lover; and since it involves no sympathy for any of the characters, one may call it comic. Like many similar passages in the *Orlando,* however, it impinges on material of another kind; and with its light-hearted cynicism it actually reinforces the effect of the more serious stories which surround it.

The coherence of Ariosto's irony is apparent when we turn to the outstanding example of pathos in the poem, the episode which gave him his title. *Orlando Furioso,* that is *Orlando Mad,* is clearly an ironic extension of Boiardo's title *Orlando Innamorato, Orlando in Love:* love, says Ariosto, is madness; and he illustrates the axiom in Canto XXIII, depicting, step by step, the process by which Orlando's jealous passion for Angelica destroys every vestige of his reason and so of his humanity. Here, more fully than in any other scene, the poet allows us to enter into the emotions of one of his characters, and it would be a dull reader who did not respond with something like sympathy to the pathos of Orlando's experience. Yet the term *pathos* by itself does not really cover our final reaction to the episode either. Not only does the hero's madness illustrate a cool, unemotional comment on the nature of love, but it leads to some rather unattractive violence, and in the end it is cured. Furthermore, at the very moment of his derangement we are aware that this is the direct result of a series of comic episodes in which Angelica has made fools of half a dozen great men who sought her love (Sacrapant, for example), only to make a fool of herself by giving her hand to that poor little nobody Medoro. The whole context of Orlando's love is ironic, then, so that while we sympathize with his suffering, we can also smile with Ariosto at his folly. This is the equivocal effect which may be called pathetic irony.

The third variety of Ariosto's irony is the most difficult to explain and illustrate. The view which he sometimes takes of violent action is an aspect of the *Orlando* which is quite uncongenial to the modern mind; yet precisely because violence puts the greatest strain on irony as a solvent and a harmonizing power, it may be said to have the greatest value as evidence of the poem's peculiar ironic orientation. Clearly, Ariosto does not enjoy bloodshed and horror for themselves, but he feels the need to include them in a world where nothing of importance is overlooked and the sting of evil is drawn by reconciliation rather than denial. The point is nowhere better made than in the story of Zerbino and Isabella, told in Cantos XXIV and XXIX (in passages which our brief volume must omit). Each of these virtuous and faithful lovers meets a violent death.

In Isabella's sight, Zerbino is slain by a ruffian who gives the fatal wound with an enchanted sword:

> The prince so earnest was, he felt no smart;
> Yet ran the blood out of his breast amain,
> And of his curats all the former part
> With crimson stream of blood it did distain:
> So have I seen her hand that to mine heart
> Hath been a cause of anguish and much pain,
> When she a purple seam or flower hath drawn
> In silver kirtle or in sleeve of lawn.

At such a moment Ariosto might be accused of heartless triviality, comparing the blood of the dying warrior with that of his own mistress, Alessandra Benucci, when she has pricked her finger at her embroidery; but for a reader whose ironic expectations have been conditioned by all of the *Orlando* which precedes the comparison, there is a mordant pleasure in recognizing the relationship, which diminishes the horror without denying it. And the death of Isabella puts the same problem in even bolder terms. Without Zerbino to protect her, she falls into the hands of Rodomont, a brutal misogynist who is ready to seduce her; she sees that only her death will save her from his advances, and so she resorts to dissimulation. Pretending to have made a magic salve which can protect him from any wound he may ever receive, she offers it in return for her freedom; with equal dissimulation he agrees, planning to keep both medicine and doctor for himself. But knowing what he plans, she persuades him, one night when he is overlaid with wine, to prove the powers of her salve by cutting off her head after she has rubbed her neck with the concoction. So Rodomont, victor and victim, draws his sword and does what she has bidden, with one blow:

> The head where love and all the graces dwelt
> By heedless hand is from the body severed:
> Alas, whose heart at such hap could not melt?
> Yea, that is more, the head cut off endeavored

To show what pleasure of her death it felt
And how she still in her first love persevered:
Thrice from the floor the head was seen rebound,
Thrice it was heard Zerbino's name to sound.

This passage has been described as an artistic blemish which seriously disfigures the *Orlando Furioso,* and perhaps there is only one answer to such a criticism in the end: when you read Ariosto, either you believe or you do not believe in the ironic continuum which is his magic salve.

R. G.

Chronology

1525 Ariosto's house built in Ferrara.

1532 The definitive edition of the *Orlando Furioso*.

1533 The death of Ariosto in Ferrara.

1549 Simone Fornari's *Spositione sopra l'Orlando Furioso*.

1558–1603 Elizabeth I Queen of England.

1560 The birth of Sir John Harington.

1583 Harington married and settled at Kelston, Somersetshire.

1591 The first edition of Harington's translation of the *Orlando Furioso*.

1596 The first edition of Harington's *Metamorphosis of Ajax*.

1599 Harington knighted in Ireland by Lord Essex.

1607 The second edition of Harington's *Orlando Furioso*.

1612 The death of Harington.

1634 The third edition of Harington's *Orlando Furioso*.

Note on the Present Text

HE 1607 edition of Harington's *Orlando Furioso* was set up, page by page, from the 1591 edition, and the 1634 edition, page by page, from that of 1607. In 1607, however, the translator himself made numerous small changes within the lines of the poem, changes which were kept in 1634; for the most part he seems to have made them in order to improve the regularity of the meter rather than the accuracy of his version. At the same time, his revised text contains a certain number of readings which are clearly inferior to those of 1591, perhaps through oversight.

The present edition, which modernizes punctuation and spelling (except in some proper names), is based on Harington's revised text; but there are some dozens of cases where I have gone back to the wording of 1591. The passages selected are primarily intended to show the quality and character of Ariosto's poem, but it is hoped that they may also serve as background reading for students of Spenser's *Faerie Queene*. The border on the title page reproduces that of the 1591 edition; the illustrations with the cantos are from the edition of 1634.

The First Canto

O F DAMES, of knights, of arms, of love's delight,
Of courtesies, of high attempts I speak,
Then when the Moors transported all their might
On Afric seas, the force of France to break:
Incited by the youthful heat and spite
Of Agramant their king, that vowed to wreak
The death of King Trayano,[1] lately slain,
Upon the Roman Emperor Charlemain.

I will no less Orlando's acts declare,
A tale in prose ne verse yet sung or said,
Who fell bestraught with love, a hap most rare
To one that erst was counted wise and staid.
If my sweet saint[2] that causeth my like care
My slender muse afford some gracious aid,
I make no doubt but I shall have the skill
As much as I have promised to fulfill.

Vouchsafe, O prince of most renownèd race,[3]
The ornament and hope of this our time,
T'accept this gift presented to your grace
By me your servant rudely here in rhyme.
And though I paper pay and ink in place
Of deeper debt, yet take it for no crime;
It may suffice a poor and humble debtor
To say, an if he could, it should be better.

Here shall you find, among the worthy peers
Whose praises I prepare to tell in verse,
Rogero; him from whom of ancient years
Your princely stem's derivèd I rehearse,
Whose noble mind by princely acts appears,
Whose worthy fame even to the sky doth pierce;
So you vouchsafe my lowly style and base
Among your high conceits a little place.

Orlando,[4] who long time had lovèd dear
Angelica the fair and for her sake
About the world, in nations far and near,
Did high attempts perform and undertake,
Returned with her into the West that year
That Charles his power against the Turks did make,
And with the force of Germany and France
Near Pyren alps his standard did advance,

To make the kings of Afric and of Spain[5]
Repent their rash attempts and foolish vaunts,
One having brought from Afric in his train
All able men to carry sword or lance,
The other moved the Spaniards now again
To overthrow the goodly realm of France;
And hither, as I said, Orlando went,
But of his coming straight he did repent.

For here (behold how human judgments err
And how the wiser sort are oft mistaken)
His lady whom he guarded had so far
Nor had in fights nor dangers great forsaken,
Without the dint of sword or open war,
Amid his friends away from him was taken;
For Charles the Great, a valiant prince and wise,
Did this to quench a broil that did arise.

Between Orlando and Renaldo late
There fell about Angelica some brawl,
And each of them began the t'other hate,
This lady's love had made them both so thrall;
But Charles, who much mislikes that such debate
Between such friends should rise on cause so small,
To Namus of Bavier in keeping gave her
And suffered neither of them both to have her,

But promised he would presently bestow
The damsel fair on him that in that fight
The plainest proof should of his prowess show
And danger most the pagans with his might.
But aye the while, the Christians take the blow,
Their soldiers slain, their captains put to flight;
The duke himself[6] a pris'ner there was taken;
His tent was quite abandoned and forsaken.

Where when the damsel fair a while had stayed
That for the victor pointed was a prey,
She took her horse, ne further time delayed,
But secretly conveyed herself away;
For she foresaw and was full sore afraid
That this to Charles would prove a dismal day.
And riding through a wood, she happed to meet
A knight that came against her on his feet,

His curats on, his helmet not undone,
His sword and target ready to the same;
And through the wood so swiftly he did run
As they that go half-naked for a game.
But never did a shepherd's daughter shun
More speedily a snake that on her came
Than fair Angelica did take her flight
Whenas she once had knowledge of the knight.

This valiant knight was Lord of Clarimont,[7]
Duke Ammon's son, as you shall understand,
Who, having lost his horse of good account
That by mishap was slipped out of his hand,
He followed him, in hope again to mount,
Until this lady's sight did make him stand,
Whose face and shape proportioned were so well
They seemed the house where love itself did dwell.

But she, that shuns Renaldo all she may,
Upon her horse's neck doth lay the rein;
Through thick and thin she gallopeth away,
Ne makes she choice of beaten way or plain,
But gives her palfrey leave to choose the way;
And being moved with fear and with disdain,
Now up, now down, she never leaves to ride
Till she arrivèd by a river side.

Fast by the stream Ferraw[8] she sees anon,
Who noyed in part with dust and part with sweat,
Out of the battle hither came alone,
With drink his thirst, with air to suage his heat;
And minding back again to have been gone,
He was detained with an unlooked-for let:
Into the stream by hap his helmet fell,
And how to get it out he cannot tell.

And hearing now the noise and mournful cry
Of one with piteous voice demanding aid,
Seeing the damsel eke approaching nigh
That nought but help against Renaldo prayed,
What wight it was he guessèd by and by,
Though looking pale like one that had been fraid;
And though she had not late been in his sight,
He thought it was Angelica the bright.

And being both a stout and courteous knight,
And love a little kindling in his breast,
He promised straight to aid her all he might
And to perform whatever she request;
And though he want an helmet, yet to fight
With bold Renaldo he will do his best;
And both the one the other straight defied,
Oft having either other's value tried.

Between them two a combat fierce began,
With strokes that might have pierced the hardest rocks.
While they thus fight on foot and man to man,
And give and take so hard and heavy knocks,
Away the damsel posteth all she can;
Their pain and travail she requites with mocks.
So hard she rode while they were at their fight
That she was clean escapèd out of sight.

When they long time contended had in vain
Who should remain the master in the field,
And that with force, with cunning, nor with pain
The t'one of them could make the other yield,
Renaldo first did move the knight of Spain,
Although he used such courtesy but seld,
To make a truce; ne was he to be blamèd,
For love his heart to other fight inflamèd.

"You thought," said he, "to hinder me alone,
But you have hurt yourself as much or more.
You see the fair Angelica is gone:
So soon we leese that erst we sought so sore.
Had you me ta'en or slain, your gain were none
Sith you were ne'er the near your love therefor;
For while we two have made this little stay, .
She lets us both alone and goes her way.

"But if you love the lady, as you say,
Then let us both agree to find her out;
To have her first will be our wisest way,
And when of holding her there is no doubt,
Then by consent let her remain his prey
That with his sword can prove himself most stout.
I see not else, after our long debate,
How either of us can amend his state."

Ferraw, that felt small pleasure in the fight,
Agreed a sound and friendly league to make;
They lay aside all wrath and malice quite;
And at the parting from the running lake
The pagan would not let the Christian knight
To follow him on foot, for manners' sake,
But prays him mount behind his horse's back;
And so they seek the damsel by the track.

O ancient knights of true and noble heart:
They rivals were, one faith they lived not under,
Beside they felt their bodies shrewdly smart
Of blows late given, and yet (behold a wonder)
Through thick and thin, suspicion set apart,
Like friends they ride, and parted not asunder
Until the horse, with double spurring drivèd,
Unto a way which parts in two arrivèd.

And being neither able to descry
Which way was gone Angelica the bright,
Because the track of horses' feet, whereby
They seek her out, appear alike in sight,
They part, and either will his fortune try;
The left hand one, the other takes the right.
The Spaniard, when he wandered had a while,
Came whence he went; the way did him beguile.

He was arrived but there, with all his pain,
Where in the ford he let his helmet fall;
And of his lady, whom he loved in vain,
He now had little hope or none at all.
His helmet now he thinks to get again
And seeks it out, but seek it while he shall,
It was so deeply sunken in the sand
He cannot get it out at any hand.

Hard by the bank a tall young poplar grew,
Which he cut down, thereof a pole to make,
With which each place in feeling and in view
To find his skull he up and down doth rake.
But lo, a hap unlooked-for doth ensue:
While he such needless, fruitless pain doth take,
He saw a knight arise out of the brook,
Breast-high, with visage grim and angry look.

The knight was armed at all points save the head,
And in his hand he held the helmet plain,
That very helmet that such care had bred
In him that late had sought it with such pain;
And looking grimly on Ferraw, he said,
"Ah, faithless wretch, in promise false and vain,
It grieves thee now this helmet so to miss
That should of right be rendered long ere this.

"Remember, cruel pagan, when you killèd
Me, brother to Angelica the bright,[9]
You said you would, as I then dying willèd,
Mine armor drown when finished were the fight.
Now if that fortune have the thing fulfillèd
Which thou thyself shouldst have performed in right,
Grieve not thyself; or if thou wilt be grievèd,
Grieve that thy promise cannot be believèd.

Here she at last herself in safety thought
As being from Renaldo many a mile;
Tired with annoy the heat and travel brought,
She thinks it best with sleep the time beguile,
And having first a place convenient sought,
She lets her horse refresh his limbs the while,
Who fed upon the banks well-clothed with grass
And drank the river water clear as glass.

Hard by the brook an arbor she descried
Wherein grew fair and very fragrant flowers,
With roses sweet and other trees beside
Wherewith the place adorns the native bowers,
So fencèd in with shades on either side,
Safe from the heat of late or early hours;
The boughs and leaves so cunningly were mixed
No sun, no light could enter them betwixt.

Within, the tender herbs a bed do make,
Inviting folk to take their rest and ease;
Here means this lady fair a nap to take
And falls to sleep, the place so well doth please.
Nor long she lay but her a noise did wake;
The trampling of a horse did her disease,
And looking out as secret as she might,
To come all armed she saw a comely knight.

She knows not yet if he be foe or friend,
'Twixt hope and fear she doubtfully doth stand,
And what he means to do she doth attend,
And who it was she fain would understand.
The knight did to the river side descend,
And resting down his head upon his hand,
All in a muse he sitteth still alone
Like one transformed into a marble stone.

He tarried in this muse an hour and more,
With look cast down in sad and heavy guise;
At last he did lament his hap so sore,
Yet in so sweet and comely mournful wise,
So hard a heart no tiger ever bore
But would have heard such plaints with wat'rish eyes.
His heart did seem a mountain full of flame,
His cheeks a stream of tears to quench the same.

"Alas," said he, "what means this diverse passion?
I burn as fire, and yet as frost I freeze;
I still lament, and never move compassion;
I come too late and all my labor leese.
I had but words and looks for show and fashion,
But others get the game and gainful fees.
If neither fruit nor flower come to my part,
Why should her love consume my careful heart?

"Like to the rose I count the virgin pure
That grow'th on native stem in garden fair,
Which while it stands with walls environed sure,
Where herdmen with their herds cannot repair,
To favor it, it seemeth to allure
The morning dew, the heat, the earth, the air;
Young gallant men and lovely dames delight
In their sweet scent and in their pleasing sight.

"But when at once 'tis gatherèd and gone
From proper stalk where late before it grew,
The love, the liking little is or none;
But favor, grace, and beauty all adieu.
So when a virgin grants to one alone
The precious flower for which so many sue,
Well he that getteth it may love her best,
But she forgoes the love of all the rest.

"She may deserve his love, but others' hate,
To whom of love she showed herself so scant.
Oh then my cruel fortune or my fate!
Others have store, but I am starved with want.
Then leave to love this lady so ungrate:
Nay, live to love (behold, I soon recant);
Yea, first let life from these my limbs be rent
Ere I to change my love shall give consent."

If some perhaps desirous are to know
What wight it was with sorrow so oppressed,
'Twas Sacrapant that was afflicted so,
And love had bred this torment in his breast:
That tickling wound, that flatt'ring cruel foe,
Most happy they that know and have it least.
The love of her, I say, procured his woe,
And she had heard and knew it long ago.

Her love allured him from the eastern land
Unto the western shores where sets the sun,
And here he heard how by Orlando's hand
A passage safe from th'Indies she had won;
Her sequestration he did understand
That Charles had made, and how the same was done
To make the knights more venturous and bold
In fighting for the flower-de-luce of gold.

And furthermore himself had present been
When Charles his men were overthrown and slain.
Since then he traveled far to find this queen,
But hitherto it hath been all in vain,
Now much despair and little hope between.
So ruefully thereof he doth complain,
And with such wailing words his woes rehearsed,
As might the hardest stony heart have pierced.

And while in this most doleful state he bides,
And sighs full oft, and sheddeth many a tear,
And speaks these same, and many words besides
Which I to tell for want of time forbear,
His noble fortune so for him provides
That all this came into his mistress' ear;
And in one moment he prevailèd more
Than he had done in many years before.

Angelica with great attention heard
The moan and plaint that him tormented sore,
Who long had lovèd her with great regard,
As she had trial many years before;
Yet as a marble pillar cold and hard
She not inclines to pity him the more,
Like one that all the world doth much disdain
And deemeth none worthy her love to gain.

But being now with danger compassed round,
She thought it best to take him for her guide,
For one that were in water almost drowned
Were very stout if for no help he cried;
If she let pass the fortune now she found,
She thinks to want the like another tide;
And furthermore for certain this she knew,
That Sacrapant had been her lover true.

Ne meant she tho to quench the raging fires
That aye consumed his faithful loving heart,
Ne yet with that a lover most desires
T'assuage the pain in all or yet in part;
She means he first shall pull her from the briars,
And feed him then with words and women's art
To make him first of all to serve her turn;
That done, to wonted coyness to return.

Unto the river side she doth descend,
And toward him most goddesslike she came,
And said, "All peace to thee, my dearest friend,"
With modest look, and called him by his name;
And further said, "The gods and you defend
My chastity, mine honor, and my fame,
And never grant by their divine permission
That I gave cause of any such suspicion."

With how great joy a mother's mind is filled
To see a son for whom she long hath mourned,
Whom she heard late in battle to be killed
And saw the troops without him home returned,
Such joy had Sacrapant when he beheld
His lady dear; his tears to smiles are turned
To see her beauty rare, her comely favor,
Her princely presence, and her stately havior.

Like one all ravished with her heavenly face
Unto his lovèd lady he doth run,
Who was content in arms him to embrace,
Which she perhaps at home would not have done;
But doubting now the dangerous time and place,
She must go forward as she hath begun,
In hope by his good service and assistance
To make her home return without resistance.

And in most lovely manner she doth tell
The strange adventures and the divers chance
That since they two did part, to her befell,
Both on the way and since she came to France,
And how Orlando usèd her right well,
Defending her from danger and mischance,
And that his noble force and magnanimity
Had still preserved the flower of her virginity.

It might be true, but sure it was incredible
To tell to one that were discreet and wise;
But unto Sacrapant it seemèd possible
Because that love had dazzled so his eyes.
Love causeth what is seen to seem invisible
And makes of things not seen a shape to rise;
It is a proverb usèd long ago,
We soon believe the thing we would have so.

But to himself thus Sacrapant doth say,
"Be't that my lord of Anglant[11] were so mad
To take no pleasure of so fair a prey
When he both time and place and power had,
Yet am not I obligèd any way
To imitate a precedent so bad;
I'll rather take my pleasure while I may
Than wail my want of wit another day.

"I'll gather now the fresh and fragrant rose,
Whose beauty may with standing still be spent;
One cannot do a thing, as I suppose,
That better can a woman's mind content.
Well may they seem much grievèd for a glose
And weep and wail and dolefully lament;
There shall no foolish plaints nor fainèd ire
Hinder me to incarnate my desire."

This said, forthwith he did himself prepare
T'assault the fort that eas'ly would be won;
But lo! a sudden hap that bred new care
And made him cease his enterprise begun,
For of an enemy he was aware.
He clasped his helmet late before undone,
And armèd all, he mounteth on his beast
And standeth ready with his spear in rest.

Behold, a warrior whom he did not know
Came down the wood in semblance like a knight;
The furniture was all as white as snow,
And in the helm a plume of feathers white.
King Sacrapant by proof doth plainly show
That he doth take the thing in great despite,
To be disturbed and hindered from that pleasure
That he preferred before all other treasure.

Approaching nigh, the warrior he defied
And hopes to set him quite beside the seat;
The other with such lofty words replied
As persons use in choler and in heat.
At last when glorious vaunts were laid aside,
They came to strokes, and each to do his feat
Doth couch his spear; and running thus they sped,
Their coursers both encountered head to head.

As lions meet or bulls in pastures green,
With teeth and horns, and stain with blood the field,
Such eager fight these warriors was between,
And either's spear had pierced the t'other's shield;
The sound that of these strokes had raisèd been
An echo loud along the vale did yield.
'Twas happy that their curats were so good;
The lances else had piercèd to the blood.

For quite unable now about to wheel,
They butt like rams the one the other's head,
Whereof the pagan's horse such pain did feel
That ere long space had passed, he fell down dead;
The t'other's horse a little gan to reel,
But being spurred, full quickly up he sped.
The pagan's horse thus overthrown and slain
Fell backward greatly to his master's pain.

That unknown champion seeing th'other down,
His horse upon him lying dead in view,
Expecting in this fight no more renown,
Determined not the battle to renew,
But by the way that leadeth from the town
The first appointed journey doth pursue
And was now ridden half a mile at least
Before the pagan parted from his beast.

Like as the tiller of the fruitful ground
With sudden storm and tempest is astonished,
Who sees the flash and hears the thunder's sound,
And for their master's sakes the cattle punished,
Or when by hap a fair old pine he found
By force of raging winds his leaves diminished:
So stood amazed the pagan in the place,
His lady present at the woeful case.

He fetched a sigh most deeply from his heart,
Not that he had put out of joint or lamèd
His arm, his leg, or any other part,
But chiefly he his evil fortune blamèd
At such a time to hap so overthwart,
Before his love to make him so ashamèd;
And had not she some cause of speech found out,
He had remainèd speechless out of doubt.

"My lord," said she, "what ails you be so sad?
The want was not in you but in your steed,
For whom a stable or a pasture had
Been fitter than a course at tilt indeed;
Nor is that adverse party very glad,
As well appears, that parted with such speed,
For in my judgment they be said to yield
That first leave off and do depart the field."

Thus while she gives him comfort all she may,
Behold there came a messenger in post,
Blowing his horn and riding down the way
Where he before his horse and honor lost;
And coming nearer, he of them doth pray
To tell if they had seen pass by that coast
A champion armed at all points like a knight,
The shield, the horse, and armor all of white.

"I have both seen the knight and felt his force,"
Said Sacrapant, "for here before you came,
He cast me down and also killed my horse,
Ne know I (that doth grieve me most) his name."
"Sir," quoth the post, "the name I will not force
To tell sith you desire to know the same:
First, know that you were conquered in this fight
By valor of a damsel fair and bright,

"Of passing strength, but of more passing hue,
And Bradamant[12] this damsel fair is namèd;
She was the wight whose meeting you may rue
And all your life hereafter be ashamèd."
This said, he turned his horse and bade adieu;
But Sacrapant, with high disdain enflamèd,
Was first so wroth and then so shamed thereto
He knew not what to say nor what to do.

And after he had stayed a while and mused
That at a woman's hands he had receivèd
Such a disgrace as could not be excused,
Nor how he might revenge it he perceivèd,
With thought hereof his mind was so confused
He stood like one of wit and sense bereavèd.
At last he go'th a better place to find;
He takes her horse and makes her mount behind.

Now having rode a mile or thereabout,
They heard a noise, a trampling on the ground;
They thought it was some company or rout
That causèd in the woods so great a sound.
At last they see a warlike horse and stout,
With gilded barb that cost full many a pound;
No hedge, no ditch, no wood, no water was
That stoppèd him where he was bent to pass.

Angelica, casting her eye aside,
"Except," said she, "mine eyes all dazzled be,
I have that famous horse Bayardo spied
Come trotting down the woods, as seems to me.
How well for us our fortune doth provide!
It is the very same, I know 'tis he.
On one poor nag to ride we two were loath,
And here he cometh fit to serve us both."

King Sacrapant alighted by and by
And thinks to take him gently by the rein,
But with his heels the horse doth straight reply,
As who should say his rule he did disdain.
It happy was he stood the beast not nigh,
For if he had, it had been to his pain,
For why such force the horse had in his heel
He would have burst a mountain all of steel.

But to the damsel gently he doth go,
In humble manner and in lowly sort:
A spaniel after absence fawneth so
And seeks to make his master play and sport.
For Bayard called to mind the damsel tho
When she unto Albracca did resort
And used to feed him for his master's sake,
Whom she then loved, and he did her forsake.[13]

She takes the bridle boldly in her hand
And stroked his breast and neck with art and skill;
The horse that had great wit to understand,
Like to a lamb by her he standeth still;
And while Bayardo gently there did stand,
The pagan got him up and had his will,
And she that erst to ride behind was fain
Into her saddle mounted now again.

And being newly settled in her seat,
She saw a man on foot all armèd run;
Straight in her mind she gan to chafe and fret
Because she knew it was Duke Ammon's son.[14]
Most earnestly he sued her love to get;
More earnestly she seeks his love to shun.
Once she loved him, he hated her as much;
And now he loves, she hates, his hap was such.

The cause of this first from two fountains grew,
Like in the taste but in effects unlike,
Placed in Ardenna, each in other's view.
Who tastes the one, love's dart his heart doth strike;
Contrary of the other doth ensue:
Who drink thereof their lovers shall mislike.
Renaldo drank of one, and love him painèd;
She drunk the other and his love disdainèd.[15]

The liquor thus with secret venom mingled
Makes her to stand so stiffly in the nay,
On whom Renaldo's heart was wholly kindled,
Though scarce to look on him she can away;
But from his sight desiring to be singled,
With soft low voice the pagan she doth pray
That he approach no nearer to this knight,
But fly away with all the speed he might.

"Why then," quoth he, "make you so small esteem
Of me, as though that I to him should yield?
So weak and faint my forces do you deem
That safe from him yourself I cannot shield?
Then you forget Albracca, it should seem,
And that same night when I amid the field,
Alone, unarmèd, did defend you then
Against King Agrican[16] and all his men."

"No, sir," said she; ne knows she what to say,
Because Renaldo now approached so nigh,
And threatened so the pagan in the way
When under him his horse he did espy
And saw the damsel taken as a prey,
In whose defence he means to live and die.—
But what fell out between these warriors fierce
Within the second book I do rehearse.

1. Father of Agramant, the King of Barbary.

2. Alessandra Benucci, whom Ariosto loved and eventually married.

3. Ariosto's first patron, Cardinal Ippolito d'Este, the brother of Duke Alfonso of Ferrara.

4. In this stanza and those that follow Ariosto alludes to various episodes in Matteo Boiardo's *Orlando Innamorato,* the unfinished poem of which the *Orlando Furioso* is a sequel.

5. Agramant and Marsilio, respectively.

6. Namus.

7. Renaldo.

8. A Saracen of Spain.

9. Argalia, whose ghost is referring to an episode in the *Orlando Innamorato.*

10. By the life of his mother.

11. Orlando.

12. The sister of Renaldo and lover of Rogero (Ruggiero in the Italian).

13. Renaldo had been among those attacking Albracca, the city of Angelica's father, when his horse Bayardo fell into her hands.

14. Renaldo.

15. These effects of the river (not fountain) of love and the fountain of hate are recounted in the *Orlando Innamorato*.

16. King of Tartary, who led the attack on Albracca.

The Second Canto

O BLIND god Love, why tak'st thou such delight
With darts of divers force our hearts to wound?
By thy too much abusing of thy might
This discord great in human hearts is found.
When I would wade the shallow ford aright,
Thou draw'st me to the deep to have me drowned;
From those love me my love thou dost recall
And place it where I find no love at all.

Thou mak'st most fair unto Renaldo seem
Angelica that takes him for a foe,
And when that she of him did well esteem,
Then he disliked and did refuse her tho,
Which makes her now of him the less to deem;
Thus, as they say, she renders *quid pro quo*.[1]
She hateth him and doth detest him so
She first will die ere she will with him go.

Renaldo, full of stately courage, cried,
"Down, thief, from off my horse, down by and by.
So robbed to be I never can abide,
But they that do it dearly shall aby.
Also this lady you must leave beside;
Else one of us in her defense will die.
A horse so good and such a goodly dame
To leave unto a thief it were a shame."

"What! me a thief! Thou in thy throat dost lie,"
Quoth Sacrapant, that was as hot as he.
"Thief to thyself! Thy malice I defie,
For as I hear, the name is due to thee;[2]
But if thou dare thy might and manhood try,
Come take this lady or this horse from me,
Though I allow in this of thine opinion
That of the world she is the matchless minion."

Like as two mastiff dogs with hungry maws,
Moved first to hate, from hate to raging ire,
Approach with grinning teeth and grisly jaws,
With staring eyes, as red as flaming fire;
At last they bite and scratch with teeth and claws
And tear themselves and tumble in the mire:
So after biting and reproachful words
Did these two worthy warriors draw their swords.

One was on foot, the t'other on a horse;
You think perhaps the horseman vantage had.
No, sure, no whit; he would have wished to scorse,
For why at last to light he must be glad;
The beast did know thus much by nature's force,
To hurt his master were a service bad.
The pagan could not nor with spur nor hand
Make him unto his mind to go or stand.

He stops when he should make a full career;
He runs or trots when he would have him rest;
At last to throw his rider in the mire
He plungeth with his head beneath his breast.
But Sacrapant, that now had small desire
At such a time to tame so proud a beast,
Did work so well at last, by sleight and force,
On his left side he lighted from his horse.

When from Bayardo's over-furious might
The pagan had himself dischargèd so,
With naked swords there was a noble fight;
Sometimes they lie aloft, sometimes alow,
And from their blows the fire flies out in sight.
I think that Vulcan's hammers beat more slow,
Where he within the mountain Aetna's chaps
Doth forge for Jove the fearful thunderclaps.

Sometimes they proffer; then they pause a while;
Sometime strike out, like masters of the play;
Now stand upright; now stoop another while;
Now open lie; then cover all they may;
Now ward; then with a slip the blow beguile;
Now forward step; now back a little way;
Now round about; and where the t'one gives place,
There still the other presseth in his place.

Renaldo did the pagan prince invade
And strike at once with all the might he could;
The other doth oppose against the blade
A shield of bone and steel of temper good.
But through the same a way Fusberta[3] made,
And of the blow resounded all the wood;
The steel, the bone like ice in pieces broke,
And left his arm benumbèd with the stroke.

Which when the fair and fearful damsel saw
And how great damage did ensue thereby,
She lookèd pale for anguish and for awe,
Like those by doom that are condemned to die;
She thinks it best herself from hence withdraw,
Else will Renaldo take her by and by,
The same Renaldo whom she hateth so,
Though love of her procurèd all his woe.

Unto the wood she turns her horse in haste
And takes a little narrow path and blind;
Her fearful looks ofttimes she back doth cast,
Still doubting lest Renaldo came behind;
And when that she a little way had passed,
Alow the vale a hermit she did find,
A weak old man, with beard along his breast,
In show devout and holier than the rest.[4]

He seemed like one with fasts and age consumèd,
He rode upon a slothful-going ass,
And by his look a man would have presumèd
That of his conscience[5] scrupulous he was;
Yet her young face his old sight so illumèd
Whenas he saw the damsel by to pass,
Though weak and faint as such an age behovèd,
That charity his courage somewhat movèd.

The damsel of the hermit asked the way
That might unto some hav'n town lead most near,
That she might part from France without delay
Where once Renaldo's name she might not hear.
The friar, that could enchant, doth all he may
To comfort her and make her of good cheer,
And to her safety promising to look,
Out of his bag forthwith he drew a book:

A book of skill and learning so profound
That of a leaf he had not made an end
But that there rose a sprite from underground
Whom like a page he doth of errands send.
This sprite by words of secret virtue bound
Goes where these knights their combat did intend;
And while they two were fighting very hard,
He enters them between without regard.

"Good sirs," quoth he, "for court'sy sake me show
When one of you the t'other shall have slain,
And after all the travail you bestow,
What guerdon you expect for all your pain.
Behold, Orlando striking ne'er a blow
Nor breaking staff, while you strive here in vain,
To Parisward the lady fair doth carry,
While you on fighting undiscreetly tarry.

"I saw from hence a mile, or thereabout,
Orlando with Angelica alone;
And as for you, they jest and make a flout,
That fight where praise and profit can be none.
'Twere best you quickly went to seek them out
Before that any farther they be gone;
Within the walls of Paris if they get,
Your eye on her again you shall not set."

Whenas the knights this message had receivèd,
They both remained amazèd, dumb, and sad
To hear Orlando had them so deceivèd,
Of whom before great jealousy they had;
But good Renaldo so great grief conceivèd
That for the time, like one all raging mad,
He sware, without regard of God or man,
That he will kill Orlando if he can.

And seeing where his horse still stood untied,
He thither goes; such haste he made away
He offers not the pagan leave to ride
Nor at the parting once adieu doth say.
Now Bayard felt his master's spurs in side
And gallops main ne maketh any stay;
No rivers, rocks, no hedge nor ditches wide
Could stay his course or make him step aside.

Nor marvel if Renaldo made some haste
To mount again upon his horse's back;
You heard before how many days had passed
That by his absence he had felt great lack.
The horse, that had of human wit some taste,
Ran not away for any jadish knack;
His going only was to this intent,
To guide his master where the lady went.[6]

The horse had spied her when she took her flight
First from the tent as he thereby did stand,
And followed her and kept her long in sight
As then by hap out of his master's hand
(His master did not long before alight
To combat with a baron[7] hand to hand);
The horse pursued the damsel all about
And holp his master still to find her out.

He followed her through valley, hill, and plain,
Through woods and thickets, for his master's sake,
Whom he permitted not to touch the rein
For fear lest he some other way should take,
By which Renaldo, though with mickle pain,
Twice found her out; twice she did him forsake,
For first Ferraw, then Sacrapant withstood
That by twice finding her he did no good.

Bayardo trusting to the lying sprite
Whose false but likely tale so late he heard,
And doubting not it was both true and right,
He doth his duty now with due regard.
Renaldo, pricked with love and raging spite,
Doth prick apace, and all to Parisward;
To Parisward he maketh so great shift
The wind itself seems not to go so swift.

Such haste he made Orlando out to find
That scant he ceased to travel all the night,
So deeply stuck the story in his mind
That was of late devisèd by the sprite;
Betimes and late as first he had assigned,
He rode until he saw the town in sight
Where Charles, whose chance all christened hearts did rue,
With the small relics of his power withdrew.

And for he looks to be assaulted then
Or else besieged, he useth all his care
To store himself with victual and with men;
The walls eke of the town he doth repair
And take advice both how and where and when
For his defence each thing he may prepare;
An army new to make he doth intend
And for new soldiers into England send.

He minds to take the field again ere long
And try the hap of war another day,
And all in haste to make himself more strong
He sends Renaldo England's aid to pray.
Renaldo thought the emperor did him wrong
To send him in such haste and grant no stay;
Not that ill will to th'island he did carry,
But for another cause he fain would tarry.

Yet now, although full sore against his mind
As loath to leave the lady he so lovèd,
Whom he in Paris hopèd had to find,
Because t'obey his prince it him behovèd
He taketh this embassage thus assigned;
And having straight all other lets removèd,
He posted first to Callis[8] with great haste
And thence embarked ere half next day was passed.

Against the mariners' and master's minds,
Such haste he made to have returnèd back,
He takes the sea though swelling with great winds
And threat'ning ruin manifest and wrack;
Fierce Boreas, that himself despisèd finds,
Doth beat on seas with tempest foul and black,
By force whereof the waves were raised so high
The very tops were sprinkled all thereby.

The mariners take in their greater sail,
And by the wind they lie, but all in vain;
Then back again they bend without avail;
Now they are out, they cannot in again.
"No," said the wind, "my force shall so prevail
Your bold attempts shall put you to some pain."
It was a folly any more to strive;
Needs must they follow as the wind did drive.

In the foreship sometimes the blast doth blow
Straight in the poop; the seas break to the skies;
Needs must they bear a sail, though very low,
To void the waves that higher still did rise.
But sith my web so divers now doth grow,
To weave with many threads I must devise;
I leave Renaldo in this dangerous place
And of his sister speak a little space.

I mean the noble damsel Bradamant,
Of Ammon daughter and Dame Beatrice,
In whose rare mind no noble part did want,
So full of value and so void of vice
King Charles and France of her might rightly vaunt;
So chaste, so fair, so faithful and so wise,
And in the feats of arms of so great fame
A man might guess by that of whence she came.

There was a knight enamored on this dame
That out of Afric came with Agramant,
Rogero hight; so was his father's name
(His mother was the child of Agolant).
The damsel, that of worthy lineage came
And had a heart not made of adamant,
Disdainèd not the love of such a knight
Although he had but seld been in her sight.[9]

Long travel and great pain she had endurèd
And rid alone her lover to have found,
Ne would she think her safety more assurèd
If with an army she were guarded round.
You heard before how she by force procurèd
King Sacrapant to fall and kiss the ground.
The wood she passed and after that the mountain,
Until at last she saw a goodly fountain:

A goodly fountain running in a field
All full of trees whose leaves do never fade,
Which did to passengers great pleasure yield,
The running stream so sweet a murmur made;
Upon the south a hill the sun did shield;
The ground gave flowers, the grove a grateful shade.
Now here the dame, casting her eye aside,
A man at arms fast by the brook descried.

A man at arms she spièd by the brook,
Whose banks with flowers of divers hue were clad,
Of which sweet place he so small pleasure took
His face did show his heart was nothing glad;
His targe and helmet were not far to look,
Upon a tree where tied his horse he had;
His eyes were swoll'n with tears, his mind oppressèd
With bitter thoughts that had his heart distressèd.

The damsel fair, enticed by deep desire
That all, but chiefly women, have to know
All strangers' states, doth earnestly require
The doleful knight his inward grief to show,
Who marking well her manner and attire,
Her courteous speech with him prevailèd so
He tells his state, esteeming by the sight
That needs she must have been some noble knight.

"Good sir," said he, "you first must understand
I servèd Charles against the King of Spain;
I horsemen had and footmen in my band
In ambush placed the Spanish king t'have slain;
I brought the fairest lady in this land
And my best lovèd with me in my train,
When suddenly, ere I thereof was ware,
There came a horseman that procured my care,

"Perhaps a man or some infernal sprite
In human shape, I cannot certain say;
But this I say, he took the damsel bright.
Even as a falcon seizeth on his prey,
So he my loving lady did affright
And so affrighted bare her quite away;
And when I thought to rescue her by force,
Aloft in air he mounted with his horse:

"Even as a rav'nous kite that doth espy
A little chicken wand'ring from the other
Doth catch him straight and carries him on high,
That now repents he was not with his mother.
What could I do? My horse wants wings to fly;
Scant could he set one leg before the t'other,
He traveled had before so many days
Among the painful hills and stony ways.

"But like to one that were his wit beside
I leave my men to do my first intent,
Not caring of myself what should betide,
So strongly to my fancy was I bent,
And took the blind god Cupid for my guide;
By ways as blind to seek my love I went;
And though my sense, my guide, my way were blind,
Yet on I go in hope my love to find.

"A se'nnight space abating but a day,
About the woods and mountains I did range,
In savage deserts wild and void of way
Where human steps were rare and very strange.
Fast by the desert place a plain there lay
That showèd from the rest but little change,
Save only that a castle full of wonder
Did stand in rocks that had been clov'n asunder.

"This castle shines like flaming fire afar,
Not made of lime and stone as ours are here;
And still as I approached a little narre,
More wonderful the building doth appear.
It is a fort impregnable by war,
Compacted all of metal shining clear.
The fiends of Hell this fort of steel did make
Of metal tempered in the Stygian lake.

"The towers are all of steel and polished bright;
There is on them no spot of any rust;
It shines by day; by dark it giveth light.
Here dwells this robber wicked and unjust,
And what he gets against all laws and right
The lawless wretch abuseth here by lust;
And here he keeps my fair and faithful lover,
Without all hope that I may her recover.

"Ah, woe was me, in vain I sought to help;
I see the place that keeps that I love best,
Even as a fox that crying hears her whelp
Now borne aloft into the eagle's nest,
About the tree she goes and fain would help,
But is constrained for want of wings to rest.
The rock so steep, the castle is so high
None can get in except they learn to fly.

"And as I tarried in the plain, behold,
I saw two knights come riding down the plain,
Led by desire and hope to win this hold,
But their desire and hope was all in vain.
Gradasso was the first, of courage bold,
A king of Serican that held the reign;
Rogero next, a man of noble nation,
Of years but young, but of great estimation.

"A little dwarf they had to be their guide,
Who told me that they came to try their force
Against the champion that doth use to ride
Out of this castle on the wingèd horse;
Which when I heard, to them for help I cried
And prayed them of my case to take remorse
And that they would, if 'twere their chance to win,
Set free my love that there was lockèd in.

"And all my grief to them I did unfold,
Affirming with my tears my tale too true.
No sooner I my heavy hap had told,
But they were come within the castle's view.
I stood aloof the battle to behold
And prayed to God good fortune might ensue.
Beneath the castle lies a little plain,
Exceeding not an arrowshot or twain.

"And as they talked who first should fight or last,
They were arrivèd to the castle hill.
At length Gradasso (whether lots were cast
Or that Rogero yielded to his will)
Doth take his horn and blew therewith a blast
The noise whereof the castle walls did fill;
And straight with greater speed than can be guessed
Came out the rider of the flying beast.

"And as we see strange cranes are wont to do,
First stalk a while ere they their wings can find,
Then soar from ground not past a yard or two,
Till in their wings they gathered have the wind;
At last they mount the very clouds unto,
Trianglewise according to their kind:
So by degrees this mage begins to fly;
The bird of Jove[10] can hardly mount so high.

"And when he sees his time and thinks it best,
He falleth down like lead in fearful guise.
Even as the falcon doth the fowl arrest,
The duck and mallard from the brook that rise:
So he, descending with his spear in rest,
Doth pierce the air in strange and monstrous wise;
And ere Gradasso were thereof admonished,
He felt a stripe that made him half astonished.

"The mage upon Gradasso brake his spear,
Who strikes in vain upon the air and wind;
Away he flew without or hurt or fear
And leaves Gradasso many a pace behind.
This fierce encounter was so hard to bear
That good Alfana to the ground inclined:
This same Alfana was Gradasso's mare,
The fair'st and best that ever saddle bare.

"Aloft the stars the sorc'rer doth ascend
And wheels about, and down he comes again;
And on Rogero he his force doth bend
That had compassion on Gradasso's pain.
So sore th'assault Rogero did offend
His horse the force thereof could not sustain;
And when to strike again he made account,
He saw his foe up to the clouds to mount.

"Sometimes the mage Rogero doth assail;
Straightway Gradasso he doth set upon;
And oft they strike again without avail,
So quickly he at whom they strike is gone.
He winds about as ships do under sail;
His sails are wings, and rest he gives them none,
But sets upon them in so sudden wise
That he amazed and dazzled both their eyes.

"Between this one aloft and two alow
This conflict did no little space endure,
Until at last the night began to grow,
With misty clouds making the world obscure.
I saw this sight, the truth thereof I know,
I present was thereat; yet am I sure
That very few except the wiser sort
Will credence give to such a strange report.

"This heav'nly, hellish warrior bare a shield
On his left arm that had a silken case;
I cannot any cause or reason yield
Why he would keep it covered so long space;
It had such force that whoso it beheld,
Such shining light it striketh in their face
That down they fall with eyes and senses closèd
And leave their corpse of him to be disposèd.

"The target like the carbuncle doth shine;
Such light was never seen with mortal eye;
It makes to ground the lookers-on decline,
Be they far off or be they standing nigh;
And as it closed their sight, it closèd mine,
That in a trance no little space was I.
At last when I awaked and rose again,
The air was dark, and voided was the plain.

"The sorcerer hath ta'en them, I surmise,
Into his castle, as is likely most,
And by this light that dazzled all our eyes
My hope is gone; their liberty is lost.
This is the truth, ne do I aught devise;
You hear the same; I felt it to my cost;
Now judge if I have reason to complain
That have and do endure such endless pain."

Whenas this knight his doleful tale had done,
He sate him down all cheerless in the place:
This was Earl Pinnabel, Anselmus' son,
Born in Maganza of that wicked race,
Who like the rest so lewd a course did run
He holp the more his lineage to deface;
For only virtue nobleness doth dignify,
And vicious life a lineage base doth signify.

The lady fair, attentive all this while,
Doth harken unto this Maganzese tale;
Rogero's name sometime doth make her smile;
Sometime again for fear she looketh pale;
But hearing how a sorc'rer base and vile
Should in a castle so detain him thrall,
She pitied him, and in her mind she fretted
And oft desired to hear the tale repeated.

When at the last the whole she understood,
She said, "Sir knight, mourn not, but take some pleasure;
Perhaps our meeting may be to your good
And turn your enemy unto displeasure.
Show me this fort, for why it frets my blood
So foul a prison holds so fair a treasure;
And if good fortune favor mine intent,
You will right well suppose your travail spent."

"Ah," said the knight, "should I return again,
To pass these mountains hard and overthwart?
Though for myself it is but little pain
To toil my body, having lost my heart,
For you to go whereas you may be slain
Or taken pris'ner were a foolish part;
Which if it hap, yet me you cannot blame,
Because I give you warning of the same."

This said, he riseth up his horse to take,
The noble lady on the way to guide,
Who means to venture for Rogero's sake
Or death or thralldom or whate'er betide.
But lo! a messenger great haste doth make
That comes behind, and "Tarry ho!" he cried.
This was the post that told to Sacrapant
How she that foiled him was Dame Bradamant.

This messenger brought tidings in great post
Both from Narbona and from Mompeleere[11]
How they were up in arms along the coast
Of Aquamort and all that dwellèd near,
And how Marsilia's men their hearts had lost
Because of her no tidings they could hear;
And for her absence made them ill apayed,
They sent to have her presence and her aid.

These towns and others many to the same
Between the streams of Rodon and of Vare
The emp'ror had assigned this worthy dame,
Committing them unto her trust and care.
Her noble value gat her all this fame
Because in arms herself she bravely bare,
And so the cities under her subjection
This message sent requiring her direction.

Which when she heard, it made her somewhat pause;
'Twixt yea and no she stood a pretty space.
Of one side honor and her office draws;
On th'other side love helps to plead the case.
At last she means t'ensue the present cause
And fetch Rogero from th'enchanted place,
And if her force cannot to this attain,
At least with him a pris'ner to remain.

In courteous sort her answer she contrivèd
With gracious words and sent away the post;
She longs with her new guide to have arrivèd
To that same place where both their loves were lost.
But he, perceiving now she was derivèd
From Clarimont that he detested most,
Doth hate her sore and feareth to the same
Lest she should know he of Maganza came.

There was between these houses ancient hate,
This of Maganza, that of Clarimont;
And each of them had weakened other's state
By killing men in both of great account.
This Pinnabel, a vile and wicked mate
That all his kin in vices did surmount,
Means with himself this damsel to betray,
Or else to slip aside and go his way.

And this same fancy so his head did fill
With hate, with fear, with anger, and with doubt
That he mistook the way against his will
And knew not how again to find it out,
Till in the wood he saw a little hill,
Bare on the top, where men might look about;
But Bradamant such amorous passions feels
She followeth like a spaniel at his heels.

The crafty guide, thus wand'ring in the wood,
Intending now the lady to beguile,
Said unto her forsooth he thought it good,
Sith night grew on, themselves to rest a while:
"Here is," quoth he, and showed which way it stood,
"A castle fair, and hence not many a mile;
But tarry you a little here until
I may descry the country from the hill."

This said, he mounted to the higher ground;
And standing now the highest part upon,
He cast about his eyes and lookèd round
To find some path whereby he might be gone,
When unawares a monstrous cave he found;
And strange cut out and hollowed in the stone,
Deep thirty cubits down it doth descend,
Having a fair large gate at lower end,

Such as great stately houses wont to have,
Out of which gate proceeds a shining light
That all within most lightsome makes the cave;
And all this while on this felonious knight
This noble lady due attendance gave
And never suffered him go out of sight.
She followed Pinnabel hard at his back
Because she was afeard to leese the track.

Whenas this villain traitor did espy
That his designments foolish were and vain
Either to leave her or to make her die,
He thought it best to try a further train,
Persuading her for to descend and try
What ladies fair within the cave remain:
"For why," said he, "within this little space
I saw a goodly damsel in the place,

"Both rich arrayed and very fair of hue,
Like one of noble lineage and degree;
And this her fortune made me more to rue,
That here against her will she seemed to be.
And when I thought for to descend and view
The cause of this her grief to know and see,
I was no sooner from my horse alighted
But with infernal hags I was affrighted."

The noble Bradamant, that was more stout
Than wary who it was did her persuade,
Hath such desire to help a damsel out
That straight the cave she meaneth to invade;
She finds by hap a long bough thereabout;
Thereof a pole of mighty length she made;
First with her sword she hews and pares it fit;
That done, she lets it down into the pit.

She giveth Pinnabel the bigger end
And prays him stand above and hold it fast,
And by the same intending to descend,
Upon her arms her whole weight she doth cast;
But he that to destroy her did intend
Doth ask if she would learn to leap a cast,
And laughing loosed his hands, that were together,
And wished that all the race of them were with her.

Yet great good hap the gentle damsel found,
As well deserved a mind so innocent,
For why the pole strake first upon the ground;
And though by force it shivered all and rent,
Yet were her limbs and life kept safe and sound
For all his vile and traitorous intent.
Sore was the damsel mazèd with the fall,
As in another book declare I shall.

1. Tit for tat.

2. Orlando had called Renaldo a thief in the *Orlando Innamorato*.

3. Renaldo's sword.

4. In the margin Harington identifies the hermit as a hypocrite whose figure satirizes churchmen.

5. Gilbert notes that in the Italian there is a play on the word *conscience,* which may also mean *virile member.*

6. So Harington identifies Bayardo as "man's fervent and furious appetite" which leads him to pursue pleasure on foot, "whereby is understood sensuality."

7. Rogero (Ruggiero), as told in the *Orlando Innamorato*.

8. Calais.

9. Ariosto actually says that Rogero had seen her only once before.

10. The eagle.

11. The news from Narbonne and Montpelier concerns the men of Aigues-Mortes and Marseilles since Bradamant's province, as the next stanza explains, extended from the Rhone to the Var.

The Third Canto

O H THAT my head were so well-stored with skill,
Of such a noble subject fit to treat!
Oh that my wits were equal to my will,
To frame a phrase fit for so high conceit!
Ye Muses that do hold the sacred hill,
Inspire my heart with flame of learnèd heat
While I presume in base and lowly verse
The names of glorious princes to rehearse:

Such princes as excel all princes far
In all the gifts of body and of mind,
Temp'rate in peace, victorious eke in war,
Themselves most noble, come of noble kind;
And such, except my guess do greatly err,
As are by Heav'n's eternal doom assigned
In wealth, in fame, in rule, and in prosperity
To live themselves, their children and posterity.

Nor can I now their several acts most rare
Achieved by every one of them recite,
No, though my verse with Virgil's might compare
Or I as well as Homer could endite;
With their great praise great volumes fillèd are,
With large discourse, by them that stories write.
I only mean to show what was foreshown
Long ere their persons or their deeds were known.

But first of Pinnabel a word to speak,
Who, as you heard, with traitorous intent
The bonds of all humanity did break,
For which ere long himself was after shent:
Thus while base minds their wrongs do basely wreak,
They do that once that often they repent,
And curse that time a thousand times, too late,
When they pursued their unrevengèd hate.

With fainting heart (for sin is full of fear),
By stealing steps from hence he doth depart,
And as he goes, he prieth here and there;
His fearful look bewrays his guilty heart,
Nor yet his dread doth move him to forbear
To heap more sin upon this ill desert.
Appalled with fear but touched with no remorse,
Supposing she was slain, he takes her horse.

But let him go until another time,
For I do mean hereafter you shall hear
How he was dealt with when his double crime,
In secret wrought, most open did appear.
Now unto Bradamant I bend my rhyme,
Who with her fall was yet of heavy cheer
And had been taught a gambol for the nonce
To give her death and burial at once.

Now when she came unto herself again
And had recovered memory and sense,
She gets her on her feet, although with pain,
In mind to seek some way to get fro thence;
When lo, before her face she seeth plain
A stately portal built with great expense,
And next behind the same she might descry
A larger room and fairer to the eye.

This was a church most solemn and devout
That stands on marble pillars small and round,
And raised by art on arches all about
That made each voice to yield a double sound.
A lightsome lamp that never goeth out
Did burn on altar standing in the ground,
That though the rooms were large and wide in space,
The lamp did serve to lighten all the place.

The noble damsel, full of rev'rent fear
Whenas herself in sacred place she sees,
As one that still a godly mind did bear
Begins to pray to Him upon her knees
Whose holy side was pierced with cruel spear
And who to save our lives His own did leese;
And while she stays devoutly at her prayer,
The sage Melissa doth to her repair,

Her gown ungirt, her hair about her head,
Much like a priest or prophetess arrayed;
And in her book a little while she read
And after thus unto the damsel said,
"O thou by God's appointment hither led,
O Bradamant, most wise and worthy maid,
I long have lookèd here for this thy coming,
Foretold thereof by prophet Merlin's cunning.

"Here is the tomb that Merlin erst did make
By force of secret skill and hidden art,[1]
In which sometimes the Lady of the Lake,
That with her beauty had bewitched his heart,
Did make him enter fondly for her sake,
From whence he never after could depart;
And he was by a woman overreachèd
That unto others prophesied and preachèd.

"His carcass dead within this stone is bound,
But with dead corpse the living soul doth dwell,
And shall until it hear the trumpet sound
That brings reward of doing ill or well.
His voice doth live and answer and expound
And things both present, past, and future tell,
Resolving men of every doubtful case
That for his counsel come unto this place.

"About a month, or little more or less,
It is since I repaired to Merlin's grave,
Of him, about the study I profess,
Some precepts and instructions to have;
And, for I willing was, I must confess,
To meet you at your coming to this cave,
For which he did prefix this certain day,
This movèd me of purpose here to stay."

Duke Ammon's daughter[2] silent stands and still
The while the wise Melissa to her spake,
Astonishèd at this unusual skill
And doubting if she were asleep or wake;
A modest shame with grace her eyes doth fill,
With which downcast, this answer she doth make:
"Alas, what good or merit is in me
That prophets should my coming so foresee?"

And glad of this adventure unexpected,
She followeth her guide with great delight;
And straight she saw the stately tomb erected
Of marble pure that held his bones and sprite;
And that which one would little have suspected,
The very marble was so clear and bright
That though the sun no light unto it gave,
The tomb itself did lighten all the cave.

For whether be the nature of some stone
A darksome place with lightsomeness to fill,
Or were it done by magic art alone
Or else by help of mathematic skill
To make transparencies to meet in one
And so convey the sunbeams where you will:
But sure it was most curious to behold,
Set forth with carvèd works and gilt with gold.

Now when the damsel was approachèd nigher
To this strange tomb where Merlin's bones were placed,
Forth of the stones that shine like flaming fire
His lively voice such speeches out doth cast:
"Let fortune ever favor thy desire,
O Bradamant, thou noble maid and chaste,
From out whose womb an issue shall proceed
That all the world in glory shall exceed.

"The noble blood that came of ancient Troy,
By two clear springs in thee together mixed,
Shall breed the flower, the jewel, and the joy
Of all on whom the sun his beams hath fixed
'Twixt those that heat and those that cold annoy,
From Tage to Inde, Danub and Nile betwixt,
Emp'rors and kings, and dukes and lords for aye;
Of this thy lineage carry shall the sway.

"And many a captain brave and worthy knight
Shall issue from this stock, that shall restore
By warlike feats the glory shining bright
That Italy possessèd heretofore;
And magistrates to maintain peace and right
As Numa and Augustus did before,
To cherish virtue, vice so to assuage
As shall to us bring back the Golden Age.

"Wherefore sith God hath by predestination
Appointed thee to be Rogero's wife
And means to bless thine heirs and generation
With all the graces granted in this life,
Persist thou firm in thy determination,
And stoutly overcome each storm of strife,
And work his worthy punishment and pain
That doth thy life's delight from thee detain."

This said, the prophet Merlin holds his peace
And gives Melissa time to work her will,
Who when she did perceive the voice to cease,
She purposeth by practice of her skill
To show the damsel part of that increase
That should with fame the world hereafter fill;
And for this purpose she did then assemble
A troop of sprites their persons to resemble,

Who straight, by words of secret virtue bound,
In numbers great unto the cave repair,
Of whence I know not, whether underground
Or else of those that wander in the air.
Then thrice she draws about a circle round,
And thrice she hallows it with secret prayer;
Then opens she a triple claspèd book,
And softly whisp'ring in it she doth look.

This done, she takes the damsel by the hand,
Exhorting her she should not be afraid,
And in a circle causeth her to stand,
And for her more security and aid
And, as it were, for more assurèd band
Upon her head some characters she laid;
Then having done her due and solemn rites,
She doth begin to call upon the sprites.

Behold, a crew of them come rushing in,
In sundry shapes with persons great and tall,
And now they fillèd all the room within
So readily they came unto her call,
When Bradamant to fear did straight begin;
Her heart was cold, her color waxèd pall;
But yet the circle kept her like a wall
So that she needed not to fear at all.

Howbeit, Melissa causèd them be gone
From thence unto the next adjoining cave
And thence to come before them one by one,
The better notice of their names to have,
That at more leisure they may talk thereon
Whenas occasion so may seem to crave:
"Although," quoth she, "this short time cannot serve
To speak of every one as they deserve.[3]

"Lo, here the first, thy first-begotten son,[4]
That bears thy favor and his father's name,
By whom the Lombards shall in fight be won
To Desiderius their king's great shame;
Who shall at Pontyr make the streams to run
With blood in fields adjoining to the same
And shall revenge the deeds and minds unpure
Of such as did his father's fall procure.

"And for this noble act among the rest
The emperor shall give him in reward
The honors great of Calaon and Est,
By which his family shall be preferred.
The next Uberto is whose valiant breast
Shall be unto the Holy Church a guard,
Defending it with valiant heart and hand
To th'honor of Hesperian[5] arms and land.

"Alberto he is named that third comes in,
Whose triumphs are most famous everywhere;
Then his son Hugo that did Milan win
And for his crest two vipers used to bear;
Next Atso is and next to him of kin
That erst of Lombardy the crown shall wear;
Then Albertasso by whose means are won
The Beringers both father and the son.

"To him shall Othon's favor[6] so incline
He shall in marriage give to him his daughter.
Now Hugo comes again, O happy line!
And happy man that saved so great a slaughter!
When at Christ's vicar's rule Rome did repine,
He daunteth them and so restored them after:
The which, by wit without the dint of sword,
He shall effect in Othon's time the Third.

"Now Fulko comes that to his brother gave
His land in Italy which was not small
And dwelt in Almany his land to save
Of Samsony[7] that unto him did fall,
A dukedom great that did with castles brave
Accrue to him for want of issue male;
By him that noble house is held and cherishèd
That but for him would be extinct and perishèd.

"Then cometh Atso, that misliketh war,
But yet his sons Bertold and Albertasse
With second Henry shall be still at jar
And bring the Dutchmen to a woeful pass.
Next young Renaldo, shining like a star,
Shall be unto the Church a wall of brass
And work the utter overthrow and loss
Of wicked Fred'rike namèd Barbarosse.

"Behold, another Atso shall possess
Verona with a stately territory,
Of Othon and Honorius no less
Shall be a marquis made to his great glory.
It would be long their names all to express
That shall protect the sacred consistory
And in most valorous and martial manner
Display and eke defend the Church's banner.

"Obyso next and Fulko you may view
With Henries two, the father and the son,
Both Guelfs that fruitful Umbria shall subdue
And keep the dukedom there by conquest won.
Behold him that the good state doth renew
Of Italy that late was quite undone,
Called Atso Fifth that bravely overthrew
The cruel Esselino and him slew:

"That cruel Esselino that was thought
To have been gotten by some wicked devil,
That never any goodness had been taught,
But sold his soul to sin and doing evil;
Comparing with the cruel acts he wrought,
Fierce Nero were but mild and Sylla civil.
Beside this Atso shall in time to come
The power of Second Fred'rike overcome.

"And then he shall his brother Albandrine
Unto the Florentines for money gage,
And Othon with the faction Ghibelline
He shall suppress amid the furious rage,
And raise the Church, nor letting it decline
But spending to defend it all his age;
For which good service he shall justly merit
The dukedom of Ferrara to inherit.

"Next him Renaldo now ensu'th whose lot
Shall be at Naples to be made away,
A death his virtuous deeds deservèd not;
But woe to them that guiltless blood betray.
Now followeth a worthy crew and knot,
Whose acts alone to tell would spend a day:
Obyso, Nicholas, and Aldbrandine,
Whose noble deeds shall honor much their line.

"Then Nicholas is he that next ensu'th,
That ruled in tender years both near and far,
That finds and eke revengeth their untruth
That sought his state by civil strife to mar;
The sports and exercises of his youth
Are blows and fights and dangers great and war,
Which makes that ere to manly state he came,
For martial deeds he gets the only name.[8]

"Lo, Lionel, the glory of his age,[9]
Maintaining peace and quiet all his time
And keeping that with ease by wisdom sage
To which some others by much pain do climb;
That fettered fury and rebukèd rage;
That locks up Mars in walls of stone and lime;
That all his wit, his care, and travail bent
To make his subjects live in state content.

"Now Herc'les comes, an Hercules indeed,
Whose deeds shall merit ever-during fame,
That by his pains his country's ease shall breed
And put his enemies to flight and shame;
Sharp to devise, to execute with speed,
Both stout t'attempt and patient to the same,
No prince shall ever rule his country better,
No prince had ever country more his debtor.

"Not only that he shall their moorish grounds
By great expense to pasture firm reduce;
Not that the town with wall environ round
And store with things behooveful to their use;
Not that when war in each place shall abound,
He shall maintain them peaceably in truce;
Not that he shall according to their asking
Disburden them of payments and of tasking;

"But that he shall more and above all these
Leave them behind him such a worthy race
As search within the circuit of the seas,
You shall not find two to supply their place.
So shall the one the other strive to please,
So shall the one the other's love embrace
As may for loving brotherly regard
With Castor and with Pollux be compared.

"The elder of these two Alfonso hight,
The next of them Hippolyto we call:[10]
Both passing stout and valiant in fight,
Both passing wise and provident withal,
And both in due defence of country's right
Shall seem a bulwark and a brazen wall;
They both shall have of enemies good store;
They both shall still subdue them evermore.

"Their mother[11] (if I may a mother name),
One more like Progne and Medea fell,
Unto her endless infamy and shame
Against her son Alfonso shall rebel
And join with Venice force (for this to blame),
Though for the same ere long they paid full well;
For those they thought to hurt, they did this good,
To make the ground more fruitful with their blood.

"Not far fro thence the Spanish soldier hirèd
By pastor's purse and in that pastor's pay,
That with a forcible assault aspirèd
To take a fort and eke the captain slay;
But lo, he comes, and they perforce retirèd
And have so short a pleasure of this prey
Scarce one of them in life is left abiding
To carry notice of so heavy tiding.

"His wit and valor shall him so advance
To have the honor of Romagna field,
Where by his means unto the force of France
The Pope and Spaniards forcèd are to yield;
And there in Christian blood, O fatal chance!
Shall horses swim, such numbers shall be killed;
Nor shall not men enough alive remain
To bury those that are in battle slain.

"The while his brother under card'nal's cap
Shall cover, nay, shall show a prudent head,
Hippolyto I mean, who shall have hap
With band of men but small, yet wisely led,
To give to the Venetians such a clap
As few the like in stories have been read,
To take three times five galleys at one tide
And barks and boats a thousand more beside.[12]

"Behold two Sigismonds, both wise and grave,
Alfonso next, whose fame is talked of rife,
With his five sons, then Herc'les that shall have
The King of France's daughter to his wife,
That towards him herself shall so behave
Shall make him live most happy all his life.
Hippolyto it is that now comes in
Not least for praise and glory of his kin.

"Next Francis namèd Third, Alfonsos two,
With many others worthy of renown,
The which to name might find one work to do
From Phoebus' rising to his going down.
Now therefore, if you will consent thereto,
I here will end and send the spirits down."
To this the worthy damsel said not nay,
And straight the spirits vanished all away.

Then Bradamant, that all well markèd had
Of whom herself should be the ancient mother,
Did say to learn she would be very glad
What two those were that differed from the other,[13]
That came with backward steps and looked so sad
Upon the good Alfonso and his brother.
Melissa sighs, misliking that suggestion
Which put it in her heart to ask this question.

And then as in a trance these words she spake:
"O thou more worthy son of worthy sire,
They are thy blood; on them compassion take;
Let grace assuage though justice kindle ire."
Then unto Bradamant, as new awake,
"I must," said she, "deny you this desire.
I say no more; content you with the sweet;
For you this sour morsel is not meet.

"Tomorrow when the sun at break of day
With light shall dim the light of every star,
I mean myself to guide you on your way
So as I shall be sure you shall not err.
The place whereas your love is forced to stay
Is from the salt seashore not very far,
That were you passed a mile beyond this wood,
The other way would easy be and good."

Of this night's stay the damsel was content,
And in the cave with her she doth remain,
And most thereof in Merlin's tomb she spent,
Whose voice with talk did her still entertain,
Embold'ning her to give her free consent
To love where she should sure be loved again.
Now gan the messenger of day to crow,
Whenas her guide and she away did go.

The way they went was dark and unaccessible,
By secret vaults and hollows of the hill;
To find it out had been a thing impossible
But with a guide of knowledge great and skill.
At last they came unto a path more passable,
By which they cease not to ascend until
They quite had left the dark and loathsome place
And saw the beams of Phoebus' cheerful face.

And while that up this hill they slowly stalk,
With pausing, panting oft, and taking wind,
To make less weary seem their weary walk
Melissa still doth store of matter find,
And now of this and then of that doth talk;
But chiefly she the damsel puts in mind
Of her Rogero, how he had been trainèd
Into the prison where he now remainèd.

"Atlanta that magician strange is he
That holdeth him, I trust, unto his cost;
But had you Pallas' strength or Mars'," quoth she,
"And eke of armèd men a mighty host,
Yet to attempt by force to set him free
Your travail and your labor all were lost.
Art must be won by art, and not by might;
Force cannot free your well-belovèd knight.

"For first the castle mounted is on high,
Impregnable with walls all over steeled;
And next, the horse he rides hath wings to fly
And gallops in the air as in the field;
And last, he dazzleth every mortal eye
By hidden force of his enchanted shield,
With light whereof men's sense are so dazèd
With sight thereof they fall down all amazèd.

"In all the world one only mean hath been,
And is yet still, to work so rare a feat:
A ring there is which from an Indian queen [14]
Was stole sometime, of price and virtue great.
This ring can make a man to go unseen;
This ring can all enchantments quite defeat.
King Agramant hath sent his secretary
Unto Rogero this same ring to carry.

"Brunello is his name that hath the ring,
Most lewd and false, but politic and wise,
And put in trust especial by his king
With it Rogero's safety to devise;
Which sith I wish not he, but you should bring,
To bind him to you by this enterprise,
And for I would not have the Turk [15] protect him
Because I know he greatly doth affect him,

"Do therefore this when you do meet this man,
Whose marks I wish in memory you bear:
His stature is two cubits and a span;
His head is long and gray and thin of hair;
His nose is short and flat, his color wan,
With beetle brow, eyes wat'ry not with tear;
His beard grows on his face without all stint;
And to conclude, his look is all asquint.

"Now whenas you this comely man shall meet,
As sure you shall within a day or two,
You may with courteous words him seem to greet
And tell him partly what you mean to do;
But speak not of the ring although you see't,
For so you may the matter all undo.
Then he great courtesy to you will offer
And straight his company to you will proffer.

"But when unto the castle you come nigh,
Then see you set upon him on the way
And take away the ring and make him die,
Nor give him any time lest he convey
The ring into his mouth and so thereby
Out of your sight he vanish quite away."
The worthy damsel marks her speeches well,
And so the one the other bids farewell.

Next day she happed Brunello to espy;
She knew him straight; she found him at her inn;
She grows to question with him by and by,
And he to lie doth by and by begin;
And she dissembles too and doth deny
Her country, stock, and name and sex and kin.
Brunello pleasantly doth talk and tipple,
Not knowing he did halt before a cripple.

Now when they almost broken had their fast,
She marking more his fingers than his eyes,
When much good talk between them two had passed,
The most whereof were false and forgèd lies,
Behold, mine host came unto them in haste
And told them news that made them sooner rise.—
But here I mean to make a little pause
Before I tell what was thereof the cause.

1. Harington points out that Merlin's tomb is in Wales and has been transferred to France by poetic license.

2. Bradamant.

3. The account of the Este family which follows imitates Virgil's account of the Julian house in the *Aeneid*, Book VI.

4. The younger Ruggiero, placed in the ninth century.

5. Italian.

6. The favor of Emperor Otto I, who founded the Holy Roman Empire in 962.

7. Saxony.

8. At this point Harington omits several stanzas on the growth of Ferrara's power under Nicolò III in the early fifteenth century.

9. With Leonello's name Ariosto couples that of his successor Borso, to whom, rather than to Leonello, the rest of the stanza applies in the Italian.

10. Cardinal Ippolito d'Este and his brother Duke Alfonso were successively Ariosto's patrons.

11. The Church under Julius II.

12. This stanza alludes to Ippolito's naval victory at Polesella in 1509.

13. Ferdinando and Giulio, the younger brothers of Alfonso and Ippolito, who conspired against the duke and were imprisoned for life.

14. Angelica, from whom Brunello stole the ring in the *Orlando Innamorato*.

15. The Saracen Agramant.

The Fourth Canto

THOUGH he that useth craft and simulation
  Doth seldom bend his acts to honest ends,
But rather of an evil inclination
His wit and skill to others' mischief bends,
Yet sith in this our worldly habitation
We do not ever dwell among our friends,
Dissembling doubtless oftentimes may save
Men's lives, their fame and goods, and all they have.

If man by long acquaintance and great proof
To trust some one man scant can be allurèd,
To whom he may in presence or aloof
Unfold the secrets of his mind assurèd,
Then doth this damsel merit no reproof
That with Brunello, to all fraud inurèd,
Doth frame herself to counterfeit a while,
For to deceive deceivers is no guile.

Now while these two did to confer begin,
She to his fingers having still an eye,
The host and other servants of the inn
Came on the sudden with a woeful cry;
And some did gaze without and some within,
As when men see a comet in the sky;
The cause of this their wond'ring and their crying
Was that they saw an armèd horseman flying.

And straight by th'host and others they were told
How one that had in magic art great skill
Not far from thence had made a stately hold
Of shining steel, and placed it on a hill,
To which he bringeth ladies young and old,
And men and maids according to his will;
And when within that castle they have been,
They never after have been heard or seen.

No sooner can he spy a pretty maid
But straight he takes her up into the air,
The which his custom makes them all afraid
That either are or think that they be fair.
Those hardy knights that went to give them aid,
Of which sort many hither did repair,
Went like the beasts to the sick lion's den;
For all went in, but none returned again.

This tale in worthy Bradamant did breed
A kind of pleasure and confusèd joy
In hope, which after she performed indeed,
The sight of her belovèd to enjoy;
She prayed the host procure a guide with speed,
As though each little stay did breed annoy;
She swears that in her heart she longed to wrastle
With him that kept the captives in his castle.

"Because that you, sir knight, should want no guide,"
Brunello said, "I will myself be he.
I know the way and somewhat have beside
By which may fortune you may pleasured be":
He meant the ring of force and virtue tried,
Although he meant not she the same should see.
"Great thanks," quoth she, "that you will take the pain,"
In hope hereby the precious ring to gain.

Thus each from other hiding their intent,
They forward set like friends by break of day;
Brunello sometime foremost of them went,
Sometime behind, as chancèd on the way.
Now had they certain hours in travel spent
When they arrivèd where the castle lay,
Whereas Mount Pyrene stands above the plain
So high as may discover France and Spain.

Whenas the castle did in sight appear
So strange, so fair, so stately, and so high,
In which that knight whom she esteemed so dear,
With many others, prisoner did lie,
She thought her fittest time drew very near
To take the ring and make Brunello die;
Wherefore with open force she doth assail him,
Whose strength with age and fear soon gan to fail him.

Her meaning was the caitiff to have killed,
But unto that her noble heart said nay;
Small praise would come from blood so basely spilled;
She means to get the ring another way.
But first she bound him where he willed or nilled,
And though with tears he did for pity pray,
Yet left she him unto a tree fast tied,
And with the ring away she straight did ride.

And being in the green fast by the tower,
Straight, as the fashion was, her horn she blew.
Out came that armèd knight that present hour,
And seeing there a challenger in view,
He seemeth to assault her with great power;
But by the ring she all his falsehood knew.
She saw he carried neither sword nor spear
Nor any weapon that one need to fear.[1]

He only carried at his saddlebow
A shield all wrappèd in a crimson case
And read a book by which he made to show
Some strange and strong illusions in the place;
And many that these cunnings did not know
He had deceived and ta'en in little space
And caused both swords and lances to appear
When neither sword nor lances them were near.

But yet the beast he rode was not of art,
But gotten of a griffith and a mare,
And like a griffith had the former part,
As wings and head and claws that hideous are
And passing strength and force and vent'rous heart;
But all the rest may with a horse compare.
Such beasts as these the hills of Rifee[2] yield,
Though in those parts they have been seen but seld.

This monster rare from farthest regions brought
This rare magician ordered with such skill
That in one month or little more he taught
The savage monster to obey his will;
And though by conjurations strange he wrought
In other things his fancy to fulfill,
As cunning men still try each strange conclusion,
Yet in this griffith horse was one collusion.

The lady fair, protected by the ring,
Found all his sleights, although she seemed not so,
Her purpose to the better pass to bring;
And first she seems to ward a coming blow,
And then to strike, and oft to curse the wing
That carried still away her flying foe;
And sith to fight on horseback did not boot,
She seems as in a rage to light on foot.

The necromancer, as his manner is,
Disclosèd at the last his shining shield,
Supposing that the virtue would not miss
To make her, as it had done others, yield:
So have I seen a crafty cat ere this
Play with a silly mouse of house or field
And let it go a while for sport and play,
But kill at last and bear it quite away.

I say that he the cat, the other mice
Resembled had in every former fight,
But now this ring had made this one so wise
That when she saw the strange enchanted light,
She falleth not of force but of device,
As though she were astonied at the sight,
And lay like one of life and sense bereavèd,
By which the poor magician was deceivèd.

For straight he lighted from the flying horse
To take her as he had done many mo;
The shield and book in which was all his force
He left behind him at his saddlebow;
But thinking to have found a senseless corse
Amazed and dead, he finds it nothing so;
For up she starts; so quite the case was altered
That with the cord he brought himself was haltered.

And when with those self bonds she had him tied
By which he thought before her to have snarèd,
She strong and young, he withered, old, and dried
(Alas, an unmeet match to be comparèd),
Forthwith determining he should have died,
To strike his head from shoulders she preparèd,
Till she was moved to mercy with his tears
And with the sight of white and hoary hairs.

For when he saw his force was overlaid
And that her strength was not to be withstood,
"Oh pardon life, thou heav'nly wight," he said.
"No honor comes by spilling agèd blood":
Which words to mercy moved the noble maid,
Whose mind was always merciful and good.
Then why he built the castle she demanded
And what he was to tell her him commanded.

With woeful words the old man thus replied,
"I made this castle for no ill intention,
For covetise or any fault beside,
Or that I lovèd rapine or contention,
But to prevent a danger shall betide
A gentle knight I framèd this invention,
Who, as the heavens hath showed me, in short season
Shall die in Christian state by filthy treason.[3]

"Rogero namèd is this worthy youth,
Whose good and safety fain I would advance;
My name Atlanta is, to tell you truth;
I bred him of a child till his hard chance
And valiant mind, that breeds, alas, my ruth,
With Agramant enticed him into France;
And I, that like mine own child alway loved him,
From France and danger fain would have removed him.

"By art and help of many a hellish elf
This castle for Rogero I did build,
And took him, as I meant to take thyself,
But that with greater art I was beguiled;
From dainty fare and other worldly pelf
Because he should not think himself exiled,
For company I brought him worthy wights,
Both men and women, ladies fair and knights.

"They have all plenty of desired pleasure;
I bend to their contentment all my care;
For them I spend my travail and my treasure;
For music, clothes and games and dainty fare,
As heart can think and mouth require with measure,
Great store for them within this castle are.
Well had I travailed, well my time bestowèd,
But you have marred the fruits that I have sowèd.

"But if your mind be gracious as your look,
If stony heart bide not in tender breast,
Behold, I offer thee my shield and book
And flying horse; and grant my just request,
Some two or three or all the knights I took
I give thee free; let but Rogero rest,
Whose health, whose wealth, whose safety and welfare
Have ever been, and ever shall, my care."

"Your care," quoth she, "is very ill-bestown
In thraldom vile to keep a worthy wight;
As for your gifts, you offer but mine own
Sith by my conquest you are mine in right.
Those dangers great you say to be foreshown
And upon him in time to come must light,
With figures cast and heavenly planets viewèd,
Cannot be known or cannot be eschewèd.

"How can you others' harms foresee so far
And not prevent your own that were so nigh?
I certain shall suppose your art doth err,
And for the rest, the end the truth shall try.
I now intend your matter all to mar
And that before these bonds I will untie,
You shall set free and loose your pris'ners all
Whom in this castle you detainèd thrall."

Whenas the poor old man was so distressed
That needs he must for fear and dread obey
And that this same imperious dame's behest
Could neither bear denial nor delay,
To do as she commands he deems it best
And therefore takes th'enchanted place away;
He breaks some hollow fuming pots of stone,
And straight the walls and buildings all were gone.

This done, himself eke vanished out of sight
As did the castle at that present hour;
Then ladies, lords, and many a worthy knight
Were straight released from his enchanted power,
And some there were had taken such delight
In those so stately lodgings of that tower
That they esteemed that liberty a pain
And wished that pleasant slavery again.

Here were at freedom set among the rest
Gradasso, Sacrapant,[4] two kings of name,
Prasildo and Iroldo, that from th'East
Into this country with Renaldo came.
Here Bradamant found him she lovèd best,
Her dear Rogero of renownèd fame,
Who after certain notice of her had
Did show to see her he was very glad:

As one of whom he great account did make
And thought himself to her most highly bound
Since she put off her helmet for his sake
And in her head received a grievous wound.
'Twere long to tell what toil they both did take
Both night and day each other to have found,
But till this present time they had no meeting
Nor giv'n by word nor writing any greeting.

Now when before him present he beheld
Her that from danger had him sole redeemèd,
His heart with so great joy and mirth was filled
The happiest wight on earth himself he deemèd;
And crystal tears from her fair eyes distilled,
Embracing him whom she most dear esteemèd,
As oft we see a strong and sudden passion
Bring forth effects quite of another fashion.

The griffith horse the while upon the plain
Stood with the target at his saddlebow;
The damsel thought to take him by the rein,
But then he mounteth up and, like a crow
Chased by a dog, forthwith descends again
And standeth still or soareth very low;
And when that some come nigh in hope to take him,
He flies away that none can overtake him.

But near unto Rogero soon he stayed,
Which by Atlanta's care was sole procurèd,
Who for Rogero's danger was afraid
And thinks his safety never well assurèd;
Wherefore he sent this monster for his aid
And by this means from Europe him allurèd.
To his welfare his cares and thoughts he bendeth;
To succor and preserve him he intendeth.

Rogero from his horse forthwith alighted
(The horse he rode on was Frontino namèd)
And with this flying horse was so delighted
That though he saw him wanton and untamèd,
Yet up he leaped and soon was sore affrighted;
He finds he would not to his mind be framèd,
For in the air the griffith soared so high
As doth the falcon that at fowl doth fly.

The damsel fair, that now beheld her dear
Borne far away by force of monster's wing,
Was sorrowful and of so heavy cheer
That to their course her wits she scant could bring;
The tale of Ganymede she once did hear,
Whom poets fain to tend the heavenly king,[5]
She doubts may true of her Rogero be
That was as comely and as fair as he.

As long as eyesight could at all prevail,
So long she viewed him still in all and part;
But when his distance made the sight to fail,
At least she followed him in mind and heart.
To sob, to sigh, to weep, lament, and wail
She never leaves these chances overthwart;
And seeing plain her love and she were parted,
She took Frontino and away departed.

Now was Rogero mounted up so high
He seemed to be a mote or little prick,
For no man could distinguish him by eye
Except his sight were passing fine and quick.
All southerly this griffith horse doth fly:
Was never jade that served man such a trick!
But let him on his way, God speed him well,
For of Renaldo somewhat I must tell:

Who all the while with raging tempest strivèd,
Borne where himself nor no man else did know,
By cruel stormy winds and weather drivèd
That days and nights surceasèd not to blow;
At last in Scotland weary he arrivèd
Where woods of Caledony first do show,
A famous wood wherein in times of old
Brave deeds were done by vent'rous knights and bold.

Here have those famous knights great honor won
At whose rare worth the world itself did wonder;
Here were most valiant acts achieved and done
By knights that dwelt there near or far asunder;
And many a man hath here been quite undone
Whose feeble force his enemy was under.
Here were, as provèd is by ancient charter,
The famous Tristram, Lancelot, and Sir Arthur.

At this same wood Renaldo from his fleet,
Well-mounted on his Bayard's back, did part;
He points his men at Berwick him to meet
The while himself alone with valiant heart,
Sometime on horseback, sometime on his feet,
Doth march in mind to do some worthy part.
But seeing now the night came on so fast,
Unto an abbey he repairs at last.

The abbot and his monks with comely grace,
As holy men of human manners skillèd,
Did welcome him and in a little space
With costly fare his empty stomach fillèd.
Renaldo straight inquirèd of the place
What feats of arms had there been late fulfillèd
And where a man by valiant acts may show
If his exploits deserve dispraise or no.

They said that in that wood and forest find
Adventures strange and feats of arms he might,
But as the place, so are the actions blind,
That oft their doings never come to light;
"But if," say they, "we may persuade your mind
Attempt an action worthy of a knight,
Where if you pass the peril and the pain,
Eternal fame shall unto you remain.

"For if you would perform an act indeed
Whereby great name and honor may be won,
Then this would be the best and noblest deed
That late or long time past was ever done:
Our prince's daughter standeth now in need
Of great defence, a danger great to shun,
Against a knight, Lurcanio by name,
That seeks to take away her life and fame.

"This knight hath her unto the king accusèd,
I think of malice rather than of right,
That he hath seen how she herself abusèd
And closely took her lover up by night.
Now by the laws that in this land are usèd,
Except she have a champion that by might
Within a month Lurcanio prove a liar,
She shall be straight condemnèd to the fire.

"The Scottish law that breedeth all this strife
Appoints that all of base or better sort
That take a man, except she be his wife,
And spends her time with him in Venus' sport
By cruel torment finish shall her life,
Except she find some knight that will support
That she the heinous act hath not committed,
But that in law she ought to be acquitted.

"The king for fair Genevra takes great thought,
Both for her safety and her estimation,
And seeks by all good means that may be wrought
For her defence, and maketh proclamation
That by whose help from danger she is brought,
Provided he be one of noble nation,
Shall have the goodly damsel for his wife
With livings large to keep him all his life.

"But if within this month that now ensu'th
(So little time for her defence is left her)
No knight will come that will defend her truth,
Then friends and fame and life will be bereft her;
This enterprise would much commend your youth,
The praise whereof would last a great while after,
And from Atlanta's pillars[6] unto Ind
A fairer lady you shall never find.

"Now then, beside the honor and the praise,
To have a state may make you live content,
The prince's love, that helpeth many ways,
Whose honor now is half-consumed and spent;
Again, true knights should help at all essays
When any harm to ladies fair is meant;
The very law of knighthood hath commanded
To grant this aid that we have now demanded."

Renaldo paused, and after thus he spake:
"Why then," said he, "must this fair damsel die
That for her true and secret lover's sake
Did condescend within his arms to lie?
Accursed be they that such a law did make;
Accursed be they that mean to live thereby;
Nay rather point a punishment and pain
For such as do their lovers true disdain.

"If fair Genevra had her friend or no
I stand not now the matter to decide;
Yea I would praise her had she done it so
That by her foes it had not been espied.
Be as be may, my meaning is to go
To fight for her, if I may have a guide
That will but show me where is her accuser,
And I shall quickly prove he doth abuse her.

"I know not if the fact she have committed,
Nor can I say in this the certain sure;
But this I say, it ought to be remitted
Much rather than she should distress endure.
I further say they were but meanly witted
That did so strait a statute first procure;
I also say this law they ought recall,
In place thereof a better to install.

"Sith like desire the fancies doth possess
Both of the male and of the female gender
To do that thing that fools count great excess[7]
And quench the flame that Cupid doth engender,
To grant the men more scope, the women less,
Is law for which no reason we can render;
Men using many never are ashamèd,
But women using one or two are blamèd.

"This law, I say, is partial and nought
And doth to women plain and open wrong;
I trust in God they shall be better taught
And that this law shall be revoked ere long."
The abbot and his monks in word and thought
Allowed Renaldo's speech, both old and young;
They all condemn the law and partly blame
The king that may and mendeth not the same.

Next morning when Renaldo doth perceive
The sun appear and stars their heads to hide,
He thanks them for his cheer and taketh leave
And takes a target-bearer for his guide
For fear lest unknown paths should him deceive;
Himself all armèd doth on Bayard ride,
And to the Scottish court he goes a stranger
For to defend the damsel fair from danger.

And for they thought to take a way more nigh,
They leave the common way a mile or twain,
When suddenly they heard a piteous cry
Well like to one that fearèd to be slain.
In haste they spur their horses by and by
Along the vale, and looking down the plain,
A maid between two murderers they saw
That meant to take her life against all law.

The caitiffs put the damsel in great fear
And showed that they were come to end her days,
Which made her weep and shed full many a tear;
To move their minds she trieth many ways,
And though the fact a while they did forbear,
Yet now they had removèd all delays,
Whenas Renaldo came unto her aid
And made the malefactors sore afraid.

Away they fled and left the wench alone,
For dread of death appalled and sore affrighted,
Who all her cause of danger and of moan
Unto Renaldo straight would have recited;
But so great haste he maketh to be gone
He gave no ear nor from his horse alighted,
But to ensue the journey first assigned him
He caused the guide to take her up behind him.

And now on horseback marking well her face
And marking more her gesture and behavior,
Her pleasing speech, and modest sober grace,
She now hath won a great deal more his favor;
And after he had rode a little space,
To tell her hard adventure he would have her;
And she began with humble voice and low
As more at large hereafter I will show.

1. Harington believes that in the following episode the magician Atlanta "may signify Cupid, or that fond fancy we call love."

2. The Rhiphaean Mountains in northern Scythia.

3. Atlanta's explanation summarizes several passages in the *Orlando Innamorato*.

4. We are not told how Sacrapant, left without a horse in Canto II, has reached Atlanta's castle before Bradamant.

5. Jove, who in the form of an eagle carried off Ganymede and made him his cup-bearer.

6. The Pillars of Hercules, Gibraltar and Ceuta.

7. Harington comments, "Wise men should count it a greater, notwithstanding good Renaldo's opinion."

The Fifth Canto

WE SEE the rest of living creatures all,
    Both birds and beasts that on the earth do dwell,
Live most in peace, or if they hap to brawl,
The male and female still agreeth well;
The fierce, the faint, the greater, nor the small
Against the law of nature will rebel;
The savage lions, bears, and bulls most wild
Unto their females show themselves most mild.

What fiend of Hell, what rage reigns here so rife,
Disturbing still the state of human hearts?
How comes it that we find 'twixt man and wife
Continual jars bred by injurious parts?
The undefilèd bed[1] is filled by strife
And tears that grow of words unkind and thwarts;
Nay oft all care and fear is so exilèd
Their guilty hands with blood have been defilèd.

No doubt they are accursed and past all grace
And such as have of God nor man no fear
That dare to strike a damsel in the face
Or of her head to minish but a hair;
But who with knife or poison would unlace
Their line of life or flesh in pieces tear,
No man nor made of flesh and blood I deem him,
But sure some hound of Hell I do esteem him.

Such were these thieves that would the damsel kill
That by Renaldo's coming was recoverèd;
They secretly had brought her down the hill
In hope their fact could never be discoverèd;
Yet such is God, so good His gracious will
That when she lookèd least, she was deliverèd,
And with a cheerful heart, that late was sorry,
She doth begin to tell the woeful story.

"Good sir," said she, "my conscience to discharge,
The greatest tyranny I shall you tell
That erst in Thebes, in Athens, or in Arge[2]
Was ever wrought, or where worst tyrants dwell;
My voice and skill would fail to tell at large
The filthy fact, for I believe it well;
Upon this country Phoebus shines more cold
Because he doth such wicked acts behold.

"Men seek, we see, and have in every age,
To foil their foes and tread them in the dust;
But there to wreak their rancor and their rage
Where they are loved is foul and too unjust.
Love should prevail just anger to assuage;
If love bring death, whereto can women trust?
Yet love did breed my danger and my fear,
As you shall hear if you will give me ear.

"For ent'ring first into my tender spring
Of youthful years, unto the court I came
And servèd there the daughter of our king
And kept a place of honor with good fame
Till love (alas, that love such care should bring)
Envied my state and sought to do me shame;
Love made the Duke of Alban seem to me
The fairest wight that erst mine eye did see.

"And for I thought he loved me all above,
I bent myself to hold and love him best;
But now I find that hard it is to prove
By sight or speech what bides in secret breast.
While I, poor I, did thus believe and love,
He gets my body, bed, and all the rest.
Not thinking this might breed my mistress wrong,
E'en in her chamber this I practised long,

"Where all the things of greatest value lay
And where Genevra sleeps herself sometime;
There at a window we did find a way
In secret sort to cover this our crime;
Here when my love and I were bent to play,
I taught him by a scale of cord to climb,
And at the window I myself would stand
And let the ladder down into his hand.

"So oft we meet together at this sport
As fair Genevra's absence gives us leave,
Who used to other chambers to resort
In summer time, and this for heat to leave;
And this we carried in so secret sort
As none there was our doings did perceive,
For why this window standeth out of sight
Where none do come by day nor yet by night.

" 'Twixt us this use continued many days;
Yea many months we used this privy train;
Love set my heart on fire so many ways
That still my liking lasted to my pain.
I might have found by certain strange delays
That he but little loved and much did fain,
For all his sleights were not so closely coverèd
But that they might full eas'ly be discoverèd.

"At last my duke did seem enflamèd sore
On fair Genevra; neither can I tell
If now this love began or was before
That I did come to court with her to dwell.
But look if I were subject to his lore,
And look if he my love requited well:
He asked my aid herein, no whit ashamèd
To tell me how of her he was enflamèd.

"Not all of love, but partly of ambition
He bears in hand his mind is only bent;
Because of her great state and high condition
To have her for his wife is his intent.
He nothing doubteth of the king's permission
Had he obtained Genevra's free assent;
Ne was it hard for him to take in hand
That was the second person in the land.

"He sware to me, if I would be so kind
His high attempt to further and assist,
That at his hands I should great favor find
And of the king procure me what me list;
How he would ever keep it in his mind
And in his former love to me persist,
And notwithstanding wife and all the rest,
I should be sure that he would love me best.

"I straight consented to his fond request,
As ready his commandment to obey
And thinking still my time employèd best
When I had pleased his fancy any way;
And when I found a time, then was I prest
To talk of him and good of him to say;
I usèd all my art, my wit, and pain
Genevra's love and liking to obtain.

"God know'th how glad I was to work his will,
How diligent I followed his direction;
I spared no time, no travail, nor no skill
To this my duke to kindle her affection.
But always this attempt succeeded ill;
Love had her heart already in subjection;
A comely knight did fair Genevra please,
Come to this country from beyond the seas.

"From Italy for service, as I hear,
Unto the court he and his brother came;
In tourneys and in tilt he had no peer;
All Britain soon was fillèd with his fame.
Our king did love him well and hold him dear
And did by princely gifts confirm the same;
Fair castles, towns, and lordships him he gave
And made him great, such power great princes have.

"Our sovereign much, his daughter liked him more,
And Ariodant this worthy knight is namèd;
So brave in deeds of arms himself he bore
No lady of his love need be ashamèd.
The hill of Sicil³ burneth not so sore,
Nor is the Mount Vesuvio so inflamèd
As Ariodantè's heart was set on fire,
Genevra's beauty kindling his desire.

"His certain love by signs most certain found
Caused that my suit unwillingly was heard;
She well perceived his love sincere and sound,
Inclining to his suit with great regard.
In vain I seek my duke's love to expound;
The more I seek to make, the more I marred;
For while with words I seek to praise and grace him,
No less with works she striveth to deface him.

"Thus being oft repulsed, so evil sped I,
To my too much belovèd duke I went
And told him how her heart was fixed already,
How on the stranger all her mind was bent,
And prayed him now, sith there was no remedy,
That to surcease his suit he would consent,
For Ariodant so loved the princely maid
That by no means his flames could be allayed.

"When Polynesso (so the duke we call)
This tale unpleasant oftentime had heard
And of himself had found his hopes were small
When with my words her deeds he had compared,
Grieved with repulse and vexèd therewithal
To see this stranger thus to be preferred,
The love that late his heart so sore had burnèd
Was coolèd all and into hatred turnèd:

"Intending by some vile and subtle train
To part Genevra from her faithful lover
And plant so great mislike between them twain,
Yet with so cunning show the same to cover
That her good name he will so foul distain
Alive nor dead she never shall recover.
But lest he might in this attempt be thwarted,
To none at all his secret he imparted.

"Now thus resolved, 'Dalinda fair,' quoth he
(I so am called), 'you know though trees be topped
And shrouded low, yet sprout young shoots, we see,
And issue from that head so lately lopped:
So in my love it fareth now with me.
Though by repulse cut short and shrewdly cropped,
The parèd tops such buds of love do render
That still I prove new passions there engender.

" 'Ne do I deem so dear the great delight
As I disdain I should be so reject;
And lest this grief should overcome me quite
Because I fail to bring it to effect,
To please my fond conceit this very night
I pray thee, dear, to do as I direct:
When fair Genevra to her bed is gone,
Take thou the clothes she ware and put them on.

" 'As she is wont her golden hair to dress,
In stately sort to wind it on her wire,
So you her person lively to express
May dress your own and wear her head attire;
Her gorgets and her jewels rich, no less,
You may put on t'accomplish my desire;
And when unto the window I ascend,
I will my coming there you do attend.

" 'Thus I may pass my fancy's foolish fit,
And thus,' quoth he, 'myself I would deceive.'
And I that had no reason nor no wit
His shameful drift, though open, to perceive,
Did wear my mistress' robes that served me fit
And stood at window there him to receive;
And of the fraud I was no whit aware
Till that fell out that causèd all my care.

"Of late 'twixt him and Ariodant had passed
About Genevra fair these words or such,
For why there was good friendship in times past
Between them two, till love their hearts did touch;
The duke such kind of speeches out did cast
He said to Ariodant he marveled much
That, seeing he did always well regard him,
He should again so thanklessly reward him.

" 'I know you see, for needs it must be seen,
The good consent and matrimonial love
That long between Genevr' and me hath been,
For whom I mean ere long the king to move.
Why should you fondly thrust yourself between?
Why should you rove your reach so far above?
For if my case were yours, I would forbear,
Or if I knew that you so lovèd were.'

" 'And I much more,' the other straight replies,
'Do marvel you, sir duke, are so unkind
That know our love and see it with your eyes,
Except that willfulness have made you blind,
That no man can more surèd knots devise
Than her to me and me to her do bind,
Into this suit so rashly are intruded,
Still finding from all hope you are excluded.

" 'Why bear you not to me the like respect
As my good will requireth at your hand?
Since that our love is grown to this effect,
We mean to knit ourselves in wedding's band;
Which to fulfill ere long I do expect,
For know I am, though not in rents or land,
Yet in my prince's grace no whit inferior
And in his daughter's greatly your superior.'

" 'Well,' said the duke, 'errors are hardly movèd
That love doth breed in unadvisèd breast;
Each thinks himself to be the best belovèd,
And yet but one of us is lovèd best;
Wherefore, to have the matter plainly provèd
Which should proceed in love and which should rest,
Let us agree that victor he remain
That of her liking showeth signs most plain.

" 'I will be bound to you by solemn oath
Your secrets all and counsel to conceal,
So you likewise will plight to me your troth
The thing I show you never to reveal.'
To try the matter thus they greèd both
And from this doom hereafter not repeal;
But on the Bible first they were deposèd
That this their speech should never be disclosèd.

"And first the stranger doth his state reveal
And tell the truth in hope to end the strife,
How she had promised him in woe and weal
To live with him and love him all her life
And how with writing with her hand and seal
She had confirmèd she would be his wife,
Except she were forbidden by her father,
For then to live unmarried she had rather.

"And furthermore he nothing doubts, he said,
Of his good service so plain proof to show
As that the king shall nothing be afraid
On such a knight his daughter to bestow,
And how in this he needeth little aid
As finding still his favor greater grow;
He doubts not he will grant his liking after
That he shall know it pleaseth to his daughter.

" 'And thus, you see, so sound stands my estate
That I myself in thought can wish no more;
Who seeks her now is sure to come too late,
For that he seeks is granted me before;
Now only rests in marriage holy state
To knit the knot that must dure evermore.
And for her praise I need not to declare it,
As knowing none to whom I may compare it.'

"Thus Ariodant a tale most true declarèd
And what reward he hopèd for his pain;
But my false duke, that him had foully snarèd
And found by my great folly such a train,
Doth swear all this might no way be comparèd
With his, no, though himself did judge remain;
'For I,' quoth he, 'can show signs so express
As you yourself inferior shall confess.

" 'Alas,' quoth he, 'I see you do not know
How cunningly these women can dissemble;
They least do love where they make greatest show,
And not to be the thing they most resemble.
But other favors I receive, I trow,
Whenas we two do secretly assemble,
As I will tell you, though I should conceal it,
Because you promise never to reveal it.

" 'The truth is this, that I full oft have seen
Her ivory corpse and been with her all night
And naked lain her naked arms between
And full enjoyed the fruits of love's delight.
Now judge who hath in greatest favor been,
To which of us she doth pertain in right;
And then give place, and yield to me mine own
Sith by just proofs I now have made it known.'

" 'Just proofs?' quoth Ariodant. 'Nay, shameful lies.
Nor will I credit give to any word.
Is this the finest tale you can devise?
What, hoped you that with this I would be dored?
No, no, but sith a slander foul doth rise
By thee to her, maintain it with thy sword:
I call thee lying traitor to thy face
And mean to prove it in this present place.'

" 'Tush,' quoth the duke, 'it were a foolish part
For you to fight with me that am your friend,
Sith plain to show, without deceit or art,
As much as I have said I do intend.'
These words did gripe poor Ariodantè's heart,
Down all his limbs a shivering doth descend,
And still he stood with eyes cast down on ground
Like one would fall into a deadly sound.

"With woeful mind, with pale and cheerless face,
With trembling voice that came from bitter thought,
He said he much desired to see this place
Where such strange feats and miracles were wrought.
'Hath fair Genevra granted you this grace
That I,' quoth he, 'so oft in vain have sought?
Now sure, except I see it in my view,
I never will believe it can be true.'

"The duke did say he would with all his heart
Both show where and how the thing was done,
And straight from him to me he doth depart,
Whom to his purpose wholly he had won;
With both of us he play'th so well his part
That both of us thereby were quite undone.
First he tells him that he would have him placèd
Among some houses fall'n and quite defacèd;

"Some ruined houses stood opposed direct
Against the window where he doth ascend.
But Ariodant discreetly doth suspect
That this false duke some mischief did intend,
And thought that all did tend to this effect
By treachery to bring him to his end,
That sure he had devisèd this pretence
With mind to kill him ere he parted thence.

"Thus though to see this sight he thought it long,
Yet took he care all mischief to prevent;
And if perhap they offer force or wrong,
By force the same for to resist he meant.
He had a brother valiant and strong,
Lurcanio called, and straight for him he sent,
Not doubting but alone by his assistance
Against twice twenty men to make resistance.

"He bids his brother take his sword in hand
And go into a place that he would guide
And in a corner closely there to stand
Aloof from t'other threescore paces wide;
The cause he would not let him understand
But prays him there in secret sort to bide
Until such time he happed to hear him call;
Else, if he loved him, not to stir at all.

"His brother would not his request deny;
And so went Ariodant into his place
And undiscovered closely there did lie
Till having lookèd there a little space,
The crafty duke to come he might descry
That meant the chaste Genevra to deface;
Who having made to me his wonted signs,
I let him down the ladder made of lines.

"The gown I wáre was white and richly set
With aglets, pearl, and lace of gold well-garnishèd;
My stately tresses covered with a net
Of beaten gold most pure and brightly varnishèd.
Not thus content, the veil aloft I set
Which only princes wear; thus stately harnishèd
And under Cupid's banner bent to fight,
All unawares I stood in all their sight;

"For why Lurcanio either taking care
Lest Ariodant should in some danger go
Or that he sought, as all desirous are,
The counsels of his dearest friend to know,
Close out of sight, by secret steps and ware
Hard at his heels his brother followed so
Till he was nearer come by fifty paces,[4]
And there again himself he newly places.

"But I, that thought no ill, securely came
Unto the open window as I said,
For once or twice before I did the same
And had no hurt, which made me less afraid.
I cannot boast, except I boast of shame:
When in her robes I had myself arrayed,
Methought before I was not much unlike her,
But certain now I seemèd very like her.

"But Ariodant, that stood so far aloof,
Was more deceived by distance of the place
And straight believed against his own behoof,
Seeing her clothes, that he had seen her face.
Now let those judge that partly know by proof
The woeful plight of Ariodantè's case
When Polynesso came, my faithless friend,
In both their sights the ladder to ascend.

"I, that his coming willingly did wait
And, he once come, thought nothing went amiss,
Embraced him kindly at the first receipt,
His lips, his cheeks, and all his face did kiss;
And he the more to color his deceit
Did use me kinder than he had ere this.
This sight much care to Ariodantè brought,
Thinking Genevra with the duke was nought.

"The grief and sorrow sinketh so profound
Into his heart he straight resolves to die;
He puts the pommel of his sword on ground
And means himself upon the point to lie;
Which when Lurcanio saw and plainly found,
That all this while was closely standing by
And Polynesso's coming did discern,
Though who it was he never yet could learn,

"He held his brother for the present time
That else himself for grief had surely slain,
Who had he not stood nigh and come betime,
His words and speeches had been all in vain.
'What, shall,' quoth he, 'a faithless woman's crime
Cause you to die or put yourself to pain?
Nay, let them go, and cursed be all their kind,[5]
Aye borne like clouds with every blast of wind.

" 'You rather should some just revenge devise
As she deserves, to bring her to confusion,
Sith we have plainly seen with both our eyes
Her filthy fact appear without collusion.
Love those that love again if you be wise,
For of my counsel this is the conclusion:
Put up your sword against yourself preparèd,
And let her sin be to the king declarèd.'

"His brother's words in Ariodantè's mind
Seem for the time to make some small impression,
But still the cureless wound remained behind;
Despair had of his heart the full possession;
And though he knew the thing he had assigned
Contrary to a Christian knight's profession,[6]
Yet here on earth he torment felt so sore
In Hell itself he thought there was no more.

"And seeming now, after a little pause,
Unto his brother's counsel to consent,
He from the court next day himself withdraws
And makes none privy unto his intent.
His brother and the duke both knew the cause,
But neither knew the place whereto he went;
Divers thereof most diversely did judge,
Some by good will persuaded, some by grudge.

"Sev'n days entire about for him they sought;
Sev'n days entire no news of him was found;
The eighth a peasant to Genevra brought
These news, that in the sea he saw him drowned.
Not that the waters were with tempest wrought;
Not that his ship was stricken on the ground.
How then? 'Forsooth,' quoth he, and therewith wept,
'Down from a rock into the sea he lept.'

"And further he unto Genevra told
How he met Ariodant upon the way
Who made him go with him for to behold
The woeful act that he would do that day,
And chargèd him the matter to unfold
And to his prince's daughter thus to say,
Had he been blind, he had full happy been;
His death should show that he too much had seen.

" 'There stands a rock against the Irish isle;
From thence into the sea himself he cast.
I stood and lookèd after him a while;
The height and steepness made me sore aghast.
I thence have traveled hither many a mile
To show you plainly how the matter passed.'
Whenas the clown his tale had verified,
Genevra's heart was th'roughly terrified.

"O Lord, what woeful words by her were spoken,
Laid all alone upon her restless bed!
Oft did she strike her guiltless breast in token
Of that great grief that inwardly was bred;
Her golden tresses all were rent and broken,
Recounting still those woeful words he said:
How that the cause his cruel death was such
Was only this, that he had seen too much.

"The rumor of his death spread far and near,
And how for sorrow he himself had killèd;
The king was sad, the court of heavy cheer;
By lords and ladies many tears were spillèd;
His brother most, as loving him most dear,
Had so his mind with sorrow overfillèd
That he was scantly able to refrain
With his own hands himself for to have slain.

"And oftentimes repeating in his thought
The filthy fact he saw the other night,
Which, as you heard, the duke and I had wrought,
I little looking it would come to light,
And that the same his brother's death had brought,
On fair Genevra he doth wreak his spite,
Not caring, so did wrath him overwhelm,
To leese the king's good will and all his realm.

"The king and nobles sitting in the hall
Right pensive all for Ariodant's destruction,
Lurcanio undertakes before them all
To give them perfect notice and instruction
Who was the cause of Ariodantè's fall;
And having made some little introduction,
He said it was unchaste Genevra's crime
That made him kill himself before his time:

" 'What should I seek to hide his good intent?
His love was such as greater none could be;
He hoped to have your highness' free assent
When you his value and his worth should see;
But while a plain and honest way he went,
Behold, he saw another climb the tree,
And in the midst of all his hope and suit
Another took the pleasure and the fruit.'

"He further said, not that he had surmisèd,
But that his eyes had seen Genevra stand
And at a window, as they had devisèd,
Let down a ladder to her lover's hand,
But in such sort he had himself disguisèd
That who it was he could not understand;
And for due proof of this his accusation
He bids the combat straight by proclamation.

"How sore the king was grieved to hear these news
I leave it as a thing not hard to guess.
Lurcanio plain his daughter doth accuse,
Of whom the king did look for nothing less;
And this the more his fear and care renews
That on this point the laws are so express:
Except by combat it be proved a lie,
Needs must Genevra be condemned to die.

"How hard the Scottish law is in this case
I do not doubt but you have heard it told,
How she that doth another man embrace
Beside her husband, be she young or old,
Must die, except within two fortnights' space
She find a champion stout that will uphold
That unto her no punishment is due,
But he that doth accuse her is untrue.

"The king, of crime that thinks Genevra clear,
Makes offer her to wed to any knight
That will in arms defend his daughter dear
And prove her innocent in open fight.
Yet for all this no champion doth appear,
Such fear they have of this Lurcanio's might:
One gazeth on another as they stand,
But none of them the combat takes in hand.

"And further, by ill fortune and mischance,
Her brother Zerbin now is absent thence
And gone to Spain, I think, or else to France,
Who were he here, she could not want defence,
Or if perhap so lucky were her chance
To send him notice of her need from hence;
Had she the presence of her noble brother,
She could not need the aid of any other.

"The king, that means to make a certain trial
If fair Genevra guilty be or no
(For still she stiffly stood in the denial
Of this that wrought her undeservèd woe),
Examines all her maids, but they reply all
That of the matter nothing they did know;
Which made me seek for to prevent the danger
The duke and I might have about the stranger.

"And thus for him more than myself afraid,
So faithful love to this false duke I bare,
I gave him notice of these things and said
That he had need for both of us beware.
He praised my constant love and farther prayed
That I would credit him and take no care;
He points two men, but both to me unknown,
To bring me to a castle of his own.

"Now, sir, I think you find by this effect
How soundly I did love him from my heart
And how I proved by plain course and direct
My meaning was not any ways to start;
Now mark if he to me bare like respect,
And mark if he requited my desert:
Alas, how shall a silly wench attain
By loving truly to be loved again?

"This wicked duke, ungrateful and perjurèd,
Beginneth now of me to have mistrust;
His guilty conscience could not be assurèd
How to conceal his wicked acts unjust
Except my death, though causeless, be procurèd:
So hard his heart, so lawless was his lust.
He said he would me to his castle send,
But that same castle should have been mine end.

"He willed my guides, when they were past that hill
And to the thick a little way descended,
That there, to quite my love, they should me kill;
Which, as you saw, they to have done intended
Had not your happy coming stopped their will,
That (God and you be thanked) I was defended."
This tale Dalinda to Renaldo told,
And all the while their journey on they hold.

This strange adventure luckily befell
To good Renaldo, for that now he found,
By this Dalinda that this tale did tell,
Genevra's mind unspotted, clear, and sound;
And now his courage was confirmèd well
That wanted erst a true and certain ground,
For though before for her he meant to fight,
Yet rather now for to defend the right.

To great St. Andrews town he maketh haste
Whereas the king was set with all his train,
Most careful waiting for the trumpet's blast
That must pronounce his daughter's joy or pain.
But now Renaldo spurrèd had so fast
He was arrived within a mile or twain;
And through the village as he then was riding,
He met a page that brought them fresher tiding:

How there was come a warrior all disguisèd
That meant to prove Lurcanio said untrue,
His colors and his armor well devisèd
In manner and in making very new;
And though that sundry sundrily surmisèd,
Yet who it was for certain no man knew.
His page, demanded of his master's name,
Did swear he never heard it since he came.

Now came Renaldo to the city wall,
And at the gate but little time he stayed,
The porter was so ready at his call.
But poor Dalinda now grew sore afraid;
Renaldo bids her not to fear at all,
For why he would her pardon beg, he said.
So thrusting in among the thickest rout,
He saw them stand on scaffolds all about.

It straight was told him by the standers-by
How there was thither come a stranger knight
That meant Genevra's innocence to try,
And that already was begun the fight,
And how the green that next the wall did lie
Was railed about of purpose for the sight.
This news did make Renaldo hasten in
And leave behind Dalinda at her inn.

He told her he would come again ere long
And spurs his horse that made an open lane;
He piercèd in the thickest press among
Whereas these valiant knights had giv'n and ta'en
Full many strokes, with sturdy hand and strong.
Lurcanio thinks to bring Genevra's bane;
The other means the lady to defend,
Whom, though unknown, they favor and commend.

There was Duke Polynesso bravely mounted
Upon a courser of an exc'lent race;
Six knights among the better sort accounted
On foot in arms do marshal well the place.
The duke by office all the rest surmounted,
High Constable, as always in such case,
Who of Genevra's danger was as glad
As all the rest were sorrowful and sad.

Now had Renaldo made an open way
And was arrivèd there in lucky hour
To cause the combat to surcease and stay
Which these two knights applied with all their power.
Renaldo in the court appeared that day
Of noble chivalry the very flower;
For first the prince's audience he prayed;
Then with great expectation thus he said:

"Send, noble prince," quoth he, "send by and by,
And cause forthwith that they surcease the fight;
For know that whichsoe'er of these doth die,
It certain is he dies against all right.
One thinks he tells the truth and tells a lie
And is deceived by error in his sight;
And look what cause his brother's death procurèd,
That very same hath him to fight allurèd.

"The t'other of a nature good and kind,
Not knowing if he hold the right or no,
To die or to defend her hath assigned
Lest so rare beauty should be spillèd so.
I harmless hope to save the faultless mind
And those that mischief mind, to work them woe.
But first, O prince, to stay the fight give order
Before my speech proceedeth any farder."

Renaldo's person, with the tale he told,
Moved so the king that straight without delay
The knights were bidden both their hands to hold;
The combat for a time was caused to stay.
Then he again, with voice and courage bold,
The secret of the matter doth bewray,
Declaring plain how Polynesso's lust
Was first contriver of this deed unjust,

And proff'reth of this speech to make a proof
By combat hand to hand with sword and spear.
The duke was called that stood not far aloof
And scantly able to conceal his fear.
He first denies, as was for his behoof,
And straight to battle both agreèd were;
They both were armed; the place before was ready;
Now must they fight, there could be no remedy.

How was the king, how were the people glad
That fair Genevra faultless there did stand
As God's great goodness now revealèd had
And should be provèd by Renaldo's hand;
All thought the duke of mind and manners bad,
The proud'st and cruel'st man in all the land;
It likely was, as every one surmisèd,
That this deceit by him should be devisèd.

Now Polynesso stands with doubtful breast,
With fainting heart, with pale dismayèd face;
Their trumpets blew; they set their spears in rest;
Renaldo cometh on a mighty pace,
For at this fight he finish will the feast,
And where to strike him he designs a place.
His very first encounter was so fierce
Renaldo's spear the t'other's sides did pierce.

And having overthrown the duke by force,
As one unable so great strokes to bide,
And cast him clean six paces from his horse,
Himself alights and th'other's helm untied,
Who making no resistance, like a corse,
With faint low voice for mercy now he cried
And plain confessed with this his later breath
The fault that brought him this deservèd death.

No sooner had he made this last confession
But that his life did fail him with his voice.
Genevra's double scape of foul oppression
In life and fame did make the king rejoice;
In lieu of her, to leese his crown's possession
He would have wished, if such had been his choice;
To leese his realm he could have been no sadder;
To get it lost he could have been no gladder.

The combat done, Renaldo straight untied
His beaver, when the king, that knew his face,
Gave thanks to God that did so well provide
So doubtless help in such a dangerous case.
That unknown knight stood all this while aside
And saw the matters passèd in the place;
And everyone did muse and marvel much
What wight it was whose courtesy was such.

The king did ask his name because he meant
With kingly gifts his service to reward,
Affirming plainly that his good intent
Deservèd thanks and very great regard.
The knight with much entreaty did assent,
And to disarm himself he straight prepared.—
But who it was if you vouchsafe to look,
I will declare it in another book.

1. The nuptial bed.
2. A literal translation of the Italian would read, "in Thebes or Argos or Mycenae."
3. Etna.
4. That is, he was now ten paces from Ariodant.
5. Harington notes, "Not all womenkind, but faithless women."
6. Harington explains, "For despair is the damnablest thing that may be, by the rules of Christian religion."

The Sixth Canto

Most wretched he that thinks by doing ill
His evil deeds long to conceal and hide,
For though the voice and tongues of men be still,
By fowls or beasts his sins shall be descried;
And God oft worketh by His secret will
That sin itself the sinner so doth guide
That of his own accord, without request,
He makes his wicked doings manifest.

The graceless wight, Duke Polynesso, thought
His former fault should sure have been concealèd
If that Dalinda unto death were brought,
By whom alone the same could be revealèd.
Thus making worse the thing before was nought,
He hurt the wound which time perhaps had healèd;
And weening with more sin the less to mend,
He hastened on his well-deservèd end,

And lost at once his life, his state, and friends,
And honor too, a loss as great or more.
Now, as I said, that unknown knight intends,
Sith everyone to know him sought so sore
And sith the king did promise large amends,
To show his face which they saw oft before;
And Ariodant most lovely did appear
Whom they thought dead as you before did hear.

He whom Genevra woefully did wail,
He whom Lurcanio deemèd to be dead,
He whom the king and court did so bewail,
He that to all the realm such care had bred
Doth live; the clown's report in this did fail,
On which false ground the rumor false was spread.
And yet in this the peasant did not mock;
He saw him leap down headlong from the rock.

But as we see men oft with rash intent
Are desperate and do resolve to die,
And straight do change that fancy and repent
When unto death they do approach more nigh:
So Ariodant to drown himself that meant,
Now plunged in sea, repented by and by,
And being of his limbs able and strong,
Unto the shore he swam again ere long.

And much dispraising in his inward thought
This fond conceit that late his mind possessed,
At last a blind and narrow path him brought,
All tired and wet, to be a hermit's guest,
With whom to stay in secret sort he sought,
Both that he might his former grief digest
And learn the truth, if this same clown's report
Were by Genevra ta'en in grief or sport.

There first he heard how she conceived such grief
As almost brought her life to woeful end;
He found of her they had so good belief
They thought she would not in such sort offend;
He further heard, except she had relief
By one that would her innocence defend,
It was great doubt Lurcanio's accusation
Would bring her to a speedy condemnation.

And look, how love before his heart enragèd,
So now did wrath enflame; and though he knew well
To wreak his harm his brother's life was gagèd,
He nath'less thought his act so foul and cruel
That this his anger could not be assuagèd,
Unto his flame love found such store of fuel;
And this the more increased his wrath begun,
To hear how everyone the fight did shun;

For why Lurcanio was so stout and wise,
Except it were for to defend the truth,
Men thought he would not so the king despise
And hazard life to bring Genevra's ruth,
Which causèd everyone his friend advise
To shun the fight that must maintain untruth.
But Ariodant after long disputation
Means to withstand his brother's accusation.

"Alas," quoth he, "I never shall abide
Her through my cause to die in woe and pain;
For danger or for death what may betide,
Be she once dead, my life cannot remain.
She is my saint; in her my bliss doth bide;
Her golden rays my eyes' light still maintain;
Fall back, fall edge, and be it wrong or right,
In her defence I am resolved to fight.

"I take the wrong, but yet I'll take the wrong;
And die I shall, yet if I die I care not.
But then alas, by law she dies ere long:
O cruel laws so sweet a wight that spare not!
Yet this small joy I find these griefs among,
That Polynesso to defend her dare not,
And she shall find how little she was lovèd
Of him that to defend her never movèd.

"And she shall see me dead there for her sake,
To whom so great a damage she hath done;
And of my brother just revengement take
I shall, by whom this strife was first begun;
For there at least my death plain proof shall make
That he this while a foolish thread hath spun;
He thinketh to avenge his brother's ill
The while himself his brother there shall kill."

And thus resolved, he gets him armor new,
New horse, and all things new that needful been,
All clad in black, a sad and mournful hue;
And crossed with wreath of yellow and of green,
A stranger bare his shield that neither knew
His master's name nor him before had seen;
And thus as I before rehearsed disguisèd,
He met his brother as he had devisèd.

I told you what success the matter had,
How Ariodant himself did then discover,
For whom the king himself was even as glad
As late before his daughter to recover;
And since he thought in joyful times and sad
No man could show himself a truer lover
Than he that, after so great wrong, intended
Against his brother her to have defended,

Both loving him by his own inclination
And prayed thereto by many a lord and knight
And chiefly by Renaldo's instigation,
He gave to Ariodant Genevra bright.
Now by the duke's attaint and condemnation
Albania came to be the king's in right,
Which duchy, falling in so lucky hour,
Was given unto the damsel for her dower.

Renaldo for Dalinda's pardon prayed,
Who for her error did so sore repent
That straight she vowed, with honest mind and staid,
To live her life in prayer and penitent;
Away she packed nor further time delayed;
In Dacia[1] to a nunn'ry there she went.
But to Rogero now I must repair
That all this while did gallop in the air,

Who, though he were of mind and courage stout
And would not eas'ly fear or be dismayed,
Yet doubtless now his mind was full of doubt;
His heart was now appalled and sore afraid.
Far from Europa he had traveled out,
And yet his flying horse could not be stayed,
But passed the pillars twelvescore leagues and more
Pitched there by Herc'les many years before.

This griffith horse, a bird most huge and rare,
Doth pierce the sky with so great force of wing
That with that noble bird he may compare
Whom poets fain Jove's lightning down to bring,
To whom all other birds inferior are
Because they take the eagle for their king.
Scarce seemeth from the clouds to go so swift
The thunderbolt sent by the lightning's drift.

When long this monster strange had kept his race,
Straight as a line bending to neither side,
He spied an island distant little space
To which he bends in purpose there to bide;
Much like in semblance was it to the place
Where Arethusa used herself to hide[2]
And seeks so long her love to have beguiled
Till at the last she found herself with child.

A fairer place they saw not all the while
That they had traveled in the air aloft;
In all the world was not a fairer isle
If all the world to find the same were sought.
Here, having traveled many a hundred mile,
Rogero by his bird to rest was brought
In pastures green and hills with cool fresh air,
Clear rivers, shady banks, and meadows fair.

Here divers groves there were of dainty shade;
Of palm or orange trees, of cedars tall,
Of sundry fruits and flowers that never fade
The show was fair, the plenty was not small,
And arbors in the thickest places made
Where little light and heat came not at all,
Where nightingales did strain their little throats,
Recording still their sweet and pleasant notes.

Amid the lily white and fragrant rose,
Preserved still fresh by warm and temp'rate air,
The fearful hare and cony careless goes;
The stag with stately head and body fair
Doth feed secure, not fearing any foes
That to his damage hither may repair;
The buck and doe doth feed among the fields,
As in great store the pleasant forest yields.

It needless was to bid Rogero light;
Whenas his horse approachèd nigh the ground,
He cast himself out of his saddle quite;
And on his feet he falleth safe and sound
And holds the horse's reins lest else he might
Fly quite away and not again be found;
And to a myrtle by the water side,
Between two other trees, his beast he tied.

And finding thereabout a little brook
That near unto a shady mountain stands,
His helmet from his head forthwith he took,
His shield from arm, his gauntlet from his hands;
And from the higher places he doth look
Full oft to sea, full oft to fruitful lands,
And seeks the cool and pleasant air to take
That doth among the leaves a murmur make.

Oft with the water of that crystal well
He seeks to quench his thirst and suage his heat,
With which his veins enflamed did rise and swell
And caused his other parts to fry in sweat.
Well may it seem a marvel that I tell,
Yet will I once again the same repeat:
He traveled had above three thousand mile
And not put off his armor all the while.

Behold, his horse he lately tièd there,
Among the boughs in shady place to bide,
Strave to go loose and started back for fear
And pulls the tree to which the reins were tied,
In which, as by the sequel shall appear,
A human soul itself did strangely hide;
With all his strength the steed strives to be loosèd,
By force whereof the myrtle sore was bruisèd.

And as an arm of tree from body rent
By peasant's strength with many a sturdy stroke,
When in the fire the moisture all is spent,
The empty places filled with air and smoke
Do boil and strive and find at last a vent
When of the brand a shiver out is broke:[3]
So did the tree strive, bend, writhe, wring, and break,
Till at a little hole it thus did speak:

"Right courteous knight (for so I may you deem
And must you call, not knowing other name),
If so you are as gracious as you seem,
Then let your friendly deed confirm the same;
Unloose this monster sent, as I esteem,
To add some farther torment to my shame.
Alas, mine inward griefs were such before
By outward plagues they need be made no more."

Rogero mazèd lookèd round about
If any man or woman he might see;
At last he was resolvèd of his doubt;
He found the voice was of the myrtle tree;
With which abashed, though he were wise and stout,
He said, "I humbly pray thee pardon me,
Whether thou be some human ghost or sprite
Or power divine that in this wood hast right.

"Not willfulness, but ignorance did breed
Thine injury, mine error in this case,
And made me do this unadvisèd deed
By which unwares thy leaves I did deface;
But let thy speech so far forth now proceed
To tell me how thou art that in this place
Dost dwell in tree amid the desert field,
As God from hail and tempest thee may shield.

"And if that I for this amends may make,
Or now or after, or by pain or art,
I swear to thee by her and for her sake
That holds of me and shall the better part[4]
That I shall not surcease all pains to take
To work thy joy or to assuage thy smart."
This said, he saw again the myrtle shake,
And then again he heard that thus it spake:

"Sir knight, your courtesy doth me constrain
To show to you the thing that you desire,
Although I sweat, as you may see, with pain,
Like greenest boughs upon the flaming fire.
I will discover unto you her train
(Woe worth the time that ever I came nigh her)
That did for malice and by magic strange
My lively shape to lifeless branches change.[5]

"I was an earl; Astolfo was my name,
Well-known in France in time of war and peace;
Orlando's cousin and Renald's, whose fame
While time shall last, in earth shall never cease,
Of Othon, King of English Isle, I came
And should succeed him after his decease,
Both comely, young, careless of worldly pelf,
To none an enemy but to myself.

"For as we turnèd from the Eastern Isles
Whose banks are worn with surge of Indian wave,
Where I and many more with witching wiles
Were straight enclosèd in a hollow cave
Until Orlando did avenge the guiles
And found by force a mean his friends to save,
We westward went upon the shore and sand
That lieth on the north side of the land.

"And as we traveled homeward on our way,
As chance did lead or destiny us drive,
It was our fortune once on break of day
Hard by Alcina's castle to arrive,
Where she alone, to sport herself and play,
Such kind of gins for fishes did contrive
That though we saw no net, no bait, no hook,
Yet still we saw that store of fish she took.

"The dolphin strong, the tunny good of taste,
The mullet, sturgeon, salmon (princely fish),
With porpoise, seals, and thornpool came as fast
As she was pleasèd to command or wish;
And still she took of each kind as they passed,
Some strange for show, some dainty for the dish,
The horsefish and the huge and monstrous whales
Whose mighty members harnessed are with scales.

"Among the rest that were too long to count
We saw the fish that men balena call;
Twelve yards above the water did amount
His mighty back, the monster is so tall;
And for it stood so still, we made account
It had been land, but were deceivèd all;
We were deceived, well I may rue the while;
It was so huge we thought it was an isle.

"I say this potent witch Alcina took
All sorts of fish without or net or aid,
But only reading in a little book
Or mumbling words, I know not what she said;
But seeing me, so well she liked my look
That at her sport but little time she stayed,
But sought forthwith to trap me by her skill,
Which straight fell out according to her will.

"For toward me with pleasant cheer she came,
In modest manner and in comely sort,
And did withal her speech demurely frame
And prayed me to her lodging to resort;
Or if I would be partner of her game,
She offered me to show me all the sport
And all the kinds of fish in seas that were,
Some great, some small, some smooth, and some with hair.

" 'And if you list a mermaid fair to see
That can with song the raging storms appease,
At yond same little bank you may,' quoth she,
'To which we two will safely pass with ease.'
The bank which she pretends to show to me
Was that same fish, the monster of the seas;
And I that too much lovèd to adventure
Upon the fish's back with her did enter.

"My cousins Dudon and Renaldo beckoned
To draw me thence; I heard not what they said,
But of their speech and signs I little reckoned;
I had not wit enough to be afraid.
But soon my courage was appalled and weakened;
I straight was fain in vain to cry for aid;
The monstrous fish that seemed to me an isle
Straight bare me from the shore full many a mile.

"There was Renaldo like to have been drowned,
Who swam to save me if perhaps he might;
But suddenly of him and of the ground
A misty cloud did take away the sight;
Alcina and I with seas environed round
Did travel on that monster all the night,
And then with gracious speeches she began
To give me all the comfort that she can.

"And thus at last to this place we repair,
Of which by wrong Alcina keeps possession,
Deposing forcibly the rightful heir,
Her elder lawful sister, by oppression;
The other two, more vicious than fair,
Are bastards and begotten in transgression;
I heard it told and have it not forgotten,
She and Morgana were in incest gotten.

"And as their first beginning was of sin,
So is their life ungodly and defamèd;
Of law nor justice passing not a pin,
But like the heifer wanton and untamèd,
By war they seek their sister's right to win,
Their elder sister Logistilla[6] namèd,
And have so far prevailèd with their powers
They have of hers about an hundred towers,

"And had ere this time taken all away
Save that the rest is strongly fencèd round;
For of one side the water stops the way,
On th'other side the vantage of the ground
Which with a mighty bank doth make a stay,
Much like the English and the Scottish bound;
And yet the bastard sisters do their best
And labor still to spoil her of the rest,

"And why, because they see her good and holy;
They hated her because themselves are vicious.
But to return and tell you of my folly
That turned to me so hurtful and pernicious,
I now again grew somewhat bold and jolly;
I see no cause to fear or be suspicious;
And finding she loved me by signs most plain,
I wholly bent myself to love again.

"When I her dainty members did embrace,
I deemèd then there was none other bliss;
Methought all other pleasures were but base;
Of friends nor kin I had no want nor miss;
I only wished to stand in her good grace
And have access her coral lips to kiss;
I thought myself the happiest of all creatures
To have a lady of so goodly features.

"And this the more confirmed my joy and pride,
That toward me she showed such love and care;
By night and daily I was by her side;
To do or speak against me no man dare;
I was her stay, I was her house's guide;
I did command, the rest as subjects are;
She trusted me, alone with me she talkèd;
With me within she sat, without she walkèd.

"Alas, why do I open lay my sore
Without all hope of medicine or relief?
And call to mind the fickle joy before,
Now being plunged in gulfs of endless grief?
For while I thought she loved me more and more,
Whenas I deemed my joy and bliss was chief,
Her waning love away from me was taken;
A new guest came, the old was clean forsaken.

"Then did I find full soon, though too-too late,
Her wanton, wavering, wily woman's wit,
Accustomed in a trice to love and hate;
I saw another in my seat to sit.
Her love was gone, forgone my happy state;
The mark is missed that I was wont to hit;
And I had perfect knowledge then ere long
That to a thousand she had done like wrong.

"And lest that they about the world might go
And make her wicked life and falsehood known,
In diverse places she doth them bestow
So as abroad they shall not make their moan,
Some into trees amid the field that grow,
Some into beasts, and some into a stone;
In rocks or rivers she doth hide the rest
As to her cruel fancy seemeth best.

"And you that are arrived by steps so strange
To this unfortunate and fatal isle,
Although in youthful sports a while you range
And though Alcina favor you a while,
Although you little look for any change,
Although she friendly seem on you to smile,
Yet look no less but changed at last to be
Into some brutish beast, some stone or tree.[7]

"Thus though perhap my labor is but lost,
Yet have I giv'n you good and plain advice;
Who can themselves beware by other's cost
May be accounted well among the wise;
The waves that my poor ship so sore hath tossed
You may avoid by heed and good device;
Which if you do, then your success is such
As many others could not do so much."

Rogero did with much attention hear
Astolfo's speech, and by his name he knew
To Bradamant he was of kindred near,
Which made him more his woeful state to rue;
And for her sake that lovèd him most dear,
To whom from him all love again was due,
He sought to bring him aid and some relief,
At least with comfort to assuage his grief.

Which having done, he askèd him again
The way that would to Logistilla guide;
For were it by the hills, by dale or plain,
He thither meant forthwith to run or ride.
Astolfo answered it would ask much pain,
And many a weary journey he should bide,
Because to stop this way Alcina sets
A thousand kinds of hindrances and lets.

For as the way itself is very steep,
Not passable without great toil and pain,
So she that in her mischief doth not sleep
Doth make the matter harder to attain
By placing men of arms the way to keep,
Of which she hath full many in her train.
Rogero gave Astolfo many thanks
For giving him this warning of her pranks.

And leading then the flying horse in hand,
Not daring yet to mount a beast so wild
Lest, as before I made you understand,
He might the second time have been beguiled,
He means to go to Logistilla's land,
A virtuous lady, chaste, discreet, and mild,
And to withstand Alcina tooth and nail
That upon him her force might not prevail.

But well we may commend his good intent,
Though missing that to which he did aspire;
Who judgeth of our actions by th'event,
I wish they long may want their most desire.
For though Rogero to resist her meant
And fearèd her as children fear the fire,
Yet was he taken to his hurt and shame
Even as the fly is taken in the flame.

For going on his way, behold, he spies
A house more stately than can well be told,
Whose walls do seem exalted to the skies,
From top to bottom shining all of gold,
A sight to ravish any mortal eyes;
It seemed some alchemist did make this hold;
The walls seemed all of gold, but yet I trow
All is not gold that makes a golden show.

Now though this stately sight did make him stay,
Yet thinking on the danger him foretold,
He left the easy and the beaten way
That leadeth to this rich and stately hold,
And to her house where virtue bears the sway
He bends his steps with all the haste he could;
But ere he could ascend the mountain's top,
A crew of caitiffs sought his way to stop,

A foul, deformed, a brutish, cursèd crew,[8]
In body like to antique work devisèd,
Of monstrous shape and of an ugly hue
Like masking matachinas all disguisèd;
Some look like dogs and some like apes in view;
Some dreadful look and some to be despisèd,
Young shameless folk and doting foolish agèd,
Some nak'd, some drunk, some bedlam-like enragèd.

One rides in haste a horse without a bit;
Another rides as slow an ass or cow;
The third upon a centaur's rump doth sit;
A fourth would fly with wings, but knows not how;
The fifth doth for a spear employ a spit;
Sixth blows a blast like one that gelds a sow.
Some carry ladders, others carry chains;
Some sit and sleep while others take the pains.

The captain of this honorable band,
With belly swoll'n and puffèd, blubbered face,
Because for drunkenness he could not stand,
Upon a tortoise rode a heavy pace;
His sergeants all were round about at hand,
Each one to do his office in his place;
Some wipe the sweat; with fans some make a wind;
Some stay him up before, and some behind.

Then one of these that had his feet and breast
Of manlike shape, but like unto a hound
In ears, in neck, and mouth, and all the rest,
Doth utter barking words with currish sound,
Part to command and partly to request
The valiant knight to leave the higher ground
And to repair unto Alcina's castle,
Or else they two for mastery must wrastle.

This monster, seeing his request denied,
Strake at Rogero's beaver with a lance;
But he that could no such rude jests abide
With Ballisarda⁹ smote him in the paunch.
Out came the sword a foot on th'other side,
With which he led his fellows such a dance
That some hopped headless, some cut by the knees,
And some their arms and some their ears did leese.

In vain it was their targets to oppose
Against the edge of his enchanted blade;
No steel had force to bear those fatal blows;
Unto the quick the sword a passage made.
But yet with numbers they do him enclose;
Their multitude his force did overlade;
He needs at least Briareus' hundred arms
To foil the foes that still about him swarms.

Had he remembered to unfold the shield
Atlanta carried at his saddlebow,
He might have quickly overcome the field
And caused them all without receiving blow,
Like men dismayed and blind, themselves to yield;
But he perhaps that virtue did not know,
Or if he did, perhaps he would disdain,
Where force did fail, by fraud his will to gain.

But being full resolvèd not to yield
Unto such beasts, but ere he parted thence
He would his carcass leave amid the field
And manfully would die in his defence,
Then lo, good hap that fails the forward seld
Provided him a mean to rid him hence:
There came two ladies, either like a queen,
And each of them most stately to be seen.[10]

For each of them an unicorn did ride
As white as lilies or unmolten snow,
And each of them was decked with so great pride
As might most richly set them forth to show;
But each of them was so divinely eyed
Would move a man in love with them to grow,
And each of them in all points was so choice
As in their sight a man would much rejoice.

Then both of them unto the meadow came
Whereas Rogero fought with all that rout,
And both of them those brutish beasts did blame
That sought to harm a knight so strong and stout.
Rogero, blushing now with modest shame,
Thanked them that had of danger helped him out
And straight consented with those ladies fair
Unto Alcina's castle to repair.

Those ornaments that do set forth the gate,
Embossed a little bigger than the rest,
All are enriched with stones of great estate,
The best and richest growing in the East,
In parted quadrons, with a seemly rate,
The columns diamonds as may be guessed:
I say not whether counterfeit or true,
But shine they did like diamonds in view.

About these stately pillars and between
Are wanton damsels gadding to and fro,
And as their age, so are their garments green;
The black ox hath not yet trod on their toe;
Had virtue with that beauty tempered been,
It would have made the substance like the show.
These maids with courteous speech and manners nice
Welcome Rogero to this paradise,

If so I may a paradise it name
Where love and lust have built their habitation,
Where time well-spent is counted as a shame,
No wise staid thought, no care of estimation,
Nor nought but courting, dancing, play, and game,
Disguisèd clothes, each day a sundry fashion;
No virtuous labor doth this people please,
But nice apparel, belly-cheer, and ease.

Their air is alway temperate and clear
And wants both winter's storms and summer's heat,
As though that April lasted all the year.
Someone by fountain's side doth take his seat,
And there with feignèd voice and careless cheer
Some sonnet made of love he doth repeat;
Some others, otherwhere with other fashions,
Describe unto their loves their loving passions.

And Cupid then, the captain of the crew,
Triumphs upon the captives he hath got
And, more and more his forces to renew,
Supplies with fresh the arrows he hath shot,
With which he hits, his level is so true,
And wounds full deep although it bleedeth not.
This is the place to which Rogero went
And these the things to which our youth is bent.

Then straight a stately steed of color bay,
Well-limbed and strong, was to Rogero brought,
And decked with fair caparison most gay,
With gold and pearl and jewels richly wrought;
The griffith horse, that whilom to obey
The spur and bit was by Atlanta taught,
Because his journey long requirèd rest,
Was carried to a stable to be dressed.

The ladies fair that had the knight defended
From that same wicked and ungracious band
Which, as you heard at large, before pretended
Rogero's passage stoutly to withstand,
Told now Rogero how that they intended,
Because his value great they understand,
Of him to crave his furtherance and aid
Against their foe that made them oft afraid.

"There is," quoth they, "a bridge amid our way,
To which we are already very nigh,
Where one Erifila[11] doth all she may
To damage and annoy the passers-by;
A giantess she is; she lives by prey;
Her fashions are to fight, deceive, and lie;
Her teeth be long, her visage rough with hair;
Her nails be sharp, and scratching like a bear.

"The harm is great this monster vile doth do
To stop the way that but for her were free;
She spills and spoils, she cares not what nor who,
That grief to hear and pity is to see;
And for to add more hatred her unto,
Know this, that all yon monsters you did see
Are to this monster either sons or daughters
And live like her by robberies and slaughters."

Rogero thus in courteous sort replied,
"Fair ladies, gladly I accept your motion;
If other service I may do beside,
You may command, I stand at your devotion;
For this I wear this coat and blade well-tried,
Not to procure me riches or promotion,
But to defend from injury and wrong
All such as have their enemies too strong."

The ladies did Rogero greatly thank,
As well deserved so stout and brave a knight
That proffered, at the first request so frank,
Against the giantess for them to fight.
Now they drew nigh unto the river's bank
Whenas Erifila came out in sight.—
But they that in this story take some pleasure
May hear the rest of it at further leisure.

1. Denmark.

2. Probably the fountain of Arethusa on the island of Ortygia in Syracuse, where the nymph is supposed to have fled from her lover, the River Alpheus.

3. A similar comparison is used to describe the similar case of Pier delle Vigne in Dante's *Inferno,* canto 13; both Ariosto and Dante, of course, remember Polydorus, who speaks when the tree into which he has been transformed is injured in the *Aeneid,* Book III.

4. Bradamant.

5. Astolfo's account of his capture by Alcina is founded on the *Orlando Innamorato.*

6. Allegorically, reason (but Harington identifies her as "the true Christian religion").

7. Harington notes that Astolfo's metamorphosis shows "how men given over to sensuality, leese in the end the very form of men (which is reason)."

8. Harington calls them "the base conceits of men," the Seven Deadly Sins.

9. Rogero's sword, originally stolen from Orlando by Brunello.

10. Harington interprets them as "ambition and desire of advancement."

11. Allegorized by some Italian commentators and Harington as covetousness; but Ariosto himself emphasizes her pride.

The Seventh Canto

A LL they that to far countries do resort
  Shall see strange sights in earth, in seas, in skies
Which when again at home they shall report,
Their solemn tales esteemèd are as lies,
For why the fond and simple common sort
Believe but what they feel or see with eyes;
Therefore to them my tale may seem a fable
Whose wits to understand it are not able.

But careless what the simple sots surmise,
If they shall deem it a device or deed,
Yet sure to those that are discreet and wise
It will no wonder nor no passion breed;
Wherefore my tale to such I do devise
And wish them to the same to take good heed,
For some there are may fortune in this book
As in a glass their acts and haps to look.

For many men with hope and show of pleasure
Are carried far in foolish fond conceit
And waste their precious time and spend their treasure
Before they can discover this deceit.
Oh happy they that keep within their measure,
To turn their course in time and sound retreat
Before that wit, with late repentance taught,
Were better never had than so dear bought!

A little while before I did rehearse
How that Rogero by two dames was brought
To combat with Erifila the fierce,
Who for to stop the bridge and passage sought.
In vain it were for to declare in verse
How sumptuously her armor all was wrought,
All set with stones and gilt with Indian gold,
Both fit for use and pleasant to behold.

She mounted was, but not upon a steed;
Instead thereof she on a wolf doth sit,
A wolf whose match Apulia doth not breed,
Well-taught to hand although she used no bit;
And all of sandy color was her weed.
Her arms were thus, for such a champion fit:
An ugly toad was painted on her shield,
With poison swoll'n and in a sable field.

Now each the other forthwith had described,
And each with other then prepared to fight;
Then each the other scornfully defied;
Each seeks to hurt the other all he might.
But she, unable his fierce blows to bide,
Beneath the visor smitten was so right
That from her seat six paces she was heavèd
And lay like one of life and sense bereavèd.

Rogero ready was to draw his sword
To head the monster lying on the sand,
Until those dames with many a gentle word
Assuaged his heat and made him hold his hand;
He might in honor now her life afford
Sith at his mercy wholly she doth stand:
"Wherefore, sir knight, put up your blade," say they;
"Let's pass the bridge and follow on our way."

The way as yet unpleasant was and ill
Among the thorny bushes and between;
All stony, steep, ascending up the hill,
A way less pleasant seldom hath been seen;
But this once passed according to their will,
And they now mounted up upon the green;
They saw the fairest castle standing by
That ere was seen with any mortal eye.

Alcina met them at the outer gate
And came before the rest a little space
And with a count'nance full of high estate
Salutes Rogero with a goodly grace;
And all the other courtiers in like rate
Do bid Rogero welcome to the place
With so great shows of duty and of love
As if some god descended from above.

Not only was this palace for the sight
Most goodly, fair, and stately to behold,
But that the people's court'sy bred delight
Which was as great as could with tongue be told.
All were of youth and beauty shining bright;
Yet to confirm this thing I dare be bold,
That fair Alcina passed the rest as far
As doth the sun another little star:

A shape whose like in wax 'twere hard to frame
Or to express by skill of painters rare.
Her hair was long and yellow to the same,
As might with wire of beaten gold compare;
Her lovely cheeks with show of modest shame,
With roses and with lilies painted are;
Her forehead, fair and full of seemly cheer,
As smooth as polished ivory doth appear.

Within two arches of most curious fashion
Stand two black eyes that like two clear suns shined,[1]
Of steady look but apt to take compassion,
Amid which lights the naked boy and blind
Doth cast his darts that cause so many a passion
And leave a sweet and cureless wound behind;
From thence the nose in such good sort descended
As envy knows not how it may be mended;

Conjoined to which in due and comely space
Doth stand the mouth, stained with vermilion hue;
Two rows of precious pearl serve in their place
To show and shut a lip right fair to view;
Hence come the courteous words and full of grace
That mollify hard hearts and make them new;
From hence proceed those smilings sweet and nice
That seem to make an earthly paradise.

Her breast as milk, her neck as white as snow;
Her neck was round, most plump and large her breast;
Two ivory apples seemèd there to grow,
Full tender, smooth, and fittest to be pressed;
They wave like seas when winds most calm doth blow.
But Argus self might not discern the rest;
Yet by presumption well it might be guessed
That that which was concealèd was the best.

Her arms due measure of proportion bare;
Her fair white hand was to be viewèd plain;
The fingers long, the joints so curious are
As neither knot appeared nor swelling vein.
And full to perfect all those features rare,
The foot that to be seen doth sole remain,
Both slender, short, little it was and round;
A finer foot might nowhere well be found.

She had on every side prepared a net
If so she walk or laugh or sing or stand.
Rogero now the counsel doth forget
He had received late at Astolfo's hand;
He doth at nought those wholesome precepts set
That warnèd him to shun Alcina's land;
He thought no fraud, no treason, nor no guile
Could be accomp'nied with so sweet a smile.

The dame of France[2] whom he so lovèd erst
He quite forgets, so far awry he swervèd;
The tale Astolfo had to him rehearsed
He thinketh false or else by him deservèd;
Alcina's goodly shape his heart so pierced
She only seemed a mistress to be servèd;
Ne must you blame Rogero's inclination,
But rather blame the force of incantation.

Now as abroad the stately courts did sound
Of trumpets, shagbot, cornets, and of flutes,
Even so within there wants no pleasing sound
Of virginals, of viols, and of lutes,
Upon the which persons not few were found
That did record their loves and loving suits
And in some song of love and wanton verse
Their good or ill successes did rehearse.

As for the sumptuous and luxurious fare,
I think not they that Ninus did succeed
Nor Cleopatra fair, whose riot rare
To Antony such love and loss did breed,
Might with Alcina's any way compare,
Whose love did all the others' far exceed,
So deeply was she ravished in the sight
Of this so valiant and so comely knight.

The supper done and tables ta'en away,
To purposes and such like toys they went,
Each one to other secretly to say
Some word by which some pretty toy is meant;
This helped the lovers better to bewray
Each unto other what was their intent;
For when the word was hither tossed and thither,
Their last conclusion was to lie together.

These pretty kinds of amorous sports once ended,
With torches to his chamber he was brought;
On him a crew of gallant squires attended
That every way to do him honor sought.
The chamber's furniture could not be mended;
It seemed Arachne had the hangings wrought.
A banquet new was made, the which once finished,
The company by one and one diminished.

Now was Rogero couchèd in his bed
Between a pair of cambric sheets perfumèd,
And oft he harkens with his wakeful head
For her whose love his heart and soul consumèd;
Each little noise hope of her coming bred,
Which finding false, against himself he fumèd
And cursed the cause that did him so much wrong
To cause Alcina tarry thence so long.

Sometime from bed he softly doth arise
And look abroad if he might her espy;
Sometime he with himself doth thus devise,
"Now she is coming, now she draws thus nigh";
Sometime for very anger out he cries,
"What meaneth she, she doth no faster hie?"
Sometimes he casts lest any let should be
Between his hand and this desirèd tree.

But fair Alcina, when with odors sweet
She was perfumed according to her skill,
The time once come she deemèd fit and meet
When all the house were now asleep and still:
With rich embroidered slippers on her feet
She goes to give and take of joys her fill,
To him whom hope and fear so long assailèd,
Till sleep drew on and hope and fear both failèd.

Now when Astolfo's successor espied
Those earthly stars, her fair and heav'nly eyes,
As sulphur once inflamèd cannot hide,
Even so the metal in his veins that lies
So flamed that in the skin it scant could bide,
But of a sudden straight he doth arise,
Leaps out of bed, and her in arms embracèd,
Ne would he stay till she herself unlacèd.

So utterly impatient of all stay
That though her mantle was but cypress light
And next upon her smock of lawn it lay,
Yet so the champion hasted to the fight
The mantle with his fury fell away;
And now the smock remained alone in sight,
Which smock as plain her beauties all discloses
As doth a glass the lilies fair and roses.

And look how close the ivy doth embrace
The tree or branch about the which it grows,
So close the lovers couchèd in the place,
Each drawing in the breath the other blows;
But how great joys they found that little space
We well may guess, but none for certain knows;
Their sport was such, so well their leer they couth
That oft they had two tongues within one mouth.[3]

Now though they keep this close with great regard,
Yet not so close but some did find the same;
For though that virtue oft wants due reward,
Yet seldom vice wants due deservèd blame.
Rogero still was more and more preferred;
Each one to him with cap and court'sy came;
For fair Alcina being now in love
Would have him placed the others all above.

In pleasure here they spend the night and day;
They change their clothes so often as they lust;
Within they feast, they dance, disport, and play;
Abroad they hunt, they hawk, they ride, they joust;
And so while sensual life doth bear the sway,
All discipline is trodden in the dust.
Thus while Rogero here his time misspends,
He quite forgets his duty and his friends.

For while Rogero bides in feast and joy,
King Agramant doth take great care and pain;
Dame Bradamant doth suffer great annoy
And traveled far to find him, all in vain;
She little knew Alcina did enjoy
Her due delights, yet doth she mourn and plain
To think how strangely this same flying horse
Bare him away against his will by force.

In towns, in fields, in hills, in dales she sought;
In tents, in camps, in lodgings, and in caves
Oft she inquired, but yet she learnèd nought;
She passed the rivers fresh and salt sea waves;
Among the Turks she leaves him not unsought,
Gramercy ring that her from danger saves:
A ring whose virtue works a thing scant possible,
Which holding in her mouth she goes invisible.

She will not, nor she cannot think him dead,
For if a man of so great worth should die,
It would some great report or fame have bred
From East unto the West, both far and nigh.
It cannot sink nor settle in her head
Whether he be in seas, in earth, or sky;
Yet still she seeks, and her companions are
Sorrows and sighs and fears and loving care.

At last she means to turn unto the cave
Where lie the great and learnèd Merlin's bones
And at that tomb to cry so loud and rave
As shall with pity move the marble stones;
Nor till she may some certain notice have
Of her beloved, to stay her plaints and moans,
In hope to bring her purpose to effect
By doing as that prophet should direct.

Now as her course to Poitiersward[4] she bent,
Melissa, using wonted skill and art,
Encountered her, her journey to prevent,
Who knew full well and did to her impart
Both where he was and how his time he spent,
Which grieved the virtuous damsel to the heart,
That such a knight, so valiant erst and wise,
Should so be drowned in pleasure and in vice.

O poisoned hook that lurks in sugared bait![5]
O pleasures vain that in this world are found,
Which like a subtle thief do lie in wait
To swallow man in sink of sin profound!
O kings and peers, beware of this deceit
And be not in this gulf of pleasure drowned;
The time will come and must, I tell you all,
When these your joys shall bitter seem as gall.

Then turn your cloth of gold to clothes of hairs,
Your feasts to fasts, to sorrows turn your songs,
Your wanton toys and smilings into tears,
To restitution turn your doing wrongs,
Your fond secureness turn to godly fears,
And know that vengeance unto God belongs,
Who when He comes to judge the souls of men,
It will be late, alas, to mend it then.

Then shall the virtuous man shine like the sun;
Then shall the vicious man repent his pleasure;
Then one good deed of alms sincerely done
Shall be more worth than mines of Indian treasure;
Then sentence shall be giv'n which none shall shun;
Then God shall weigh and pay our deeds by measure.
Unfortunate and thrice accursèd they
Whom fond delights do make forget that day.

But to return unto my tale again:
I say Melissa took no little care
To draw Rogero by some honest train
From this same place of feasts and dainty fare,
And like a faithful friend refused no pain
To set him free from her sweet senseless snare,
To which his uncle[6] brought him with intent
His destiny thereby for to prevent.

As oft we see men are so fond and blind
To carry to their sons too much affection,
That when they seem to love, they are unkind,
For they do hate a child that spare correction:
So did Atlanta, not with evil mind,
Give to Rogero this so bad direction,
But of a purpose thereby to withdraw
His fatal end that he before foresaw.

For this he sent him past so many seas
Unto the isle that I before did name,
Esteeming less his honor than his ease,
A few years' life than everlasting fame;
For this he causèd him so well to please
Alcina, that same rich, lascivious dame,
That though his time old Nestor's life had finished,
Yet her affection should not be diminished.

But good Melissa on a ground more sure,
That loved his honor better than his weal,
By sound persuasions means him to procure
From pleasure's court to virtue's to appeal:
As leeches good that in a desp'rate cure
With steel, with flame, and oft with poison heal,
Of which although the patient do complain,
Yet at the last he thanks him for his pain.

And thus Melissa promisèd her aid
And help Rogero back again to bring,
Which much recomforted the noble maid
That loved this knight above each earthly thing;
But for the better doing this, she said,
It were behoveful that he had her ring,
Whose virtue was that whoso did it wear
Should never need the force of charms to fear.

But Bradamant, that would not only spare
Her ring to do him good, but eke her heart,
Commends the ring and him unto her care;
And so these ladies take their leave and part.
Melissa for her journey doth prepare
By her well-trièd skill in magic art
A beast that might supply her present lack,
That had one red foot and another black.

Such haste she made that by the break of day
She was arrivèd in Alcina's isle.
But straight she changed her shape and her array
That she Rogero better might beguile:
Her stature tall she makes, her head all gray;
A long white beard she takes to hide the wile;
In fine, she doth so cunningly dissemble
That she the old Atlanta doth resemble.

And in this sort she waiteth till she might
By fortune find Rogero in fit place,
Which very seldom happed, for day and night
He stood so high in fair Alcina's grace
That she could least abide of any wight
To have him absent but a minute space.
At last full early in a morning fair
She spied him walk abroad to take the air.

About his neck a carc'net rich he ware
Of precious stones, all set in gold well-tried;
His arms, that erst all warlike weapons bare,
In golden bracelets wantonly were tied;
Into his ears two rings conveyèd are
Of golden wire, at which on either side
Two Indian pearls, in making like two pears
Of passing price, were pendent at his ears.

His locks, bedewed with waters of sweet savor,
Stood curlèd round in order on his head;
He had such wanton womanish behavior
As though in Valence he had long been bred;
So changed in speech, in manners, and in favor,
So from himself beyond all reason léd
By these enchantments of this am'rous dame
He was himself in nothing but in name;

Which when the wise and kind Melissa saw,
Resembling still Atlanta's person sage
Of whom Rogero always stood in awe
Even from his tender youth to elder age,
She toward him with look austere did draw,
And with a voice abrupt as half in rage,
"Is this," quoth she, "the guerdon and the gain
I find for all my travail and my pain?

"What, was't for this that I in youth thee fed
With marrow of the bears and lions fell?
That I through caves and deserts have thee led
Where serpents of most ugly shape do dwell,
Where tigers fierce and cruel leopards bred,
And taught thee how their forces all to quell?
An Atys or Adonis for to be
Unto Alcina as I now thee see!

"Was this foreshowed by those observèd stars,
By figures and nativities oft cast,
By dreams, by oracles that never errs,
By those vain arts I studied in time past,
That thou should'st prove so rare a man in wars,
Whose famous deeds to endless praise should last,
Whose acts should honored be both far and near,
And not be matched with such another peer?

"Is this a mean or ready way, you trow,
Which other worthy men have trod before,
A Caesar or a Scipio to grow
And to increase in honor more and more?
But to the end a man may certain know
How thrall thou art unto Alcina's lore,
Thou wearest here her chains and slavish bands
With which she binds thy warlike arms and hands.

"If thou regard not thine own estimation
To which the heav'ns ordain thee if thou would,
Defraud not yet thine heirs and generation
Of which I have thee oftentime foretold,
Appointed by etern predestination,
Except thou do their due from them withhold,
Out of thy loins and bowels to proceed
Such men whose match the world did never breed.

"Let not so many a worthy soul and mind,
Framed by the wisdom of the Heav'nly King,
Be hindered of the bodies them assigned,
Whose offspring chief must of thy issue spring;
Be not unto thine own blood so unkind,
Of whose great triumphs all the world shall ring,
Whose successors, whose children and posterity
Shall help our country to her old prosperity.

"What good hath this great queen unto thee done
But many other queans can do the same?
What certain gain is by her service won
That soon doth fancy, sooner doth defame?
Wherefore, to make thee know what thou hast done
That of thy doings thou may'st have some shame,
But wear this ring, and next time you repair
To your Alcina, mark if she be fair."

Rogero all abashed and mute did stand,
With silent tongue and look for shame downcast;
The good enchantress took him by the hand,
And on his finger straight the ring she placed;
But when this ring had made him understand
His own estate, he was so sore aghast
He wished himself half buried under ground
Much rather than in such place once be found.

But she that saw her speech took good effect
And that Rogero shamèd of his sin,
She doth her person and her name detect
And as herself, not Atlant, doth begin
By counsel and advice him to direct
To rid himself from this so dangerous gin,
And gives him perfect notice and instruction
How these deceits do bring men to destruction.

She showed him plainly she was thither sent
By Bradamant that loved him in sincerity,
Who to deliver him from bondage meant
Of her that blinded him with false prosperity;
How she took Atlant's person to th'intent
Her countenance might carry more austerity.
But finding now him home reduced again,
She saith she will declare the matter plain;

And unto him forthwith she doth impart
How that fair dame that best deserved his love
Did send that ring and would have sent her heart,
If so her heart his good so far might move;
The ring this virtue had, it could subvert
All magic frauds and make them vain to prove.
Rogero, as I said, no time did linger,
But put the ring upon his little finger.

When truth appeared, Rogero hated more
Alcina's trump'ries, and did them detest,
Than he was late enamorèd before.
(O happy ring, that makes the bearer blessed!)
Now saw he that he could not see before,
How with deceits Alcina had been dressed;
Her borrowed beauties all appearèd stainèd;
The painting gone, nothing but filth remainèd.

E'en as a child that taking from the tree
An apple ripe and hides it in some place,
When he returns the same again to see
After a sev'night or a fortnight's space,
Doth scant believe it should the same fruit be
When rottenness that ripeness doth deface,
And where before delight in it he took,
Now scant he bides upon the same to look:

E'en so Rogero plainly now descried
Alcina's foul disgraces and enormity;
Because of this his ring she could not hide
By all her paintings any one deformity;
He saw most plainly that in her did bide
Unto her former beauties no conformity,
But looks so ugly that from East to West
Was not a fouler old misshapen beast.

Her face was wan, a lean and wrinkled skin;
Her stature scant three horseloaves did exceed;
Her hair was gray of hue and very thin;
Her teeth were gone, her gums served in their stead;
No space was there between her nose and chin;
Her noisome breath contagion would breed;
In fine, of her it might have well been said,
In Nestor's youth she was a pretty maid.[7]

I fear her arts are learnèd nowadays,
To counterfeit their hair and paint their skin;
But reason's ring their crafts and guiles bewrays;
No wise men of their paintings pass a pin.
Those virtues that in women merit praise
Are sober shows without, chaste thoughts within,
True faith and due obedience to their make,
And of their children honest care to take.[8]

Now though Rogero, as before I said,
Detested sore the ugly witch's sight,
Yet by Melissa's counsel wisely led,
He doth conceal the matter for a night
Till of provision he were better sped
With which he might more safely take his flight;
And taking care his meaning close to hide,
He doth forthwith his armor all provide,

And tells Alcina he would go and try
If that he were not waxen gross or no,
Because that idle he so long did lie
And never fought with any armèd foe.
His sword unto his girdle he doth tie;
With armor on, a walking he doth go,
And with a scarf about his arm he lapped
The shield that in the cypress case was wrapped.

And thus arrayed, he cometh to the stable
And took a horse, as wise Melissa taught,
A horse as black as any jet or sable,
So made as if in wax he had been wrought,
Most swift for course and strong of limbs and able;
This horse, hight Rabican, was thither brought
By Duke Astolfo, who by sorcery
Was turnèd late into a myrtle tree.

As for the griffith horse that there was by,
Melissa wisheth him to let him stand
And saith that she herself ere long would try
To make him gentle to the spur and hand,
And that she would next day a time espy
To bring it him and let him understand
How he should do with very little pain
To make him yield to spur, to rod, and rein.

She further said his flight would be suspected
Except he let the flying horse to stay.
Rogero none of all her words neglected,
But did her counsel wise and sage obey;
And so before his meaning was detected,
From this misshapen hag he stole away,
And means, if God will grant him so much grace,
To be at Logistilla's in short space.

Such men of arms as watchèd at the gate
He slew; the rest he suddenly assailèd;
Good was his hap that scaped with broken pate;
They took their heels whenas their hearts them failèd.
Alcina now had notice all too late;
Rogero was so far it nought availèd.—
But in another book shall be containèd
How him Dame Logistilla entertainèd.

1. Harington observes in the margin, "Yellow hair and black eyes is monstrous, and seldom or never seen."

2. Bradamant.

3. Harington: "This lascivious description of carnal pleasure needs not offend the chaste ears or thoughts of any, but rather shame the unchaste, that have themselves been at such kind of banquets."

4. The Italian reads, "a Pontiero."

5. This stanza and the two that follow it have no equivalent in Ariosto; Harington adds the moralization, which partially offsets his omission of many details in the Italian.

6. Atlanta.

7. Harington comments, "You see what manner of monster Alcina appeared in her own likeness, when the ring of reason had dissolved all enchantments."

8. Ariosto has no equivalent for this stanza of moralization.

The Nineteenth Canto
stanzas 17-42 of the Italian

[Medoro and his friend Cloridano, humble Saracen soldiers, have
attempted at night to retrieve the body of their fallen leader
Dardinello; but before they can accomplish this, a Christian
force encounters them, Cloridano is slain, and Medoro is left
seriously wounded on the field. Here Angelica finds him.]

For lo, a damsel came, though meanly clad
In shepherd's weeds, yet fresh and fair of favor
And such a one as in those base clothes had
A show of princely birth and high behavior;
She, finding him lie there in case so bad,
Did think it charity to be his savior.
This was, if you forget, the lady fair
That of Cataya was undoubted heir;

I showed you by what hap she gat the ring[1]
And how the same had filled her with such pride
And her into so high conceit did bring
That all her suitors now she flat denied;
She careth not for earl nor duke nor king,
Orlando she and Sacrapant defied,
But chiefly she would blush and be ashamed
If she but happed to hear Renaldo named.

So great her folly grew, so vain her pride
As she esteemèd all the world at nought,
The which when once the blind boy[2] had espied
(Not blind when any mischief may be wrought),
He will no longer this presumption bide;
And for a fit occasion long he sought,
And finding this, he thought himself now sped,
And up he draws his arrow to the head.

Now when this Indian[3] queen did there behold
A lovely youth lie dying in the place,
His body feeble in a mortal cold,
A deadly pale amid his lively face,
A kind of passion straight on her took hold
That moved her mind to pity this his case,
And much the rather when he did declare
The woeful cause that bred him all this care.

She having learned of surgery the art,
An art which still the Indians greatly prize,
Which fathers to their children do impart,
Whose knowledge in tradition chiefly lies,
Which without books the children learn by heart:
I say Angelica doth then devise,
By skill she had in juice of herbs and flowers,
For to renew Medoro's lively powers.

And calling to her mind she late had seen
An herb whose virtue was to stanch the blood,
As dittany or some such herb I ween
That for such purpose wholesome was and good,
Straightway she seeks this herb upon the green
With all the haste and diligence she could;
And finding it, she takes thereof a branch
Whose virtue was the course of blood to stanch.

Then coming back again, she met by hap
A silly shepherd seeking of his cow
That brake out of his ground at some small gap
And now was strayed he knew not where nor how;
She prays him take the herbs were in her lap
(A servitor more fit to serve a sow)
And bear her company unto the place
Where poor Medoro lay in dangerous case.

Then from their horse she and the shepherd light,
And straight between two tiles those herbs she bruised
And took the juice between her fingers bright
And so into the wound the same infused,
Whose virtue great revived Medoro's sprite
To find himself so well and kindly used
That doubt it was which most his wound did salve,
The precious surgeon or the precious salve.

And now he had recovered so much force
As what with hers and with the shepherd's aid
He clambered up upon the shepherd's horse,
Howbeit in the place so long he stayed
Until he saw his lovèd master's corse[4]
Into a grave with Cloridano's laid;
And then and not before he did agree
To do as he by her should pointed be.

From thence unto the shepherd's house she went
And made her patient eke with her to go,
And there to bide with him she was content
Till he were clearly rid of all his woe;
But in this while she felt her heart relent
With sundry qualms that wonted not be so,
And when his comely personage she saw,
A secret heat she felt her heart to gnaw.

For while she healed his wound, another dart
Did wound her thoughts, and high conceits so deep
As now therewith was ravished her proud heart,
Possessing it although she wake or sleep;
Her wound to heal there was no herb nor art,
For more and more like flame the same doth creep;
Yet her chief care is him to help and cure
That all this torment doth to her procure.

Thus while Medoro better grows and better,
She feels herself tormented more and more,
And he that for his life to her was debtor
Is he alone that plagueth her so sore;
Wherefore, though modesty a while did let her,
Yet now perforce no further she forbore
But plainly to Medoro told her grief
And at his hands as plainly asked relief.

O stout Orlando, valiant Sacrapant,
O fierce Ferraw, O hundreds more beside,
Where are those valiant acts of which you vaunt?
Where is your pomp, your glory, and your pride?
One poor Medore all your desires doth daunt,
One poor Medore doth all your power deride,
And she whom all of you have wooed in vain
To woo Medoro doth not now disdain.

She suffers poor Medoro take the flower
Which many sought but none had yet obtained;
That fragrant rose that to the present hour
Ungathered was, behold, Medoro gained;
And over her to give him perfect power
With sacred rites a marriage was ordained,
And with the veil of this so sacred order
She covers this her folly and disorder.

Now when the solemn marriage was done,
Of which god Cupid asked the banns, I trow,
She going forward as she hath begun
Continued there with him a month or mo;
From rising to the setting of the sun
With him she doth sit, talk, lie, stand, and go,
Forgetting so all maidenly sobriety
That she of him could never have satiety.

If in the house she stayed, then would she crave
Medoro in the house with her to stay;
If in the field she walk, then must she have
Medoro lead or guide her in the way;
And by a river in a shady cave
They oft did use to spend the heat of day,
Like to that cave where, shunning stormy weather,
The Trojan duke[5] and Dido met together.

Amid these joys as great as joys might be
Their manner was on every wall within,
Without on every stone or shady tree,
To grave their names with bodkin, knife, or pin:
"Angelica" and "Medore" you plain might see;
So great a glory had they both therein
"Angelica" and "Medore" in every place
With sundry knots and wreaths they interlace.

Now when she thought in this well-pleasing place
She had already made sufficient stay,
And for she longed to do Medore that grace
To give to him her kingdom of Catay
From whence she had been absent so long space,
From this poor house she means to go away;
Yet minds she, ere she go, her host to please
With whom she found such pleasure and such ease.

Angelica had since she was a girl
Worn on her arm, as for Orlando's sake,
A bracelet rich of precious stone and pearl
Which as a token she of him did take;
And though she had it of this worthy earl,
Yet did she thereof chiefest reck'ning make,
Not that the giver she did much esteem
But for the gift was rich and so did seem.

By her this bracelet many years was worn,
Not only in her time of peace and joy
But e'en when she remainèd most forlorn
And subject to each danger and annoy,
E'en then when nak'd as ever she was born,
The Orco[6] came in hope her to enjoy:
This bracelet, wanting store of coin and pence,
She gives her host as for a recompence.

Next day betime she getteth on her way
And makes Medoro sole her lord and guide;
He kept her company both night and day,
And none but he with her did go and ride.
Their meaning is at Barcelon to stay,
A port in Spain, until they may provide
A vessel that with help of oar and wind
May them transport from Spanish seas to Ind.

But ere they were arrivèd at this port,
They met a madman of his wit bestraught,
Besmeared with dirt and mire in filthy sort,
His outward sense expelled with inward thought;
This madman made them but ill-favored sport
And had made worse had he them rightly caught,
But as it was, he put them in great danger
And flies at them as dogs do at a stranger.[7]

1. In Canto X Rogero gave her the magic ring which Bradamant had
sent him by Melissa.
2. Cupid.
3. Eastern? Angelica's father was King of Cathay, or China.
4. The body of King Dardinello.
5. Aeneas.

6. A sea monster which devoured naked young women offered to propitiate the god Proteus; in Cantos VIII and X Angelica is exposed to the Orco and then rescued by Rogero.

7. Angelica, who returns to the East with her lover, disappears from the story at this point.

M. ALBAN

Art:

Anselmo Alcina

Alardo Pinabello Bra Vilan

Vilan Bra

ASTOLFO BRADAMANTE

BRA

BRADAMAN
TE

PINABELLO

The Twenty-third Canto

stanzas 100-136 of the Italian

[Meanwhile Orlando, searching for his enemy Mandricardo, reaches
the place where Medoro and Angelica have enjoyed their love.]

THUS much he prayed, and thence away he went
To seek out Mandricard, but found him not;
And for the day now more than half was spent,
The sun and season waxing somewhat hot,
A shady grove he found, and there he meant
To take some ease, but found small ease, God wot;
He thinks his thirst and heat a while to suage,
But found that set him in worse heat and rage.

For looking all about the grove, behold,
In sundry places fair ingrav'n he sees
Her name whose love he more esteems than gold,
By her own hand in barks of divers trees:
This was the place wherein before I told
Medoro used to pay his surgeon's fees,
Where she, to boast of that that was her shame,
Used oft to write hers and Medoro's name,

And then with true-love knots and pretty posies
To show how she to him by love was knit
Her inward thoughts by outward words discloses,
In her much love to show her little wit.
Orlando knew the hand and yet supposes
It was not she that had such posies writ;
And to beguile himself, "Tush, tush," quoth he,
"There may be more Angelicas than she.

"Yea, but I know too well that pretty hand;
Oft hath she sent me letters of her writing."
Then he bethinks how she might understand
His name and love by that same new inditing,
And how it might be done long time he scanned,
With this fond thought so fondly him delighting.
Thus with small hope, much fear, all malcontent
In these and such conceits the time he spent.

And aye the more he seeks out of his thought
To drive this fancy, still it doth increase,
E'en as a bird that is with birdlime caught
Doth beat her wings and strives and doth not cease
Until she hath herself all overwrought
And quite entangled in the slimy grease.
Thus on went he till him the way did bring
Unto a shady cave and pleasant spring.

This was a place wherein above the rest
This loving pair, leaving their homely host,
Spent time in sports that may not be expressed;
Here in the parching heat they tarried most,
And here Medore, that thought himself most blessed,
Wrote certain verses as in way of boast
Which in his language doubtless sounded pretty,
And thus I turn them to an English ditty:

"Ye pleasant plants, green herbs, and waters fair,
And cave with smell and grateful shadow mixed,
Where sweet Angelica, daughter and heir
Of Galafron, on whom in vain were fixed
Full many hearts, with me did oft repair
Alone and naked lay mine arms betwixt:
I, poor Medore, can yield but praise and thanks
For these great pleasures found amid your banks,

"And pray each lord whom Cupid holds in pay,
Each knight, each dame, and everyone beside,
Or gentle or mean sort that pass this way
As fancy or his fortune shall him guide,
That to the plants, herbs, spring, and cave he say,
'Long may the sun and moon maintain your pride,
And the fair crew of nymphs make such purveyance
As hither come no herds to your annoyance'."

It written was there in th'Arabian tongue,
Which tongue Orlando perfect understood
As having learned it when he was but young,
And oft the skill thereof had done him good;
But at this time it him so deeply stung
It had been well that he it never could.
And yet we see, to know men still are glad;
And yet we see, much knowledge makes men mad.

Twice, thrice, yea five times he doth read the rhyme;
And though he saw and knew the meaning plain,
Yet that his love was guilty of such crime
He will not let it sink into his brain.
Oft he perusèd it, and every time
It doth increase his sharp tormenting pain;
And aye the more he on the matter musèd,
The more his wits and senses were confusèd.

E'en then was he of wit wellnigh bestraught,
So quite he was giv'n over unto grief
(And sure if we believe as proof hath taught,
This torture is of all the rest the chief);
His sprite was dead, his courage quailed with thought;
He doth despair and look for no relief;
And sorrow did his senses so surprise
That words his tongue and tears forsook his eyes.

The raging pang remainèd still within
That would have burst out all at once too fast;
E'en so we see the water tarry in
A bottle little-mouthed and big in waist,
That though you topsy-turvy turn the brim,
The liquor bides behind with too much haste,
And with the striving oft is in such taking
As scant a man can get it out with shaking.

At last he comes unto himself anew
And in his mind another way doth frame,
That that which there was written was not true
But writ of spite his lady to defame,
Or to that end that he the same might view
And so his heart with jealousy inflame.
"Well, be't who list," quoth he, "I see this clearly:
He hath her hand resembled passing nearly."

With this small hope, with this poor little spark
He doth somedeal revive his troubled sprite;
And for it was now late and waxèd dark,
He seeks some place where he may lie that night.
At last he hears a noise of dogs that bark;
He smells some smoke and sees some candlelight;
He takes his inn, with will to sleep, not eat,
As filled with grief and with none other meat.

But lo, his hap was at that house to host
Where fair Angelica had lain before,
And where her name on every door and post
With true-love knots was joinèd to "Medore";
That knot, his name whom he detested most,
Was in his eye and thought still evermore;
He dares not ask nor once the matter touch
For knowing more of that he knows too much.

But vain it was himself so to beguile,
For why his host unaskèd by and by,
That saw his guest sit there so sad the while
And thinks to put him from his dumps thereby,
Beginneth plain without all fraud or guile,
Without concealing truth or adding lie,
To tell that tale to him without regard
Which divers had before with pleasure heard:

As thus, how at Angelica's request
He holp unto his house to bring Medore,
Who then was sorely wounded in his breast,
And she with surgery did heal his sore;
But while with her own hands the wound she dressed,
Blind Cupid wounded her as much or more,
That when her skill and herbs had cured her patient,
Her cureless wound in love made her unpatient;

So that, admit she were the greatest queen
Of fame and living in those Eastern parts,
Yet so with fancy she was overseen
To marry with a page of mean deserts.
"Thus love," quoth he, "will have his godhead seen
In famous queens' and highest princes' hearts."
This said, to end the tale, he showed the jewel
That she had giv'n him, which Orlando knew well.

This tale, and chiefly this same last conclusion,
Was e'en a hatchet to cut off all hope
When love had after many a vain collusion
Now for his farewell lent him such a rope
To hang himself and drown him in confusion;
Yet fain he would deny his sorrow scope,
And though a while to show it he forbears,
It breaketh out at last in sighs and tears.

And as it were enforced, he gives the rein
To raging grief upon his bed alone;
His eyes do shed a very shower of rain
With many a scalding sigh and bitter groan;
He slept as much as if he had then lain
Upon a bed of thorns and stuffed with stone;
And as he lay thereon and could not rest him,
The bed itself gave matter to molest him.

"Ah wretch I am," thus to himself he said;
"Shall I once hope to take repose and rest me
In that same house? yea, e'en in that same bed
Where my ungrateful love so lewdly dressed me?
Nay, let me first an hundred times be dead;
First wolves devour and vultures shall digest me."
Straight up he starts, and on he puts his clothes
And leaves the house, so much the bed he loathes.

He leaves his host, nor once doth take his leave;
He fared so ill, he bids them not farewell;
He leaves the town; his servants he doth leave;
He rides, but where he rides he cannot tell.
And when alone himself he doth perceive
To weep and wail, nay e'en to howl and yell,
He doth not cease to give his grief a vent
That inwardly so sore did him torment.

The day, the night to him were both alike;
Abroad upon the cold bare earth he lies;
No sleep, no food he takes, nor none would seek;
All sustenance he to himself denies.
Thus he began and ended half the week,
And he himself doth marvel whence his eyes
Are fed so long with such a spring of water,
And to himself thus reasons on the matter:

"No, no, these be no tears that now I shed;
These be no tears, nor can tears run so rife;
But fire of frenzy draw'th up to my head
My vital humor that should keep my life;
This stream will never cease till I be dead.
Then welcome, death, and end my fatal strife;
No comfort in this life my woe can minish
But thou, who canst both life and sorrow finish.

"These are not sighs, for sighs some respite have;
My gripes, my pangs no respite do permit;
The blindfold boy made me a seeing slave
When from her eyes my heart he first did hit.
Now all inflamed, I burn, I rage and rave
And in the midst of flame consume no whit:
Love sitting in my heart, a master cruel,
Blows with his wings, feeds with his will the fuel.

"I am not I, the man that erst I was;
Orlando, he is burièd and dead;
His most ungrateful love (ah, foolish lass)
Hath killèd Orlando and cut off his head;
I am his ghost that up and down must pass
In this tormenting hell forever led,
To be a fearful sample and a just
To all such fools as put in love their trust."

Thus wandering still in ways that have no way,
He happed again to light upon the cave
Where, in remembrance of their pleasant play,
Medoro did that epigram engrave.
To see the stones again his woes display
And her ill name and his ill hap deprave
Did on the sudden all his sense enrage
With hate, with fury, with revenge and rage.

Straightways he draweth forth his fatal blade
And hews the stones; to heave'n the shivers flee;
Accursèd was that fountain, cave, and shade,
The arbor and the flowers and every tree;
Orlando of all places havoc made
Where he those names together joined may see;
Yea, to the spring he did perpetual hurt
By filling it with leaves, boughs, stones, and dirt.

And having done this foolish, frantic feat,
He lays him down all weary on the ground,
Distempered in his body with much heat,
In mind with pains that no tongue can expound;
Three days he doth not sleep nor drink nor eat,
But lay with open eyes as in a sound;
The fourth, with rage and not with reason wakèd,
He rents his clothes and runs about stark naked.

His helmet here he flings, his pouldrons there;
He casts away his curats and his shield;
His sword he throws away, he cares not where;
He scatters all his armor in the field;
No rag about his body he doth bear
As might from cold or might from shame him shield;
And save he left behind this fatal blade,
No doubt he had therewith great havoc made.

But his surpassing force did so exceed
All common men that neither sword nor bill
Nor any other weapon he did need;
Mere strength sufficed him to do what he will.
He roots up trees as one would root a weed;
And e'en as birders laying nets with skill
Pare slender thorns away with easy strokes,
So he did play with ashes, elms, and oaks.

The herdmen and the shepherds that did hear
The hideous noise and unacquainted sound
With fear and wonder great approachèd near
To see and know what was hereof the ground.—
But now I must cut off this treatise here
Lest this my book do grow beyond his bound;
And if you take some pleasure in this text,
I will go forward with it in the next.

The Twenty-fourth Canto

stanzas 1-14 of the Italian

Whoso shall set on Cupid's snares his foot
Must seek to draw it back lest it be caught;
And madness mere in love to overshoot
The fool hath felt, the wise hath ever taught;
And though in all alike it take not root,
Yet all shall find that love's a thing of nought,
For sure it is an open sign of madness
To have another's pleasure breed thy sadness.

Now though effects prove not in all alike,
Yet all are mad in sort, all go astray
As in a wilderness where men do seek
And more and more in seeking lose their way;
Wherefore let no man this my wish mislike
In whom fond love shall carry long the sway:
I wish for due reward such doting dolts,
Like willful pris'ners, store of iron bolts.

Some man perhaps will say, "What? Soft, my friend;
You spy our faults, in your own errors blind."
And true it is; yet speak I to this end,
To bring us both into a better mind.
As for myself, I hope ere long to mend
And from these bonds in time myself unwind,
Though it had ta'en in me such root I prove it
As hard 'tis on the sudden to remove it.

I showed you in the book that went before
By what mishap Orlando waxèd mad
And lost not only care of virtue's lore,
But reason, wit, and all the sense he had;
His armor he dispersed; his clothes he tore,
The very clothes wherewith his corpse was clad;
And though he wandered all unarmed and naked,
Yet at his presence all the country quakèd.

The countrymen that heard the noise aloof
Of trees that with their fall made no small crack
Came near and saw by plain and open proof
His monstrous strength, by their so monstrous wrack;
And straight they found it best for their behoof
With all the haste they could to get them back;
For those he caught he did this lesson teach,
To keep aloof from out a madman's reach.

Away they fled, but he pursued so fast
That some he caught, and some surprised with fear
Stood still, as oft it happens, all aghast,
Not knowing how to hide themselves nor where;
Some other ploughmen, seeing what had passed,
Thought it but little wit to tarry there,
But climbed, for fear, their houses and their churches,
Not trusting strength of elms, of beech and birches.

Among the rest he takes one by his heel
And with his head knocks out another's brain,
Which causèd both of them such pain to feel
As till Doomsday they never shall complain;
Another with his fist he made to reel
Till pain itself made him past sense of pain;
And when the men fled all away afeard,
Then with like rage he set upon their hèrd.

The voice of men, the bellowings of beast
About the country raised so great a sound
As might have well been heard five leagues at least;
And all the people straight were raisèd round,
Each man providing, as he could, the best
And for the present time might then be found,
With bows, with bills, with staves and pikes and prongs
To be revenged on these outrageous wrongs.

Look how the waves are driv'n by western blast
And one and one do rise still more and more
Until their force so great be at the last
They sprinkle all the banks and beat the shore:
So now these country folk came in so fast,
By two and three, a dozen and a score,
Till at the last they grew so great a number
Their very multitude themselves did cumber.

But when they saw their force could do no good
And that his skin so strange protection had
That though they smote thereon, they drew no blood,[1]
They thought that they might worse be thought than mad
To fight with one that all them so withstood;
Wherefore they parted home dismayed and sad.
The madman went unto the nearest village,
Although he carèd not for spoil or pillage;

And finding no man there, nor small nor great,
For all were fled away from thence for awe,
As famine forced him, he sought out some meat;
And were it fine or coarse, the first he saw
In greedy sort he doth devour and eat,
Not caring if it roasted were or raw;
And when thus homely he had ta'en repast,
About the country bedlamlike he passed.

He scares both man and beast without regard;
He takes swift goats and fallow deer in chase;
Sometimes a lion fierce, a boar, a pard
He kills by strength and swiftness of his pace.
At last he came whereas a knight[2] did guard
The passage of a bridge and by the place
Had built a tower of no small work and charge,
As shall be showed hereafter more at large.

1. Long before he went mad, an enchantment had protected Orlando's body from being harmed in any way.
2. Rodomont, whose bridge Orlando passes in Canto XXIX.

The Twenty-eighth Canto
stanzas 1-84 of the Italian

[To please the misogyny of the Saracen Rodomont, his host at an
inn recounts a tale.]

You ladies, ye that ladies hold in prize,
  Give not, perdie, your ear to this same tale
The which to tell, mine host doth here devise
To make men think your virtues are but small;
Though from so base a tongue there can arise
To your sweet sex no just disgrace at all,
Fools will find fault without the cause discerning
And argue most of that they have no learning.

Turn o'er the leaf and let this tale alone:
If any think the sex by this disgraced,
I write it for no spite nor malice none,
But in my author's book[1] I find it placed;
My loyal love to ladies all is known,
In whom I see such worth to be embraced
That theirs I am and glad would be therefore
To show thereof a thousand proofs and more.

Peruse it not, or if you do it read,
Esteem it not but as an idle babble;
Regard it not, or if you take some heed,
Believe it not but as a foolish fable.
But to the matter: thus it was indeed
When all the guests were chairèd at the table
Near Rodomont (so was the pagan named),
Down sate mine host, and thus his tale he framed:

"Astolfo,[2] whilom king of Lombardy,
To whom his elder brother left his reign,
Was in his youth so fresh and fair to see
As few to such perfection could attain;
Apelles' match or Zeuxis' he might be
That such a shape could paint without much pain;
Great was his grace, and all the world so deemed it,
But yet himself of all men most esteemed it.

"He did not of his scepter take such pride,
Nor that degree that common men are under,
Nor wealth, nor friends, nor meaner kings beside
That thereabout dwelt near or far asunder,
But of his beauty, which he would not hide,
At whose rare worth he thought the world did wonder:
This was his joy, and all that he intended
To hear his comely face and shape commended.

"Among his courtiers one above the rest,
Fausto by name, by birth a Roman knight,
Who hearing oft so praised, as they know best,
His face and hands and all that praise he might:
The king did bid him tell at his request,
Near or far off, if he had seen that wight
That in all parts so perfectly was wrought;
But he was answered as he little thought.

" 'My liege,' quoth Fausto, 'plainly to declare
Both what myself doth see and others say,
But few with your rare beauty can compare,
And that same few were none were one away:
Jocundo hight, a man of beauty rare
And brother mine, excepting whom I may
Prefer your grace before all other creatures,
But he doth match or pass you for his features.'

"The king to hear such tidings strange it thought
As having still till that day kept the prize,
And with a deep desire straightways he sought
To know this man and see him with his eyes;
In fine, with Fausto so far forth he wrought
To bring him to his court he must devise,
'Although,' quoth he, 'to bring my brother to it
I shall be sure of work enough to do it.

" 'The cause is this: my brother never went
Forth of the gates of Rome scant all his life,
And such small goods as Fortune hath him lent
He hath enjoyed in quiet, free from strife,
Left by our sire; and them he hath not spent
Nor yet increased, his gains are not so rife;
And he will think it more to go to Pavy
Than some would think to th'Indies in a navy.

" 'But I shall find it hardest when I prove
To draw him from his loving wife away,
To whom he is so linked in chains of love
That all is vain if once his wife say nay;
But yet your grace is so far all above
You shall command me, certes, all I may.'
'Thanks,' quoth the king and addeth such reward
As might have movèd any to regard.

"Away he posts, arriving in few days
At Rome, and to his brother's house he went,
And with such earnest words his brother prays
That to return with him he doth consent;
Also his sister's love he so allays
That she doth hold her peace as half content,
Beside great thanks, laying before her eyes
Preferments large that hereof might arise.

"Jocundo, now resolved to go his way,
Gets men and horse against he should depart,
Sets forth himself with new and rich array
As still we see nature adorned by art;
His wife at night in bed, at board by day,
With wat'ry eyes to show a sorry heart,
Complains his absence will so sore her grieve
Till his return she doubts she shall not live.

" 'Aye me, the thought,' quoth she, 'makes me so fraid
That scant the breath abideth in my breast.'
'Peace, my sweet love and life,' Jocundo said,
And weeps as fast and comforts her his best:
'So may good fortune aye my journey aid
As I return in three score days at least;
Nor will I change the day I set thee down,
No, though the king would grant me half his crown.'

"All this might not assuage this woman's pain:
'Two months were long, yea too-too long,' she cries;
'Needs must I die before you come again,
Nor how to keep my life can I devise;
The doleful days and nights I shall sustain
From meat my mouth, from sleep will keep mine eyes.'
Now was Jocundo ready to repent
That to his brother he had giv'n consent.

"About her neck a jewel rich she ware,
A cross all set with stone in gold well-tried;
This relic late a Boem[3] pilgrim bare
And gave her father other things beside,
Which costly things he kept with no small care
Till coming from Jerusalem he died,
And her of all his goods his heir he makes;
This precious cross to her goodman she takes,

"And prays him for her sake to wear that token
And think on her. The man, that was most kind,
Received it with more joy than can be spoken
Although he needed not be put in mind,
For why no time nor no state, sound nor broken,
Nor absence long a mean should ever find
To quail his love, not only while his breath
Maintains his life, but neither after death.

"That very night that went before the morrow
That they had pointed surely to depart
Jocundo's wife was sick and sounds for sorrow
Amid his arms, so heavy was her heart;
All night they wake, and now they bid Godmorrow
And give their last farewell, and so they part:
Jocundo on his way with all his train,
His loving wife doth go to bed again.

"Scant had Jocundo rode two mile forthright
But that his cross now came into his mind,
Which on his pillow he had laid last night
And now for haste had left the same behind;
He would devise to scuse it if he might,
But no excuse sufficient could he find
But that his love must needs be much suspected
To find the precious jewel so neglected.

"When no excuse within his mind could frame
But that all seemèd frivolous and vain,
To send his man he counted it a shame;
To go himself it was but little pain;
He stayed, and when his brother did the same,
'Ride soft,' quoth he, 'till I return again;
For home again I must, there is no nay;
But I will overtake you on the way.

" 'Th'affair is such as none can do but I,
But doubt you not I will return as fast.'
Away he spurs as hard as he could hie,
Alone without or man or page for haste;
Now had the sun's new rising cleared the sky
With brightest beams ere he the stream had passed;
He hies him home and finds his wife in bed
Full sound asleep, such cares were in her head.

"He draws the curtain softly, without sound,
And saw that he would little have suspected:
His chaste and faithful yokefellow he found
Yoked with a knave, all honesty neglected.
Th'adulterer, though sleeping very sound,
Yet by his face was easily detected,
A beggar's brat bred by him from his cradle
And now was riding on his master's saddle.

"Now if he stood amazed and discontent
Believe it, ye to try that would be loath,
For he that tries it doubtless will repent
As poor Jocundo did, who was so wroth
That out he drew his sword, with just intent
For their ungrateful act to kill them both.
But lo, the love he bare her did withstand
Against his heart to make him hold his hand.

"O ribald love that such a slave could'st make
Of one that now was subject to thy force!
He could not break her sleep for pity's sake
That brake all bonds of faith without remorse;
But back he goes before they did awake,
And from his house he gets him to his horse:
Love so pricks him, and he so pricks his steed,
He overtakes his company with speed.

"His look is sad; all changèd is his cheer;
Full heavy was his heart, they well perceived;
They see no cause of grief, nor guess they near,
And they that guess most likely are deceived;
They thought he went to Rome, but you do hear
How at Corneto[4] he his hurt received;
Each man espied that love procured that passion,
But none descried the manner nor the fashion.

"His brother deems that all his grief doth grow
Because his loving wife is left alone,
But he a clean contrary cause doth know:
Her too much company did cause his moan.
He bends his brows; his looks he casts alow
With pouting lips and many a grievous groan;
In vain doth Faustus comfort seek to bring him,
For why he knows not where the shoe doth wring him.

"He gives a salve afore the sore is found;
His plasters are as poison to the smart;
He seeks to heal and wider makes the wound;
He names his wife, but her name kills his heart.
Gone was his taste; his sleeps do grow unsound;
Nature decay'th, and little helpeth art;
And that fair face that erst was of such fame
Is now so changed it seemeth not the same.

"His eyes are sunk so deep into his head
It made his nose seem bigger than it should;
His flesh doth shrink; his bones do seem to spread;
He was so changed as more cannot be told;
At last an ague makes him keep his bed
And bait at inns more often than he would;
His fair complexion now is pale and witherèd,
Much like the rose that yesterday was gatherèd.

"With this mishap was Faustus sore aggrieved,
Not only for his brother's woeful state
But fearing of his prince to be reproved
Unto whose grace he undertook so late
To show the goodliest man, as he believed,
Now grown uncouth by force of inward bate;
Yet, as they could, their way they so contrived
That at the last in Pavy they arrived.

"He would not straightway show him to the king
Lest everyone might deem his judgment small,
But sent by letters notice of the thing
And what mishap his brother did befall:
How scant alive he could him thither bring,
A secret grief so greatly did him gall
And with an ague pulled him down so sore
He seemed not now the man he was before.

"And yet behold, this noble king is glad
That he is come, and means to make him cheer
As if he were the dearest friend he had,
So sore he had desired to see him here;
Nor would the worthy-natured prince be sad
In praise of beauty to have found a peer;
He knew Jocundo's beauty had excelled
But that by this disease it was expelled.

"He placeth him to his own lodging nigh;
He visits him each day and every hour;
Great plenty of provision he doth buy;
To welcome him he bendeth all his power.
But still Jocundo languishing doth lie;
His wife's misdeed makes all his sweet seem sour;
No songs, no sights which oft he heard or saw
One dram of this his dolor could withdraw.

"Fast by his lodging was amongst the rest
A fair large room which very few did use;
Here would he walk as one that did detest
All pleasing sights and comforts all refuse;
Here the wide wound he bare within his breast
With thousand thoughts unpleasant he renews;
Yet here he found, which few would have believed,
A remedy for that which had him grieved.

"For at the upper end of this old hall
There was a place of windows void and light
Save that the lime new molten from the wall
Let in a little beam that shinèd bright;
Here did he see, which some may think a tale,
A very strange and unexpected sight;
He heard it not, but saw it in his view,
Yet could he scant believe it should be true.

"For at the chink was plainly to be seen
A chamber hanged with fair and rich array
Where none might come but such as trusty been;
The princess here in part doth spend the day;
And here he saw a dwarf embrace the queen
And strive a while, and after homely play
His skill was such that ere they went asunder
The dwarf was got aloft and she lay under.

"Jocundo standeth still as one amazed,
Supposing sure that he had seen a vision;
But seeing plain, when he a while had gazed,
It was an act and not an apparition,
'Good God!' said he, 'are this queen's eyes so dazed
To love a dwarf, more worthy of derision,
Whose husband is a prince of worthy fame,
So brave a man, such love? Now fie, for shame.'

"He now began to hold his wife excused;
His anger now a little was relented;
And though that she her body had abused
And to her servant had so soon consented,
Not her for this, but he the sex accused
That never can with one man be contented.
'If all,' quoth he, 'with one like stain are spotted,
Yet on a monster mine was not besotted.'

"The day ensuing he returnèd thither
And saw the dwarf courageous still and jolly;
Eke he another day repairèd hither,
And still he found the queen committing folly;
He oft returns, he finds them oft together;
They cease not work on days profane nor holy;
Yea, which was strange, the goodly queen complained
That of the dwarf she found she was disdained.

"One day when in the corner he had stayed,
He sees her come all sad and malcontent
Because the dwarf his coming still delayed,
For whom of purpose twice before she sent.
Once more she sends; this answer brings the maid,
'Forsooth unto his play he is so bent
That for mistrust at chess to leese a shilling
To come to you the ape's face is not willing.'

"Jocundo, who before had still been sad,
Upon this sight became of better cheer;
The pains, the plaints, the cloudy storms he had
Away were blown; the coast began to clear;
Most ruddy fair he cheerful grew and glad
That angel-like his beauty did appear,
So as the king and others thought it strange
In so short time to find so great a change.

"Now as the king desirèd much to know
The mean whereby his hurt so soon was healed,
No less Jocundo did desire to show
And would not have the thing from him concealed,
So as his choler might no greater grow
Than his had been whenas it were revealed;
But first he made him swear on his salvation
Upon the parties to use no castigation.

"He made him swear, for aught he heard or saw
Wherewith his mind might fortune be diseased,
Yet from his choler so much to withdraw
As that in show he may not seem displeased,
Nor punish it by might nor yet by law,
Nor first nor last, but hold himself appeased,
So as th'offenders might not have suspected
That their misdeeds were to his grace detected.

"The king so sure, by oath so solemn bound,
As one that little thought his queen so stained:
Jocundo first his own grief doth expound,
Why he so long so doleful had remained,
And in whose arms his own wife he had found,
And how the grief thereof so sore him pained,
Had not a salve unlooked-for been applied,
Of that conceit no doubt he should have died.

" 'But lying in your highness' house forlorn,
I saw,' quoth he, 'that minished much my moan;
For though it grievèd me to wear a horn,
It pleased me well I ware it not alone.'
This said, he brought him where the wall was torn
And showed him that that made his heart to groan,
For why the dwarf did manage with such skill,
Though she curvets, he keeps his stirrup still.

"Much did the king this foul prospect mislike
(Believe my words, I say; I need not swear);
Horn wood he was; he was about to strike
All those he met and his own flesh to tear;
His promise to have broken he was like
If of his oath he had not had some fear;
But unrevengèd all must now be borne,
For on his agnusdei he had sworn.

"Now to Jocundo gently he doth speak,
'Good brother mine, advise me what to do;
Sith I am bound by oath, I may not wreak
The fact with such revenge as longs thereto.'
'Forsooth, let's try if others be as weak,'
Jocundo said, 'and make no more ado.'
This was the counsel he did give the king,
Into their order other men to bring:

" 'We both are young and of such pleasing hue,
Not to be matched with such another pair:
What she will be so obstinately true
But will be won with youth and being fair?
If youth and beauty both do miss their due,
The want herein our purses shall repair.
Let us not spare our beauty, youth, and treasure
Till of a thousand we have had our pleasure.

" 'To see strange countries placèd far apart,
Of other women eke to make some trial
Will ease the pain that whilom pierced our heart
And salve our sore, there can be no denial.'
The king that longed to ease his newfound smart
Consented straight; and to avoid espial
Himself, the knight, two pages, and no mo
Out of the realm forthwith disguisèd go.

"Away they passed through Italy and France
And through the Flemish and the English land;
And those whose beauties highest did advance,
Those still they found most ready to their hand.
They give, they take, so lucky is their chance
To see their stock at one stay still to stand;
Some must be wooed forsooth, they were so chaste,
And some there were that wooèd them as fast.

"In countries some a month or two they tarrièd,
In some a week, in others but a day;
In all of them they find the women marrièd
Like to their wives, too gentle to say nay.
At last, because they doubt to have miscarrièd,
They mean to leave this sport and go their way;
They found it full of danger and debate
To keep their standings in another's gate.

"They do agree to take by common voice
Some one whose shape and face may please them both,
In whom without suspect they might rejoice;
'For wherefore,' quoth the king, 'should I be loath
To have yourself a partner in my choice?
I must have one, and I believe for troth
Among all womenkind there is not one
That can content herself with one alone.

" 'But of some one we two might take our pleasure
And not enforce ourselves beyond our ease,
But as they say, take meat and drink and leisure
And by our doings other not displease.
Well might that woman think she had a treasure
That had us two her appetite to please;
And though to one man faithful none remain,
No doubt but faithful they would be to twain.'

"The Roman youth much praised the prince's mind
And to perform it seemèd very fain;
Away they posted as they had assigned,
By town and city, over hill and plain,
Till at the last a pretty piece they find,
The daughter of an innkeeper in Spain,
A girl of person tall and fair of favor,
Of comely presence and of good behavior.

"She was new ent'ring in the flower and pride
Of those well-pleasing youthful years and tender;
Her father many children had beside,
And poverty had made his portion slender;
And for them all unable to provide,
It made him soon consent away to send her;
The price agreed, away the strangers carry her
Because the father money wants to marry her.

"In concord great she did with them remain,
Who took their pleasure one and one by turn,
As bellows do where Vulcan's wonted pain
By mutual blast doth make the metal burn.
Their meaning is, now they have traveled Spain,
By Syphax' realm[5] to make their home return;
And having left Valenza out of sight,
At fair Zativa[6] they did lodge at night.

"The masters go abroad to view the town,
And first the churches for devotion's sake
And then the monuments of most renown,
As travelers a common custom take;
The girl within the chamber sate her down;
The men are busied; some the beds do make,
Some care to dress their wearied horse, and some
Make ready meat against their masters come.

"In this same house the girl a Greek had spied
That in her father's house a boy had been
And slept full often sweetly by her side,
And much good sport had passèd them between;
Yet fearing lest their love should be descried,
In open talk they durst not to be seen;
But when by hap the pages down were gone,
Old love renewed, and thus they talk thereon.

"The Greek demands her whither she was going
And which of those two great estates her keeps;
She told them all (she needs no further wooing)
And how anight between them both she sleeps.
'Ah,' quoth the Greek, 'thou tellest my undoing,
My dear Fiametta,' and with that he weeps;
'With these two lords wilt thou from Spain be banished?
Are all my hopes thus into nothing vanished?

" 'My sweet designments turnèd are to sour;
My service long finds little recompence.
I made a stock, according to my power,
By hoarding up my wages and the pence
That guests did give that came in lucky hour;
I meant ere long to have departed hence
And to have asked thy sire's good will to marry thee,
And that obtained, unto a house to carry thee.'

"The wench of her hard fortune doth complain
And saith that now she doubts he sues too late;
The Greek doth sigh and sob and part doth fain;
'And shall I die,' quoth he, 'in this estate?
Let me enjoy thy sweetness once again
Before my days draw to their doleful date;
One small refreshing ere we quite depart
Will make me die with more contented heart.'

"The girl, with pity movèd, thus replies,
'Think not,' quoth she, 'but I desire the same;
But hard it is among so many eyes
Without incurring punishment and shame.'
'Ah,' quoth the Greek, 'some means thou wouldst devise,
If thou but felt a quarter of my flame,
To meet this night in some convenient place
And be together but a little space.'

" 'Tush,' answered she, 'you sue now out of season,
For every night I lie betwixt them two,
And they will quickly fear and find the treason
Sith still with one of them I have to do.'
'Well,' quoth the Greek, 'I could refute that reason
If you would put your helping hand thereto;
You must,' said he, 'some pretty scuse devise
And find occasion from them both to rise.'

"She first bethinks herself and after bad
He should return when all were sound asleep,
And learnèd him, who was thereof right glad,
To go and come what order he should keep.
Now came the Greek, as he his lesson had,
When all was hushed, as soft as he could creep,
First to the door, which opened when he pushed,
Then to the chamber, which was softly rushed.

"He takes a long and leisurable stride,
And longest on the hinder foot he stayed;
So soft he treads, although his steps were wide,
As though to tread on eggs he were afraid;
And as he goes, he gropes on either side
To find the bed with hands abroad displayed;
And having found the bottom of the bed,
He creepeth in, and forward go'th his head.

"Between Fiametta's tender thighs he came,
That lay upright as ready to receive;
At last they fell unto their merry game,
Embracing sweetly now to take their leave;
He rode in post, ne can he bait for shame;
The beast was good and would not him deceive;
He thinks her pace so easy and so sure
That all the night to ride he could endure.

"Jocundo and the king do both perceive
The bed to rock, as oft it comes to pass,
And both of them one error did deceive,
For either thought it his companion was.
Now hath the Greek taken his latter leave,
And as he came, he back again doth pass;
And Phoebus' beams did now to shine begin;
Fiametta rose and let the pages in.

"Now with Jocundo gan the king to jest:
'Brother,' quoth he, 'I doubt we do you wrong;
It were more time for you to take your rest
That have this night a journey rode so long.'
Jocundo answers him again in jest,
'O sir, you do mistake; you sing my song;
Take you your ease, and much good do your grace,
That all this night have rid a hunting pace.'

" 'I?' quoth the king. 'I would, in faith I swear,
Have lent my dog a course among the rest,
But that I found yourself so busy were
And rode so hard you could not spare the beast.'
'Well,' said the knight, 'it seemeth me to bear;
Although you brake your promise and behest,
Yet privy quips and taunts here needed none;
You might have bid me let the wench alone.'

"One urged so far, the t'other so replied
That unto bitter words their tongues were moved;
Scarce one forbare to say the t'other lied;
And plain to try whose truth should be reproved,
They called the girl the matter to decide,
Who was afraid as well it her behooved;
And she must tell, they standing face to face,
Which of them two deservèd this disgrace.

" 'Tell,' quoth the king with grim and angry sight,
'Nor fear not him nor me, but tell us true
Which of us two it was that all this night
So gallantly performèd all his due.'
Thus either deeming he did hold the right,
They lookèd both which should be found untrue.
Fiametta lowly laid herself on ground,
Doubting to die because her fault was found.

"She humbly pardon craves for her offence
And that they pity would her woeful case
That she with pity moved to recompence
His love that lasted had no little space;
And who it was she told them and of whence
Had this ill luck in this unlucky place,
How she had hoped that though they happed to wake,
Yet for his partner either would it take.

"The king and his companion greatly mused
When they had heard the practice so detected,
And their conceits not little were confused
To hear a hap so strange and unexpected;
And though no two were ever so abused,
Yet had they so all wrathful mind rejected
That down they lay and fell in such a laughter
They could not see nor speak an hour after.

"And when at last their stomachs and their eyes
Watered and ached, they laughèd had so much,
'Such shifts,' quoth they, 'these women will devise,
Do what we can, their chastity is such;
If both our cares could not for one suffice
That lay betwixt us both and did us touch,
If all our hairs were eyes, yet sure,' they said,
'We husbands of our wives should be betrayed.

" 'We had a thousand women proved before,
And none of them denièd our request
Nor would and if we tried ten thousand more,
But this one trial passeth all the rest;
Let us not then condemn our wives so sore
That are as chaste and honest as the best;
Sith they be as all other women be,
Let us turn home and well with them agree.'

"When on this point they both were thus resolved,
They gave the Greek Fiametta for his wife
And tied the knot that cannot be dissolved,
With portion large to keep them all their life;
Themselves went home and had their sins absolved
And take again their wives and end all strife."
And thus mine host the pretty story ended,
With which he pray'th them not to be offended.

The pagan prince of whom I erst made mention
Was pleasèd with this story passing well
And heard the same with heed and great attention
And praisèd it and said it did excel
And swears he thought no wit nor no invention,
No pen could write, no tongue attain to tell,
By force of eloquence or help of art,
Of women's treacheries the hundredth part.

But at the table sate another guest,
Of riper years and judgment more discreet,
Who such untruths to hear could not digest
And see their praises so trod under feet;
Wherefore his speech he presently addressed
Unto his host and said, "We daily meet
With slanders and with lying fables told,
And this is one, to say I dare be bold.

"Nor thee nor him that told thee trust I will,
No, though in other things he gospel spake;
I dare affirm it well that evil will,
Not any trial that himself could make,
Moved him of all the kind to speak so ill,
Belike for some one naughty woman's sake;
But he that would enter in women's praise
On higher steps aloft his style might raise.

"But tell me now if any one of you
That married are have not awry yet stepped?
No, scarce a man that hath not been untrue
And with some other woman hath not slept;
Nay, that is more, they woo, they seek, they sue,
They try, they tempt those that be safest kept;
Yet women seek not after men, I ween
(I mean not such as common harlots been).

"Surely the man on whom your tale you father
Cannot himself nor other men excuse
Who still to take an unknown piece had rather
Although their own were better far to choose;
But if themselves were wooed, I surely gather
Such courtesies they never would refuse
But rather strain themselves beyond their might
Such kindness with more kindness to requite.

"But be't some woman breaks chaste wedlock's laws
And leaves her husband and becomes unchaste,
Yet commonly it is not without cause;
She sees her man in sin his substance waste;
She feels that he his love from her withdraws
And hath on some perhap less worthy placed:
Who strikes with sword, the scabbard him may strike;
And sure love craveth love, like asketh like.

"Indeed in their behalf agree would I
That all wives that adult'ry do commit
Should by a law condemnèd be to die
If so their husbands guiltless be of it;
But if that men unpunished walk awry,
Doubtless in sense and reason 'tis not fit
The weaker sex should for this sin be vexed;
'Do as you would be done to,' saith the text.

"Yet when a man is bent to speak his worst
That in despite he can of women say,
He calls them but incontinent and cursed;
No greater fault he to their charge can lay.
To rob, to spoil, houses to break and burst,
Whole cities, towns, and countries to betray,
Usury, murder, all such sins appear
Proper to men; women of them are clear."

This said this grave wise man and would have told
Some story to the same, his speech to verify,
Of women that had lived till they were old
Chastely and virtuously and with sincerity
But that the cruel Turk[7] did him behold
With so grim look as did the poor man terrify
And made him hold his peace with threats and terror,
Yet hating inwardly the pagan's error.

1. The book of Archbishop Turpin, Ariosto's supposed source.

2. Not, of course, the English prince of the same name who has already appeared in Canto VI; Ariosto attaches his fiction in the present case to the historical Astolfo, King of Lombardy (see Canto XXXIII, footnote 5).

3. Bohemian.

4. A real city northwest of Rome; but here there is a pun on *corn* (horn) with reference to the horns of cuckolds.

5. Numidia.

6. Játiva in southeastern Spain.

7. Saracen.

The Thirty-second Canto

stanzas 10-110 of the Italian

[Rogero, who is a Saracen by nurture, continues to serve King Agramant in spite of being betrothed to the Christian heroine Bradamant; and he has written her that this service will require him to be away from her for fifteen or twenty days at most.]

THIS while what torments Bradamant endurèd,
Those twenty days how did she wail and mourn!
Against which time she thought herself assurèd
Her love to her and to the faith should turn;
She makes no doubt but he might have procurèd
Within that space to make his home return
(Yea though he were in prison kept or banishèd)
If troth and care of promise were not vanishèd.[1]

In this long looking she would often blame
The fiery coursers of the heavenly light;
She thought that Phoebus' wheels were out of frame
Or that his chariot was not in good plight;
Great Joshua's day[2] seemed shorter than these same,
And shorter seemed the false Amphitryon's night;[3]
Each day and night she thought was more than doubled,
So fancy blind her sense and reason troubled.

She now envies the dormouse of his rest
And wished some heavy sleep might overtake her
Wherewith she might most deadly be possessed
Till her Rogero should return to wake her;
But waking cares aye lodgèd in her breast
That her desired sleep did quite forsake her;
To sleep so long doth so much pass her power
She cannot frame her eyes to wink one hour,

But turns and tosses in her restless bed
(Alas, no turning turns her cares away);
Oft at the window she puts forth her head
To see how near it waxeth unto day;
When by the dawning darksome night is fled,
She notwithstanding stands at that same stay;
And during all the time the day doth last,
She wishes for the night again as fast.

When fifteen days were of the twenty spent,
She grows in hope that his approach is nigh;
Then from a tower with eyes to Paris bent
She waits and watches if she can descry
At least some messenger that he hath sent
May bring the news where her sweetheart doth lie
And satisfy her mind by what hard chance
He is constrained to stay so long in France.

If far aloof the shine of armor bright
Or anything resembling it she spies,
She straightway hopes it is her only knight
And wipes her face and clears her blubbered[4] eyes;
If anyone unarmed do come in sight,
It may be one from him she doth surmise;
And though by proof she find each hope untrue,
She ceaseth not for that to hope anew.

Sometime all armed she mounteth on her steed
And so rides forth in hope to meet her dear,
But soon some fancy her conceit doth feed
That he is passed some other way more near;
Then homeward hasteth she with as much speed;
Yet she at home no news of him can hear.
From day to day she passeth on this fashion,
Hither and thither tossèd with her passion.

Now when her twenty days were full expired
And that beside were passèd some days more,
Yet not Rogero come whom she desired,
Her heart with care and sorrows waxèd sore;
With cries and plaints the woods and caves she tired,
Her breasts she beat, her golden locks she tore,
Nor while these gripes of grief her heart embrace,
Doth she forbear her eyes or angel's face.

"Why then," quoth she, "beseems it me in vain
To seek him still who thus from me doth slide?
Shall I esteem of him that doth disdain
My suit and scorn the torments I abide?
Him in whose heart a hate of me doth reign,
Him that accounts his virtues so well tried
As though some goddess should from heav'n descend
Before that he his heart to love would bend?

"Though stout he is, he knows how well I love him
And how I honor him with soul and heart;
Yet can my hot affection nothing move him
To let me of his love possess some part;
And lest he might perceive it would behoove him
To ease my grief if he did know my smart,
To give me hearing of my plaint he fears
As to the charm the adder stops his ears.[5]

"Love, stop his course that doth so loosely range
And flit so fast before my sorry pace;
Or with my former state else let me change
When I sought not to track thy tedious trace.
I hope in vain; remorse to thee is strange;
Thou dost triumph upon my piteous case;
For hearts thy meat, thy drink is lovers' tears,
Their cries the music doth delight thine ears.

"But whom blame I? It was my fond desire
That first enticed me to his killing call
And made me past my reach so far aspire
That now I feel the greater is my fall;
For when aloft my wings be touched with fire,
Then farewell flight, and I am left to fall;
But still they spring, and still I upward tend,
And still I see my fall and find no end.

"Desire, quoth I? myself I was too light
To give desire an entrance in my breast,
Who when he had my reason put to flight
And of my heart himself was full possessed,
No room for joy is left or heart's delight,
Since I do harbor this unruly guest
Who though he guide me to my certain fall,
The long expectance grieves me worst of all.

"Then mine the fault be, if it be a fault,
To love a knight deserves to be belovèd,
With all good inward parts so richly fraught,
Whose virtues be so known and well approvèd;
And more, whom would not his sweet face have caught?
Myself, I must confess, his beauty movèd:
What blind, unhappy wretch were she would shun
The pleasing prospects of the precious sun!

"Beside my destiny which drew me on,
By others' sugarèd speech I was entrainèd,
As though I should by this great match anon
Another Paradise on earth have gainèd;
But now their words into the wind be gone,
And I in Purgatory am restrainèd.
Well may I Merlin curse, the false deceiver;
Yet my Rogero I shall love forever.

"I hoped of Merlin's and Melissa's promises,
Who did such stories of our race foretell:[6]
Is this the profit of believing prophecies
And giving credit to the sprites of Hell?
Alas, they might have found them better offices
Than me to flout that trusted them so well;
But all for envy have they wrought me this
So to bereave me of my former bliss."

Thus sighs and lamentations are not feignèd;
Small place was left for comfort in her breast;
Yet spite of sorrows hope was entertainèd,
And though with much ado, yet in it pressed
To ease her mourning heart when she complainèd
And giving her sometimes some little rest,
By sweet remembrance of the words he spake
When he was forced of her his leave to take.

The minding of those words did so recure
Her wounded heart that she was well content
For one month's space his absence to endure,
Yea when his days of promise quite were spent;
Yet still she looked for him, you may be sure,
And many a time that way she came and went
Till by the way at last such news she heard
That all the hope she had before was marred.

For she by chance did meet a Gascon knight
That in the wars of Africa was caught,
One that was taken captive in that fight
Then when fore Paris the great field was fought.
What she requires to know he could recite;
But careless of the other news he brought,
Of her Rogero chiefly she inquires;
To hear of him is all that she desires.

Of whom the knight could let her understand,
For in that court he late his life had led:
How Mandricard and he fought hand to hand
And how much blood on either part was shed,
And though by wounds himself in peril stand,
That he subdued his foe and left him dead.[7]
Now if with this his story he had ended,
Rogero's scuse had very well been mended.

But he proceeds to tell how one was there,
A lady hight Marfisa,[8] in the field
Whose fame for martial acts did shine most clear,
Whose beauty rare to few or none did yield;
Rogero her, she held Rogero dear;
They never were asunder or but seld;
And that they two, as everyone there saith,
The t'one the t'other plighted have their faith;

And if Rogero once were whole and sound,
Their wedding should be celebrate with speed;
That such a pair as yet was never found,
And happy they should come of such a seed;
How much it joyed the pagan princes round
To think upon the race they two should breed,
Which likely were all others to excel
In feats of arms that erst on earth did dwell.

The Gascon knight of all that he had said
Himself had reason to believe was sooth;
So general a fame thereof was spread
There were but few but had it in their mouth;
Some little kindness she did use had fed
Their foolish humor of this false untruth.
Still fame will grow if once abroad it fly
Although the ground be troth or be a lie.

They came indeed together to this fight,
And many times together they were seen,
For he was warlike, stout, and worthy knight,
And she a gallant, fair, and dainty queen;
By which suspicion, never judging right,
Did gather straight they had assurèd been,
And specially because when she departed,
To visit him she was so soon reverted.

Of just suspect their reason was but slender
If they had weighèd well their virtues rare,
Though of his wounds she seemed to be so tender
And of his danger had so great a care;
Against bad tongues no goodness can defend her,
For those most free from faults they least will spare,
But prate of them whom they have scantly known
And judge their humors to be like their own.

Now when the knight avowed the tale he told
(And yet in truth you know 'twas but a tale),
The damsel's heart was touched with shivering cold;
The little hope she had, away it stale;
Almost in sound her seat she scarce could hold;
With mourning cheer and face both wan and pale
She said no more, but mad with grief and ire,
Her horse she turned and homeward did retire.

And all in armor on her bed she lies;
She wished a thousand times she now were dead;
She bites the sheets to damp her sobs and cries,
The Gascon's news still beating in her head;
Her heart is swoll'n, and blubbered be her eyes;
With trickling tears bedewèd is her bed.
When grief would be no longer holden in,
Needs must it out, and thus it doth begin:

"Ah, wretched me, whom might a maiden find
In whom she might be bold to put her trust
Since you, Rogero mine, become unkind
And tread your faith and promise in the dust?
You, only you mine eye so far did blind
I still esteemed you faithful, true, and just.
Ah, never wench that lovèd so sincerely
Was in requital punished so severely.

"Why, my Rogero, why do you forget,
Sith you in beauty pass each other knight
And do in feats of arms such honor get
As none can match your chivalry in fight,
This golden virtue with the rest to set
By which your glorious name will shine more bright,
If as in other graces you abound,
So in your promise constancy were found?

"This is the virtue breeds most estimation,
By which all other virtues show more clear,
As things most fair do lose their commendation
Which by the want of light cannot appear.
What glory was it by false protestation
Her to deceive whose saint and god you were,
Whom your fair speeches might have made believe
That water would be carried in a sieve?

"From any heinous act wouldst thou refrain
That murd'rest her who bears thee so good will?
How wouldst thou use thy foe that thus in pain
Dost let thy friend to be tormented still?
Thou that with breach of faith thy heart doth stain,
No doubt thou dost not care for doing ill.
Well this I know, that God is ever just;
He will ere long revenge my wrongs, I trust,

"For why unthankfulness is that great sin
Which made the Devil and his angels fall,
Lost him and them the joys that they were in,
And now in Hell detains them bound and thrall;
Then mark the guerdon thou art like to win,
For why like faults like punishment do call,
In being thus unthankful unto me
That always was so faithful unto thee.

"Beside of theft thyself thou canst not quit
If theft it be to take that is not thine,
The keeping of my heart. No, that's not it:
That thou shouldst have it I do not repine;
Thyself thou stalst, which I cannot remit;
Thyself thou knowst thou art, or shouldst be, mine;
Thou knowst damnation doth to them belong
That do keep back another's right by wrong.

"Though thou, Rogero, do forsake me so,
I cannot will nor choose but love thee still;
And since there is no measure of my woe,
Death is the only way to end mine ill.
But thus to cut off life, and thou my foe,
It makes me do it with a worser will;
Yet had I died when best I did thee please,
I should have counted death no death, but ease."

When with these words she was resolved to die,
She took her sword in hand for that intent
And forced herself upon the point to lie;
Her armor then her purpose did prevent,
A better spirit[9] checked her by and by,
And in her heart this secret reason went,
"O noble lady born to so great fame,
Wilt thou thus end thy days with so great shame?

"Nay rather, if thou beest resolved to die,
Unto the camp why dost thou not repair
Where bodies of brave knights in heaps do lie?
Lo, there, to honor the directest stair,
The loss of life with glory thou mayst buy;
To die in thy Rogero's sight were fair,
And happily by him thou mayst be slain;
So he that wrought thy woe may rid thy pain.

"Thou mayst be sure Marfisa there to see
Who hath so falsely stol'n away thy friend;
If first on her thou couldst revengèd be,
With more contented mind thy days would end."
Unto this counsel she doth best agree
And onward on this journey straight doth tend.
She takes a new device that might imply
A desperation and a will to die;

The color of her bases was almost
Like to the falling whitish leaves and dry
Which when the moisture of the branch is lost,
Forsakenly about the tree doth lie,
With cypress trunks embroidered and embossed,
For cypress once but cut will always die:
A fine conceit, she thinks, to represent
In secret sort her inward discontent.

She took Astolfo's horse[10] and Goldielance
As fittest both for this her present feat;
That spear could make the bravest knight to dance
And caper, with a touch, beside his seat;
But where Astolfo had it, by what chance,
Or why he gave it need I not repeat.[11]
She took it, notwithstanding her election
Not knowing of that magical confection.[12]

Thus all alone, without both squire and page,
Thus furnishèd she set herself in way;
To Parisward she traveled in a rage
Whereas the camp of Sar'cens lately lay
And, as she thought, kept up King Charles in cage,
Not understanding how before that day
Renaldo, aiding Charles with Malagige,
Had forcèd them from thence to raise their siege.

Now had she left Mount Dordon[13] at her back
When little way behind her she descried
A gallant damsel following of her track,
A shield of gold unto her saddle tied;
Of squires and other servants none did lack,
And three brave knights were riding by her side;
But of the squires that overtook her last
She asked one what those were that by her passed.

And straight the worthy lady it was told
How from Pole Arctic that same damsel came,
Sent from a queen, with that fair shield of gold,
Unto King Charles that there was known by fame,
But so as he must this condition hold,
That on a knight he must bestow the same,
Such one as he in his imagination
For prowess deemed most worthy reputation.

For she of Iceland Isle that holds the reign
And is and knows it that she is most fair
Doth think she should her worth not little stain,
And her great fame and honor much impair,
If any knight her isle and her should gain
Except he stood so high on honor's stair
As that he were adjudged in feats of war
The primer man and passing others far.

Wherefore the cause she sends to France is this:
She thinks if she shall find one anywhere,
That in the court of France he surely is,
And therefore she doth send to seek him there.
As for those three, because you shall not miss
To know the truth, I'll tell you what they were;
They were three kings of whom great fame there go'th:
Of Norway one, one Swethland, one of Goth.[14]

These three, though far they dwell from Iceland Isle,
Yet love of that same queen hath brought them hither
(This isle is called Perduta otherwhile
Because the seamen leese it in foul weather);
These kings lived from their country in exile
And to this queen were suitors all together;
And she, that knew not well how to forbid them,
With this same pretty shift from thence she rid them.

She saith she minds to wed for her behoof
That wight that most excels in warlike action;
"And though," quoth she, "you show no little proof
Of value here, as 'twere in private faction,
Yet I must have you tried more far aloof
Before my mind can have full satisfaction;
Wherefore I mean myself and crown to yield
Alone to him that bringeth back my shield."

This is the cause that these three kings did move
Each one to come from so remote a nation
With purpose firm their utmost force to prove,
To win the golden shield with reputation
Or leese their lives for that fair lady's love
If that they failèd of their expectation.—[15]
When he had told her thus, he her forsook,
And soon his company he overtook.

The damsel rode a softer pace behind,
And so as in a while she lost their sight,
And often she revolvèd in her mind
The tale the fellow told, with small delight;
She doubts this shield bestowed in such a kind
Will be in France a cause of brawl and fight;
That this will be a means she greatly fears
To set her kin together all by th'ears.

This fancy moved her much, but more than this
That former jealous fancy did her move
That her Rogero's kindness altered is,
That on Marfisa he had placed his love;
This so possessed her sense that she did miss
Her way, nor never thought as did behoove,
Till night was almost come and sun nigh set,
Where she a lodging for herself may get.

E'en as an empty vessel that was tied
Unto the wharf with some old rotten cable,
If that the knot do hap to break or slide
So that to hold it be no longer able,
Is borne away as please the wind and tide:
So Bradamant with mind and thoughts unstable
Was in such muse as she the right way missed
And so was borne where Rabicano list.

But when she saw the sun was almost set,
She took more heed; and asking of a clown,
A shepherd that by hap thereby she met,
Where she might lodging get ere sun went down,
The shepherd made her answer that as yet
She was almost three leagues[16] from any town
Or other place where she might eat or lodge,
Save at a castle called Sir Tristram's Lodge.

But everyone that list is not assurèd,
Though he do thither come, to stay therein;
To martial feats they must be well inurèd;
With spear and shield they must their lodging win;
Such custom in the place hath long endurèd,
And many years ago it did begin;
Wherefore 'tis good that one be well advisèd
Ere such an act by him be enterprisèd.

In brief, thus is their order: if a knight
Do find the lodging void, they him receive
With promise that if more arrive that night,
Either he shall to them his lodging leave
Or else with each of them shall prove in fight
Which of them can of lodging t'other reave;
If none do come that night, he shall in quiet
Have both his horsemeat, lodging, and his diet.

If four or five do come together first,
The castle-keeper them must entertain;
Who cometh single after hath the worst,
For if he hope a lodging there to gain,
He must, according to that law accursed,
Fight with all those that did therein remain;
Likewise if one come first and more come later,
He must go fight with them yet ne'er the later.

The like case is if any maid or dame
Do come alone or else accompanièd;
Both they that first and they that latest came
Must by a jury have their beauties trièd;
Then shall the fairest of them hold the same,
But to the rest that come shall be denièd.—
Thus much the shepherd unto her did say
And with his finger showed to her the way.

About four miles[17] was distant then the place;
The damsel thither hastes with great desire,
And though that Rabicano trot apace,
Yet was the way so deep and full of mire,
The snow and drift still beating in their face,
She later came than manners good require;
But though it were as then both dark and late,
She boldly bouncèd at the castle gate.

The porter told her that the lodgings all
Were filled by knights that late before them took,
Who now stood by the fire amid the hall
And did ere long to have their supper look.
"Well," answers she, "then have they cause but small,
If they be supperless, to thank the cook;
I know," quoth she, "the custom and will keep it
And mean to win their lodging ere I sleep yet."

The porter went and did her message bold
To those great states then standing by the fire,
Who took small pleasure when they heard it told,
For thence to part they had so small desire
Now chiefly when 'twas rainy, dark, and cold;
But so their oath and order did require
That they must do it were it cold or warm,
And therefore quickly they themselves did arm.

These were those three great kings whom that same day
Dame Bradamant had seen but few hours past,
Though they had sooner finishèd their way
Because she rode so soft and they so fast.
Now when they were all armed, they make no stay
But all on horseback mount themselves at last.
No doubt but few in strength these three did pass;
Yet of those few, sure one this damsel was,

Who purposed, as it seemeth, nothing less
Than in so wet and in so cold a night
To lack a lodging and sleep supperless.
Now those within at windows see the fight;
The men themselves on horseback do address
To look thereon for why the moon gave light;[18]
And thus at last, though first 'twere somewhat late,
They did abase the bridge and ope the gate.

E'en as a secret and lascivious lover
Rejoiceth much when after long delays
And many fears in which his hope did hover
He hears at last the noise of pretty keys:
So Bradamant, that hopes not to recover
A lodging, for the which so long she stays,
Did in her mind in such like sort rejoice
Whenas she heard the watchful porter's voice.

Now when those knights and some few of their train
Were past the bridge, the dame her horse doth turn
To take the field, and then with speed again
With full career she doth on them return
And couched that spear yet never couched in vain,
For whom it hits it still doth overturn.
This spear her cousin, when he went from France,
Gave unto her; the name was Goldielance.

The valiant king of Swethland was the first
That met her, and the next the king of Goth;
The staff doth hit them full and never burst,
But from their saddles it did heave them both.
But yet the king of Norway sped the worst;
It seemed to leave his saddle he was loath;
His girses brake, and he fell upside down
In danger with the mire to choke and drown.

Thus with three blows, three kings she down did bear
And hoist their heels full high, their heads full low;
Then entered she the castle void of fear;
They stand without that night in rain and snow;
Yet ere she could get in, one caused her swear
To keep the custom which they made her know;
And then the master doth to her great honor
And entertainment great bestowèd on her.

Now when the lady did disarm her head,
Off with her helmet came her little caul,
And all her hair her shoulders overspread,
And both her sex and name was known withal,
And wonder great and admiration bred
In them that saw her make three princes fall,
For why she showed to be in all their sight
As fair in face as she was fierce in fight.

E'en as a stage set forth with pomp and pride
Where rich men cost and cunning art bestow,
When curtains be removed that all did hide,
Doth make by light of torch a glittering show,
Or as the sun that in a cloud did bide,
When that is gone, doth clearer seem to grow:
So Bradamant whenas her head was barest,
Her color and her beauty seemèd rarest.

Now stood the guests all round about the fire,
Expecting food, with talk their ears yet feeding,
While everyone doth wonder and admire
Her speech and grace, the others all exceeding,
The while her host to tell she doth desire
From whence and whom this custom was proceeding
That men were driv'n unto their great disquiet
To combat for their lodging and their diet.

"Fair dame," said he, "sometime there ruled in France
King Feramont,[19] whose son, a comely knight,
Clodian by name, by good or evil chance
Upon a lovely lady did alight;
But as we see it oftentimes doth chance
That jealousy in love mars man's delight,
Thus he of her in time so jealous grew
He durst not let her go out of his view.

"Nor ever Argus kept the milk-white cow
More straight than Clodian here did keep his wife;
Ten knights eke to this place he doth allow
Thereby for to prevent all casual strife.
Thus hope and fear between, I know not how,
As he prolongs his self-tormenting life,
The good Sir Tristram thither did repair,
And in his company a lady fair,

"Whom he had rescued but a little since
From giant's hand with whom he did her find.
Sir Tristram sought for lodging with the prince,
For then the sun was very low declined;
But as a horse with gallèd back will wince,
E'en so our Clodian with as gallèd mind,
For casting doubts and dreading every danger,
Would by no means be won to lodge a stranger.

"Whenas Sir Tristram long had prayed in vain
And still denied the thing he did demand,
'That which I cannot with your will obtain,
In spite of you,' said he, 'I will command;
I will here prove your villainy most plain
With lance in rest and with my sword in hand';
And straight he challengèd the combat then
To fight with Clodian and the other ten.

"Thus only they agreed upon the case:
If Clodian and his men were overthrown,
That all then presently should void the place
And that Sir Tristram there should lie alone.
Sir Clodian to avoid so great disgrace
The challenge took, for why excuse was none;
In fine both Clodian and his men well knocked
And from the castle that same night were locked.

"Triumphant Tristram to the castle came,
And for that night, as on his own, he seizèd,
And there he saw the prince's lovely dame
And talked with her, who him not little pleasèd.[20]
This while Sir Clodian was in part with shame
And more with thought and jealous fear diseasèd,
Disdaining not in humble sort to woo him
By message mild to send his wife unto him.

"But he, though her he do not much esteem,
For why by means of an enchanted potion
Isotta fairest unto him did seem,
To whom he vowèd had his whole devotion,
Yet for he did the jealous Clodian deem
Some plague to merit, he denied his motion
And swears it were no manners nor no reason
A lady to unlodge at such a season.

" 'But if,' saith he, 'it do his mind offend
To lie all night alone and eke abroad,
Tell him I will this other lady send
To him, that shall with him make her abode;
Now tell him that to keep this I intend
The which to win I have such pain bestowed;
'Tis reason that the fairest should remain
With him that is the strongest of us twain.'

"Clodian in mind was wond'rous malcontent,
Used so not like a prince but like a patch,
That puffing, blowing up and down he went
All night, as one were set to keep a watch;
But whether he do chafe or else lament,
He found the knight for him too hard a match.
Next day Sir Tristram let him have his wife,
And so for that time finished was the strife;

"For openly he on his honor swore
That he her honor had that night preservèd
Although discourtesies he had before
Had at his hands a great revenge deservèd.
Yet in that Clodian had lodged out of door,
He was content that penance should have servèd;
He natheless took it for no good excuse
To say that love was cause of such abuse.

"For love should gentle make rude hearts and base
And not in gentle mind breed humors vile.
Now when Sir Tristram parted from the place,
Sir Clodian meant to stay there but a while;
But to a knight that stood much in his grace
He grants the keeping of this stately pile,
Keeping one law for him and for his heirs
With everyone that to the place repairs:

"That namely ever he that was most strong
Should there be lodged, and she that was most fair,
And that the rest should take it for no wrong
To walk abroad into the open air;
This is the law which hath endurèd long,
And no man may the strength thereof impair."—
Now while the man this story did repeat,
The steward on the board did set the meat.

The board was covered in a stately hall
Whose match was scarce in all the country seen,
With goodly pictures drawn upon the wall
All round about, but chiefly on the screen;
These they did look on with delight not small
And would have quite forgot their meat, I ween,
Save that their noble host did them advise
To feed their bellies first and then their eyes.

Now as they down did at the table sit,
The master of the house began to lower
And said they did an error great commit
To lodge two ladies come in sundry hour;
Needs one must be put out, where'er it hit,
And go abroad into the cold and shower;
The fairest, sith they came not both together,
Must bide, the foulest must go try the weather.

Two aged men and women more beside
He called and bad them quickly take a view
Which of the twain should in the place abide,
And namely which of twain had fairest hue.
This jury do the matter soon decide
And gave their verdict, as it was most true,
That Bradamant passed her in hue as far
As she excelled the men in feats of war.

Then spake the knight unto the Iceland dame
Whose mind was full of timorous suspicion,
"I pray you think it not a scorn or shame,
For hence you must; there can be no remission."
Poor Ullany (so was the damsel's name)
Doth think she now is driv'n to hard condition;
Yet in her conscience true she knew it was
That Bradamant in beauty her did pass.

E'en as we see the sun obscured sometime
By sudden rising of a misty cloud
Engendered by the vapor-breathing slime
And in the middle region then embowed:
So when the damsel plainly saw that time
Her presence in the place was not allowed,
She was so changed in count'nance and in cheer
That e'en unlike herself she did appear.

But much astonied with the sudden passion,
She ready was to sound in all their sight,
But Bradamant, that would not for compassion
Permit that she should go abroad that night,
Did say this trial was of no good fashion
And that the judgment hardly could be right
When men observe not this same chief regard
As not to judge before both parts be heard;

"I, that on me do take her to defend,
Say thus, that be I fair, or less or more,
I came not as a woman, nor intend
As woman now to be adjudged therefor.
Who knows my sex except I condescend
To show the same? And one should evermore
Shun to confirm things doubtful or deny it
When chiefly others may be harmèd by it.

"Yet who can say precisely what I am?
For many men do wear their hair as long,
And you do know that as a man I came,
And all my gestures to a man belong;
Wherefore in giving me a woman's name
To both of us perhaps you may do wrong.
Your law points women, if their right be done,
By women, not by warriors, to be won.

"But yet admit it were as you do guess,
That I indeed were of the female gender,
Though that it is so I do not confess,
Should I to her my lodging then surrender
If that my beauty of the two were less?
No, sure, in that the reason were but slender:
The price that unto virtue longs of duty
Should not be ta'en away for want of beauty.

"And if your law were such that needs of force
Unto the fairest lodging should be given,
Yet at this feast I tarry would perforce,
And from my lodging I would not be driven;
Wherefore mine argument I thus enforce,
That this same match between us is not even,
For striving here with me, the case is plain
She much may leese, and little she may gain.

"And where the gain and loss unequal is,
The match is evil made in common sense;
Wherefore I think it were not much amiss
With this same law for this time to dispense;
And if that any dare mislike of this
Or seem to take the matter in offence,
I will with sword be ready to maintain
That mine advice is good and his is vain."

Thus noble Ammon's daughter, moved with pity
In her behalf who to her great disgrace
Should have been sent where neither town nor city
Was near almost in three leagues of the place,[21]
Framed her defence so stout and eke so witty
That to her reason all the rest gave place,
But chief the peril great and hazard weighing
That might have grown to them by her gainsaying.

As when the sun in summer hath most power
And that the ground with heat thereof is rivèd,
For want of rain the dry and parchèd flower
Doth fade and is as 'twere of life deprivèd,
But if in season come a fruitful shower,
It riseth up and is again revivèd:
So when the damsel this defence did hear,
She waxèd fair again, of better cheer.

And thus at last they fell unto their feast
In quiet sort, for none did come that night
To challenge any of them or molest,
No traveler, nor any wand'ring knight.
All merry were, but Bradamantè least;
Fell jealously barred her of all delight,
Her stomach so distemp'ring and her taste
She took no pleasure of that sweet repast.

When supper ended was, they all arise,
Although perhaps they would have longer sate
Save for desire they had to feed their eyes;
And now the night was spent and waxèd late,
The master of the house in seemly wise
Doth call for torches to set out his state,
And straight with torchlight fillèd was the hall.—
But what they saw, hereafter show I shall.

1. This and the following forty stanzas, as Harington himself indi-
cates, are translated by his brother Francis Harington.
2. See Joshua 10:13.
3. Zeus tripled the length of the night during which, by assuming the
form of her husband Amphitryon, he begot Hercules on Alcmene.
4. The Italian reads "begli," *beautiful*.

5. Francis Harington, not Ariosto, forgets that snakes do not have ears.

6. See Canto III.

7. This episode occurs in Canto XXX.

8. A Saracen warrior maiden who repeatedly demonstrates her prowess from Canto XVIII on.

9. Her guardian angel.

10. Rabicano.

11. Ariosto has already explained this in Canto XXIII.

12. In the texts of 1516 and 1521 Ariosto reports that she *did* know the magical properties of the lance.

13. The mountain, in central France, from which the River Dordogne flows.

14. Gothland; this is the southern part of Swethland, or Sweden.

15. Harington, following the Italian commentator Fornari, suggests that the tale of the Queen of Iceland alludes to Mary, sister of Henry VIII and Queen Dowager of France, whom Sir Charles Brandon won in marriage by overcoming four Frenchmen in the field. The parallel is as weak as the history.

16. The Italian says four leagues or six; Harington may believe that Ariosto's league is smaller than the English.

17. The Italian says some five or six miles; again, Harington may deliberately adjust the figure.

18. The moon shone, Ariosto specifically says, in spite of the rain.

19. Pharamond, traditionally the first of the kings of France, was supposed to have lived at the beginning of the fifth century, somewhat earlier than Tristram, who was a contemporary of Arthur.

20. Harington adds the information, inconsistent with the next stanza, that Tristram was pleased with Clodian's wife.

21. Ariosto tells us merely that there was no roof or shelter outside.

Grā   Rin   Brā

IL SIG.ᵒᵣ
DEL CASTELLO

BRA   MESS: ISLANDA

The Thirty-third Canto

Timagoras, Parrhasius, Polygnote,
Timant, Protogenes, Apollodore,
With Zeuxis, one for skill of special note,
Apelles eke, placed all the rest before,
Whose skill in drawing all the world doth note
And talk of still (to writers thanks therefor),
Whose works and bodies time and death did waste,
Yet spite of time and death their fames do last,

With others that in these our later days
Have lived, as Leonard and John Belline[1]
And he that carves and draws with equal praise,
Michel more than a man, angel divine,[2]
And Flores[3] whom the Flemings greatly praise,
With Raphael and Titian passing fine,
With divers others that by due desert
Do merit in this praise to have a part:

Yet all these cunning drawers with their skill
Could not attain by picture to express
What strange events should happen well or ill
In future times, no, not so much as guess.
This art is proper unto magic still,
Or to a prophet or a prophetess;
By this rare art the British Merlin painted
Strange things with which our age hath been acquainted.

He made by magic art that stately hall,
And by the selfsame art he caused to be
Strange histories engravèd on the wall,
Which, as I said, the guests desired to see.
Now when they were from supper risen all,
The pages lighted torches two or three,
Making the room to shine as bright as day,
When to his guests the owner thus did say:

"I would," quoth he, "my guests, that you should know
That these same stories that here painted are
Of future wars the sequels sad do show
That shall to Italy bring woe and care,
Whereas the French full many a bloody blow
Shall take while others they to harm prepare,
As Merlin here hath laid down, being sent
From English Arthur chief for this intent.

"King Feramont⁴ that was the first that passed
The stream of Rhine with army great of France
And being in possession quiet placed
Of all those parts, stirred with so lucky chance,
Straight in ambitious thought began to cast
His rule and scepter higher to advance;
Which that he might to pass the better bring,
He made a league with Arthur English king,

"Informing him how that his meaning was
Of Italy the rule and crown to get,
And asked his aid to bring the same to pass
Which never had achievèd been as yet.
Now Merlin, that did all men far surpass
In magic art, his purpose sought to let,
For Merlin had with Arthur so great credit
He thought all gospel was if once he said it.

"This Merlin then did first to Arthur show
And then by Arthur was of purpose sent
To Feramont of France, to let him know
The cause why he mislikèd his intent,
As namely, many mischiefs that would grow
To all that now or that hereafter meant
The like attempt, advising him abstain
From certain trouble for uncertain gain.

"And that he might his courage more appall
And quite remove him from this enterprise,
He made by magic this so stately hall,
Adornèd as you see in sumptuous wise,
And drew these histories upon the wall
That what he saw in mind, they might with eyes
And thereby know that in Italian ground
The flower-de-luce can ne'er take root profound;

"And how as often as the French shall come
As friends to aid and free them from distress,
So oft they shall their foes all overcome
And fight with honor great and good success;
But be they sure to have that place their tomb
If so they come their freedom to oppress."
Thus much the owner of the house them told
And so went on, the story to unfold:

"Lo first how Sigisbert, in hope of gain
And promises of Emperor Mauritius,
Doth pass the mountains with a mighty train,
With mind to Lombardy to be pernicious;
But Ewtar drives him back by force again
When he of such attempts is least suspicious,
So that his enterprise is quite reversèd;
Himself doth fly and leave his men dispersèd.

"Next after him the proud Clodoveus went
And had with him one hundred thousand men,
But him doth meet the Duke of Benevent
With scarce for every hundred soldiers ten,
Who doth entrap him in an ambushment
So as the French might well be likened then,
While Lombard wines too greedily they took,
To fish beguilèd with a baited hook.

"Straight Childibertus with a mighty host
Doth come with mind to wipe away this blot,
But of his gainings he may make small boast,
For of his purpose he prevailèd not;
His enterprise by heav'nly sword is crossed;
The plague doth grow among his men so hot,
What with the burning fever and the flux,
Of sixty men there scant returneth six.

"Another picture lively doth express
How that King Pepin and King Charles his son
Fought both in Italy with good success,
Not with intent that realm to overrun
But to set free Pope Steph'n from sharp distress
And wrongs that by Astolfo were him done;
One tames Astolfo that was Steph'n's oppressor;
T'other takes Desiderius his successor.[5]

"Behold another Pepin, yet a youth,
Not like his father, doth that realm invade,
And thinking to procure their woeful ruth,
Of ships and boats a mighty bridge he made;
But mark what ill success to him ensu'th:
Ere he through his great enterprise could wade,
A tempest did his massy work confound;
His bridge was broken, and his soldiers drowned.[6]

"Lo Lews of Burgundy, descending there
Where, as it seems, he taken is and bound;
And he that takes him maketh him to swear
That he shall ne'er bear arms gainst Latian ground;
Lo how he breaks his oath without all fear;
Lo how again his foes do him confound
And like a moldwarp make him lose his eyes,
A just reward for such as oaths despise.

"See here how Hugh of Arly doth great feats,
Driving the Berengars from native soil,
Forcing them twice or thrice to change their seats,
And cause the Huns and Baviers back recoil;
But greater force at last his acts defeats;
First he compounds, and after all his toil
He dies, nor after long his heir doth tarry
But yieldeth up his crown to Berengary.[7]

"Lo here another Charles,[8] that by persuasion
Of the good[9] shepherd sets on fire the fold
And kills two kings in this his fierce invasion,
Manfred and Corradin, which makes him bold;
But his own faults of his fall gave occasion;
His cruelty was such, so uncontrolled
That he and his were all killed, as they tell,
E'en at the ringing of an e'ensong bell.[10]

"Now after these about one hundred years,
For so the space between did seem to say,
From France one shall invade those famous peers
The Viscount Galeasses[11] and shall lay
Siege unto Alexandria, as appears
By those that here do stand in battle ray.
Lo how the duke, preventing every doubt,
Provideth strength within, deceit without.

"And with this wary policy proceeding,
He doth the Frenchmen at advantage take
Not finding his ambushment and not heeding,
Together with the lord of Arminake
Who dieth of his hurts with overbleeding:
Lo how the stream of blood there spilt doth make
A sanguine color in the stream of Po
By means Tanarus into it doth go.[12]

"After all these one comes that Marca hight
And three that do of Anjou house proceed;
All these to those of Naples do much spite,
Yet none of these can brag of their good speed;
For though to French they join some Latian might
Of greedy sort that with their crowns they feed,
Yet still for all their pain and their expense
Alfonse and Ferdinando[13] drive them thence.

"Lo Charles the Eight,[14] descending like a thunder
Down from the Alps with all the flower of France
And conqu'ring all, to all men's passing wonder
Not drawing once a sword nor breaking lance,
Except that rock that Typheus[15] lyeth under,
While he too high himself strave to advance;
This isle and castle both that Ischia hight
Defended was by Vasto,[16] gallant knight."

Now as the master of the castle told
And pointed out each story in his place,
It came into his fancy to unfold
The worthy praise of Alva's noble race,
Which, as for certainty they all did hold,
Wise Merlin prophesied who had the grace
To show beforehand both with tongue and pen
What accidents should hap, and where and when;

And namely that "This knight whom here you see
Defending so the castle and the rock
As though he feared not those same fires that flee
As far as Fare,[17] but them did scorn and mock:
From this same knight there shall descend," quoth he,
"Out of the root of this most worthy stock,
A knight shall win such fame and reputation
As all the world shall hold in admiration.

"Though Nereus were fair, Achilles strong,
Though Ladas swift, though Nestor was most wise
That knew so much and livèd had so long,
Though bold Ulysses could both well devise
And execute what doth to war belong,
Though Caesar's bounty praised be to the skies,
Yet place to give, all these may think no scorn,
To one that shall in Ischia Isle be born.[18]

"And if that ancient Creta may be proud
Because that Caelus' nephew[19] sprang therein,
If Thebes of Bacchus' birth doth vaunt so loud
And Hercules, if Delos of their twin,
Then may that isle no less be well allowed
To vaunt itself that hath so happy been
To have that marquis born within that place
On whom the heav'ns shall pour so great a grace.

"Thus Merlin used to tell and oft repeat
How he should be for such a time reservèd
When Roman Empire's high and stately seat
At lowest ebb should be and wellnigh starvèd,
That his rare parts again might make it great
And that by him it might be safe preservèd;
Which that you may see plainly to his glory,
Mark in this table the ensuing story.

"Lo here," said he, "how Lodwick [20] doth repent
That he had thither brought King Charles the Eight,
Which at the first he did but with intent
To weaken, not to press with so hard weight
His ancient foe; for now gainst Charles he went,
Making new leagues according to his sleight;
He thinks to take him pris'ner by the way,
But Charles by force through them doth make his way.

"But yet the soldiers that behind him stayed
Had not the like good fortune nor success,
For Ferdinando [21] grew by Mantuan aid
So strong that soon he did the French distress,
To whose great grief this marquis[22] was betrayed
By gipsen vile when he feared nothing less;
Which doth in Ferdinand so great grief breed
As doth his joy of victory exceed."

Next after these he shows them Lews the Twelfth,
That pulls out Lodwick Sforse with mighty hand
And gets by force what he had got by stealth
And plants the flower-de-luce in Milan land;[23]
Yet he no long time there in quiet dwell'th;
The great Consalvo[24] with a Spanish band
His captains and lieutenants oft repulses
And in the end from Milan quite expulses.

"Lo here (which I forgat before to show)
How Lodwick's friends and his own men betray him;
One sells his castle, never striking blow;
The Swizzers eke, that might away convey him
And had his pay and did him service owe,
For filthy lucre's sake they do betray him;
Whereby without once breaking of a lance
Two victories came to the King of France.

"Lo how by favor of this mighty king
The bastard Caesar Borgia grew full great
And doth the necks of many nobles wring
Of Italy that had most ancient seat;
Lo how this king doth eke the acorns bring
To Bulloign;[25] lo how with another feat
He doth the Genoese in fight subdue
And maketh them their late revolt to rue.

"Lo here, not far from thence, how all the field
With dead men's bones is held at Geriadad;[26]
How all the cities unto Lews do yield;
How Venice to shut up her gates is glad
And scarce herself from this great storm can shield.
Lo how the pope, his part that herein had,
Doth take away unto his great rebuke
Modone and more from good Ferrara's duke.

"At which King Lews, with rightful choler movèd,
Gives Bulloign to the Bentivols again
And thence to Breskie all his force removèd
And succors to Felsina doth ordain,
What time the Church's soldiers felt and provèd
The Frenchmen's force unto their mickle pain.
Lo after where both armies meet to fight,
Near Chassie[27] shore, to try their utmost might.

"On this side France, on that the power of Spain
United is, and deadly blows ensue;
The ditches all seemed filled with bodies slain,
A hap to make a stony heart to rue;
Long time in doubt doth victory remain;
Which way the sway would carry no man knew
Till by the virtue of Alfonse alone
The French prevail;[28] the Spanish, forced, are gone.

"Lo how the pope his lip doth bite for grief
Because the Frenchmen do Ravenna sack;
Lo how he sent to Swizzers for relief;
Lo how they come and drive the Frenchmen back;
And they that with their treason causèd chief
Of Lodowick the overthrow and wrack,
To make some mends for that they erst had done,
Unto the father's place restore the son.

"But lo a prince of France then new created
Meets with the Swizzers to their mickle cost,[29]
And so their courage quailed and force abated
As all the nation seemèd wellnigh lost;
And of their title that them antimated
Those villains vile hereafter need not boast;
Defenders of the Church, tamers of kings
They clepèd were; now clippèd are their wings.

"Lo how the French King Francis, in despite
Of all the league, fair Milan doth surprise,
Bourbon defending it from Genoa's might;
Lo while this king doth practice and devise
Some great exploit, while by foul oversight
His lawless men the town did tyrannize,
Their having too much pride and want of pity
Doth cause them suddenly to lose the city.

"Lo yet another Francis Sforse,[30] a man
Like to his grandsire both in acts and name,
Who to drive out the Frenchmen well began
And Milan did recover with great fame;
Lo France again endeavor all they can
To win with praise that they had lost with shame,
But Mantua's worthy duke on Tician stream
Cuts off his way and kept him from that realm.

"Young Frederick,[31] yet but a beardless boy
Scant having on his chin a little down,
Lo how he saves Pavia from annoy
When furiously the French besiege the town;
He makes their earnest plots turn to a toy;
The lion of the sea[32] he beateth down.
Lo here two marquises[33] both of one blood,
Both born to do their country endless good.

"The first of these is that Alfonso's son
That by the Negro erst you saw betrayed;
Behold what feats of arms by him are done,
How at their greatest need he them doth aid,
How oft he hath on Frenchmen glory won
That of his very name they seem afraid.
The t'other that so mild doth look in sight
Is lord of Vasto and Alfonso hight.

"This is that worthy knight of whom I told
Then when I did the isle of Ischia show,
Of whom I said that Merlin had foretold
To Feramont what he by skill did know,
That when this world were worn and waxen old
And Rome and Italy were brought most low,
Then he should spring who to his endless praise
Their foes should overthrow and them should raise.

"Lo how he with his cousin of Pescare
And with Colonna's prosperous aid no less
The French and Dutch that at Bycocca[34] are
Do foil and slay and drive to great distress.
Lo how again the Frenchmen do prepare
With new attempts to mend their bad success;
One camp the king in Lombardy doth make,
And with another Naples he would take.

"But she that useth men as wind doth dust,[35]
First take it up and blow it very high,
And from that highest place straight when she lust,
She throws it down whereas it first did lie:
She makes this king,[36] devoid of all mistrust,
Think he hath men an hundred thousand nigh
At Pavy siege, believing others muster;
But woe to kings whose servants are no juster.

"So while this noble prince mistrusts no harm,
His wicked captains greedy gain to win
Caused that the soldiers in the night alarm
Came to their colors slow and very thin;
Within their tents they feel their skirmish warm;
The wary Spaniards soon had entered in
With those two guides with whom they durst assay
In Hell or else in Heav'n to break a way.

"Lo how the chief nobility of France
Lie dead on ground, a cause of many tears,
How many an harquebus, a sword and lance
This stout king hath alone about his ears,
His horse slain under him by hard mischance;
And yet he nothing yields nor nothing fears
Though all the host assaulted him alone
And all the rescues and supplies were gone.

"The valiant king defends him on his feet,
Bathing his blade long time in en'mies' blood;
But virtue that with too much force doth meet
Must yield at last; it cannot be withstood.
Lo him here pris'ner; lo how in a fleet
He passeth into Spain the salt sea flood,
Whence Vasto doth the chiefest honor bring
Of the field won and of the pris'ner king.

"Thus both that host the king had thither brought
And that he meant to Naples to have sent
Were both dispersèd quite and came to nought,
Much like a lamp when all the oil is spent.
Lo how the king again so well hath wrought
He leaves his sons for pledge and homeward went;
Lo how abroad he doth new quarrels pick;
Lo how at home some do to him the like.

"Lo here the woeful murders and the rapes
That Rome doth suffer in the cruel sack,[37]
Where neither thing profane nor holy scapes
But all alike do go to spoil and wrack;
The league that should relieve sits still and gapes,
And where they should step forward, they shrink back;
Thus Peter's successor[38] by them forsaken
Is straight besiegèd and at length is taken.

"The king sends Lautrec[39] new supplies to gather,
Not that he should to Lombardy do aught
But that he might set free the Holy Father
That to so low an ebb so soon was brought;
But Lautrec should have come a little rather;
The pope's own coin hath his own freedom bought;
Lautrec attempts to conquer Naples town
And soon turns all the country upside down.

"Lo how a fair imperial navy bends
His course to succor the distressèd town,
But Doria[40] back with heave and ho them sends,
And some of them doth burn and some doth drown.
Lo fickle fortune once again intends
To change her cheer and on the French to frown;
With agues, not with swords they all are slain;
Scarce of an hundred one turns home again."

These and such stories had the stately hall
In marble rich engravèd on the screen
As were too tedious to recite them all
Though then by them they were perused and seen;
Their wonder great, their pleasure was not small,
And oft they read the writings were between
That in fair Roman letters all of gold
The circumstance of every picture told.

Now when the ladies fair and all the rest
Had seen and asked as much as they desired,
Their host doth bring them to their rooms of rest
Where sleep renews the strength of bodies tired;
Only Duke Ammon's daughter[41] could not rest;
Though bed were soft, room warm and well-attired,
Yet still she tossed from left side to the right
And could not sleep one wink all that same night.

With much ado her eyes at last she closed
Not much afore the dawning of the day;
And as she slept, she in her sleep supposed
Rogero present was and thus did say,
"My dear, what ails thee to be thus disposed
That false belief in thee doth bear such sway?
First shall the rivers to the mountains climb
Ere I will guilty be of such a crime."

Beside she thought she heard him thus to say,
"Lo I am come to be baptized, my love,
And that I seemed my coming to delay,
Another wound, and not a wound of love,
Hath been the cause of my constrainèd stay;
Suspicions vain and causeless fear remove."
With this the damsel waked, and up she started,
But found her dream and lover both departed.

Then freshly she doth her complaints renew,
And in her mind thus to herself she spake,
"Lo what I like are dreams vain and untrue,
And in a moment me do quite forsake;
But ah, what me offends is too-too true;
I dream of good, but none I find awake.
How are mine eyes, alas, in so ill taking
That closed see good and nought but evil waking?

"Sweet dream did promise me a quiet peace,
But bitter waking turneth all to war;
Sweet dream deluded me and soon did cease,
But bitter waking plagues and doth not err;
If falsehood ease and truth my pain increase,
I wish myself from truth I still might bar;
If dreams breed joy and waking cause my pain,
Aye might I dream and never wake again!

"O happy wights whom sleep doth so possess
As in six months you never open eye;
For sure such sleep is like to death, I guess,
But waking thus is not like life, think I.
How strange are then the pangs that me oppress,
That sleeping seem to live and waking die!
But if such sleep resemblance be of death,
Come, death, and close mine eyes, and stop my breath."

Now were those eastern parts of heav'n made red
Where Phoebus' beams do first begin appear,
And all the thick and rainy clouds were fled
And promisèd a morning fair and clear,
When Bradamant forsook her restless bed;
And giving for her lodging and good cheer
Right courteous thanks unto her noble host, ·
She leaves his house and minds to part in post.

But first she found how that the damsel fair,
The messenger that supped with her last night,
Was gone before with purpose to repair
To those three knights that lately felt her might
When she did cause them caper in the air,
Driv'n without stirrups from their steeds to light;
She found they had all night to their great pain
Abid the wind, the tempest, and the rain.

And that which greatly did increase their grief
Was that while those within had cheer great store,
They and their horse lacked lodging and relief;
But that which did offend their stomachs more,
And was indeed of all their sorrows chief,
Was lest the maid of whom I spake before
Would tell their mistress of their hard mischance
They had at their arrival first in France.

And having full resolvèd and designed
To die or venge the foil received last night,
To th'end the messenger might change her mind,
The messenger that Ullania hight,
Who thought their force and value far behind
The vaunts that they had made of their great might,
Therefore as soon as Bradamant they spied,
Straight each of them to combat her defied,

Not thinking, though, she should a damsel be,
For of a damsel gesture none she used.
The lady gently spake unto them three
And thought her haste the fight might have excused,
But they did urge her still so far that she
Without disgrace could not have it refused;
Wherefore she couched the golden-headed lance
And from their saddles made them all to dance.

And for that time thus ended was that fray,
For she set spurs to horse and rode so post
That ere they rose, she quite was gone away;
They that their seats had twice together lost
Were so ashamed they knew not what to say,
For why they wonted were to make their boast
No knight of France should able be to stand
Against the worst of them with spear in hand.

But Ullania further them to taunt
That Bradamant a lady was them told.
"Now, sirs," said she, "you that were wont to vaunt
From paladins to win the shield of gold,
Lo how a woman's forces can you daunt!
Now is, I hope, your lofty courage cold;
Sure for those knights you be too weak a match
When one poor damsel you can overmatch.

"What need," said she, "be further trial had?
You have already that for which you came,
Except that any of you be so mad
To join a future loss to present shame,
Or if perhaps you would be fain and glad
To end your lives by men of worthy fame:
Trow you that vanquished are by woman's hand
Renaldo or Orlando to withstand?"

Now whenas Ullany declarèd had
How that a damsel them had overthrown,
With grief and with disdain they were so mad
That scarce their wits and senses were their own;
Each one himself of armor all unclad,
Their horse turned loose, their swords away were thrown,
And vowed for penance of so great disgrace
To touch no armor in a twelve-month's space.

They further vow they ne'er will ride again,
No, not when that same year should be expired,
Although the way were mountainy or plain
And though the way were gravelly or mired;
Until they could by force of arms regain
Such horses as for service are required
And furniture for three such champions meet,
Till then they vowed to travel on their feet.

Thus willfully they walked while others rode;
But Bradamant went on, and that same night
She at a castle maketh her abode
Near to the way that leads to Paris right;
Here by her host the lady fair was showed
How Agramant was vanquished in the fight;
Good meat, good lodging, and good news she had,
Yet ate she not, nor slept, nor was she glad.

But now of her so much I must not say
That I forget my story out to tell
Of those two knights[42] that met the other day
And tied their horses at the running well;
No lands nor towns were causes of their fray
Nor who in rule nor office should excell,
But e'en that he that strongest was of twain
Should Bayard win and Durindana[43] gain.

There needs no sign of war nor trumpet's sound
To warn them when to strike or when to pause;
No heralds need to limit out the ground
Nor read them lectures of their warlike laws.
They met as they by promise firm were bound,
And each his weapon at one instant draws,
And then they laid about them strong and nimble;
Blows bred their smart, and smart their wrath did kindle.

Two blades more firm in trial and more sure
Could not in all the world have been prepared
That having been, as these were, put in ure
Would not have been in pieces burst and marred;
But both these blades were of such temper pure,
So keen, so tough, and therewithal so hard
They might a thousand times at hard edge met,
And neither blade thereby a gap would get.

Renaldo quick hither and thither goes
And oftentime was forced to change his place
And traverse ground, for why the weight he knows
Of Durindana, that would cut apace;
Gradasso ever gave the stronger blows,
But t'other still to scape them had the grace,
Or if they hit, they hit in some such part
Where though they made great sound, they caused no smart.

Renaldo, with less strength but far more art,
Strake once or twice the pagan on the arm
And with a thrust had surely pierced his heart
Save that his armor strengthened was by charm
So that no mail out of his place would start;[44]
But while each sought to do the other harm,
A sudden noise did part their earnest quarrel;
They looked and saw Bayardo in great peril.

I say they looked about and spied at length
Bayardo fighting with a monstrous fowl,
Bigger than he, her beak three yards of length,
In other shape and making like an owl,
Her talons huge and sharp and of great strength,
The feathers of her wings all black and foul,
Her eyes like fire, a long and hideous tail,
Her wings so huge they seemèd like a sail.

Perhaps it was a fowl, but I think not,
Nor ever heard I erst of such a bird;
Only so Turpin[45] calls it, well I wot,
If any will credit to him afford;
Rather I deem that Malagigi [46] got
Some sprite infernal that himself had stirred
To come in shape as I did show before,
Because the champions fierce might fight no more.

Renaldo eke himself believed the same
And with his cousin Malagige fell out
And to his charge laid not a little blame
And gave him evil language thereabout;
The t'other sware by Him that heav'ns did frame
It was not he, to put him out of doubt;
But were it fowl or were it a foul devil,
Certain to Bayard it did work much evil.

The horse, that was puissant, brake his rein
Whenas the sharpness of her claws he feels,
And what with terror moved and what with pain
He yerketh at her fiercely with his heels;
She soared aloft, and down she comes again
And strikes him so that Bayard almost reels;
And sith of other fence no mean he had,
He runs away as if he had been mad.

Unto the nearest wood he right doth run,
And still the feathered beast him held in chase
Till the thick boughs holp him her gripes to shun,
So that she gave him over in short space;
And seeing that her sport with him was done,
She soarèd up on high and left this place
And to another coast her flight doth frame
Whereas she thought to find some other game.

Gradasso and Renaldo, when they saw
The horse was fled that causèd all the fray,
Do by consent themselves from thence withdraw
To find Bayardo out and if they may;
But first each promised to observe this law,
That he that found him first of both should stay
At this same well till t'other should come thither,
And then again to fight it out together.

Thus when each had his word to th'other passed
That they would meet there at their coming back,
They after go, but Bayard ran so fast
As soon they lost the sight of any track;
Gradasso rode and therefore made more haste;
The paladin, that his good horse did lack,
Remained behind, all sad and grievèd more
And malcontent than ere he was before.

And when he traveled had about in vain,
In body weary, discontent in mind
With loss of all his travail and his pain,
He turneth to the place they first assigned
In hope the t'other would return again
And bring the horse, if so he could him find;
But when he saw his looking did not boot,
He traveled back unto the camp on foot.

But yet Gradasso's pain succeeded well,
For why a while before the light's decaying
He passèd near the place, as it befell,
Where in a cave he found him by his neighing,
Still fearing that same monstrous imp of Hell;
He takes him thence, and then but little weighing
His promise made, he turns another way
And to himself in secret thus doth say:

"Let them that list hold things in strife and war;
I mean to hold mine own with peace and ease;
Only to get this horse I came so far
And passed so many lands and many seas;
My promise breach to me shall be no bar
To keep that I so quietly do seize;
If he desire to win his horse again,
To come to India let him take the pain.

"As safe as France hath been from me now twice,[47]
So safe from him shall be my Sericane;
I thither wish him come if he be wise;
Else of Bayardo now his leave is ta'en;
If he will have him, he shall know the price;
Now mine Bayardo is and Durindane."
This said, he mounted on the steed so warly
And by another way went back to Arly,

Where finding ships new-rigged to seaward bent,
Though then at anchor in the harbor lying,
With those rich spoils to pass the seas he meant,
In all posthaste into his country hying.
Hereafter you shall hear which way he went
And of his last conflict and of his dying;[48]
Now him I leave, Renaldo, and all France
And tell you what did to Astolfo chance,

Who mounted on his stately wingèd steed,
Well-tamèd late by Logistilla's wit,
Took perfect view of France with passing speed
And saw how every town of worth did sit;
Which having well observed and marked with heed
From Rhine to Pyren mount, he thought it fit
In manner like all over Spain to ride
And many countries of the world beside.

To Aragon he passèd through Navarre,
Each man that saw him wondering at the sight;
Then Taragon he did descry not far
Upon his left hand, Biscay on his right
Where Castile, Lisbon, and Galicia are
And Cordove near, and Seville see he might,
With divers crowns, now joinèd in one reign,
Are governed by the mighty king of Spain.[49]

There saw he Gades[50] where erst by Herc'les' hand
Two pillars, marks for mariners, were placed;
Then over Atlant sea to Egypt land
And over Africa forthwith he passed
And saw where Balearic Isles do stand,
Then travelled to Eviza with like haste,
And to Arzilla-ward he thence departeth
Quite o'er that sea that it from Spagna parteth.

Oran he saw, Ippon, Morocco, Fesse,
Algiers, Buzea, and those stately towns
Whose princes with great pomp and pride possess
Of diverse provinces the stately crowns;
He saw Biserta and Tunigi no less,
And flying over many dales and downs,
He saw Capisse and Alzerbe Isle
And all the cities to the flood of Nile,

Tripoli, Bernick, Tolomit, and all
Between the sea and Atlas' woody sides;
Then on the Cereneys[51] he right doth fall
And passed Carena mounts and more besides;
Then crossing o'er the barren fields and pall
Where sands with wind do ebb and flow like tides,
The tomb of Battus[52] he doth leave behind
And Ammon's temple [53] now worn out of mind.

Then came he by another Tremisen,
That follows eke of Mahomet the law;
Unto another Ethiopia[54] then
He went, the which before he never saw,
That differs both in language and in men;
From thence he toward Nubia doth draw,
Dobada and Coallee just between,
Of which these christened and those Turkish been.

The bord'rers still are armed in heat and cold;
Senapo yet of Ethiop is the chief
And hath great store of jewels and of gold,
And much he varies not from our belief;
For he those principles most firm doth hold
That can defend from everlasting grief.
Here is it, if mine author be no liar,
Where they do use to be baptized with fire.

The duke here lighted after travel long
And to Senapo's stately court was led;
The castle was more sumptuous than strong,
And admiration more than terror bred;
The locks, bars, chains, and all that did belong
Unto the bridge and gates from foot to head,
Which we make here of iron to endure,
Was there fair wrought in massy gold most pure.

And though they have great store of metals fine,
Yet were the chambers and the lodgings here
Borne up with crystal columns that did shine
All o'er the stately court most bright and clear;
A stately border caused unto the eyne
Red, white, green, blue, and yellow to appear,
Enrichèd with divisions for the nones
Of ruby, smaragd, sapphire, topaz stones.

Most orient pearls and gems of passing price
Were sprinkled on the pavements here and there;
Hence balm doth come, hence other precious spice
Which from Jerusalem men wont to bear;
Hence cometh musk, for odors sweet and nice,
And amber pure, that some in bracelets wear;
And finally all things grow there in plenty
That in this country are esteemed most dainty.

Most true it is, else some have written lies,
The sowdan to this king doth tribute pay,
For that in this king's power alone it lies
Great Cayre and fertile Egypt to decay
Because that by those means he may devise
He may turn Nile from them another way;
This prince Senapo there is called of many,
We call him Prester John or Preter Jany.[55]

Of all the kings that ever there did reign
This king excelled in riches and in treasure,
But loss of sight made all his comforts vain
And barred him every taste of worldly pleasure;
And this did much increase his care and pain
And grievèd him indeed beyond all measure
That all his wealth and treasure not prevented
But that with famine he was aye tormented.

For when this prince as hunger mere him drew
Did but prepare himself to drink or eat,
Straight of Harpias came a cursèd crew
With mighty wings, huge paws, and bellies great,
And all the dishes quite they overthrew
And greedily devourèd all the meat;
And that they left they did so file and slaver
As few could brook the sight, but none the savor.

The cause was this why his great plague was such,
Because in youth, when men most careless are,
Finding himself to be extolled so much
And passing other kings in wealth so far,
So foul a pride his lofty heart did touch
Against his Maker he would needs move war,
To which intent a mighty power he led
Unto that mount whence Nilus hath his head.

He had been told and did it firm believe
That on that mount whose top did touch the sky
Was that same place where Adam dwelt and Eve
Before their fall did cause them thence to fly;
He hoping some rare conquest to achieve,
A mighty host preparèd by and by
With mind, so high his heart with pride did swell,
To make them tribute pay that there did dwell.

But high Jehovah their foul pride repressed,
And down he sent his angel that same night
Who slew an hundred thousand for the least
And him condemned for aye to lose his sight;
Then sent he monsters vile him to molest,
Those ugly monsters that Harpias hight,
Which so devour and so spoil all his meat
Scarce they permit him once to drink or eat.

And that which drave him into mere despair
Was that one told by way of prophecy
How those foul creatures ever should repair
Unto that place till time they might espy
A gallant knight all armèd in the air
Upon a wingèd beast aloft to fly;
And for that this unpossible he deemed,
Past hope of help himself he then esteemed.

Now when the people saw from every wall
And from each tower the strangely flying knight,
He happy thought himself that first of all
Could tell the king of this unusèd sight,
Who straight the prophecy to mind did call
And with the sudden joy forgetting quite
His trusty staff, went groping with his hand
To welcome him that now came down to land.

Astolfo, being lighted, nearer drew,
And as he was the great court ent'ring in,
Behold the king stood ready in his view
And kneeling down, to speak did thus begin:
"O heav'nly angel, O Messias new,
Though I deserve not pardon for my sin,
Yet think to us is proper to offend,
To you to pardon those that will amend.

"My guilt so heavy on my conscience lies
I dare not sue thou shouldst my sight restore,
Though well I wot that thou couldst heal mine eyes
That art of those that aye stand God before.
Let then this plague my want of sight suffice,
And let me not be starved thus evermore;
At least from me these filthy monsters drive,
And let me eat with quiet while I live.

"And I do vow a temple unto thee
Of marble fair to build here in this place
Whose gates and cover all of gold shall be,
Adorned with costly jewels in like case,
Named by thy name, and graved that men may see
Thy miracle, which no time shall deface."
Thus saith the prostrate king that nothing sees,
And gropes to have embraced Astolfo's knees.

The duke to him thus friendly doth reply:
"Nor angel I, nor new Messias am,
Nor come from Heav'n, but mortal man am I
And thrall to sin, unworthy so high name;
But for your sake my best skill I will try
To kill or drive those fowl from whence they came;
Which if I do, give God, not me, the praise,
That for your help did thither guide my ways.

"For Him your churches and your altars make
That must of duty church and altars have."
This said, he up from ground the king doth take
And went with him and other barons grave;
Straightways of meat provision new they make,
For so the hungry king in haste doth crave,
In hope that now the monsters would be quiet
And not to interrupt him at his diet.

Forthwith a sumptuous dinner was prepared
In stately sort, great store and of the best;
Senapo hopes Astolfo can him guard
From those foul fowls that did him so molest.
But lo, a sudden noise forthwith was heard;
The scent of those same viands that were dressed
Had brought them thither ere the men were able
To set down all the dishes on the table.

Of them came sev'n together in a knot
With woman's faces wan with deadly cold,
So hunger-starved as death itself might not
Be at first sight more hideous to behold;
Their wings were great, but foul black wings, God wot,
Their talons sharp to gripe but strong to hold,
A large foul paunch, a filthy tail and long
From whence there came an odor mighty strong.

As sudden heard, so sudden were they seen,
For on the table all at once they fell
And spoiled the meat and from their wombs unclean
Cast loathsome filth to see, irksome to smell;
The duke with blade of metal sharp and keen
Strikes at the monsters, thinking them to quell;
But all in vain, his bootless blade turned back
As he had smitten on a woolen sack.

Some rav'nously devoured the sweet repast
And did so eager fill their greedy gorge
That by and by they were compelled as fast
The same in beastly manner to disgorge;
The woeful king thinks now all succor past
Till good Astolfo sware by sweet Saint George,[56]
Sith force was vain, he would another way
To drive these monsters from the king assay.

The horn which ever he about him bears
He means against these monsters to employ;
He caused the king and his to stop their ears
With molten wax that no noise may them noy;
Else might his blast have bred in them such fears
To drive them thence and all the land destroy;
Then caused he them prepare another feast,
And up he gets him on his wingèd beast.

The steward that did know his mind by signs
Straightways another dinner doth address
With store of dainty meats and costly wines;
But in a trice more soon than one could guess,
The filthy flock, as famine them inclines,
Came down and seized upon the costly mess;
But straight Astolfo blew them such a blast
As on the sudden made them all aghast.

The noise into their open ears so entered
That had no means to stop them nor defence
As so their stomachs and their tastes distempered
They fled as fear expelled all other sense;
The English duke to follow them adventured,
And winding still his horn, he chased them thence
To that hill's foot whence Nilus first doth fall,
If so that Nile have any head at all.

About the bottom of this mighty mount
There is a cave descending like a well,
By which, as dwellers-by do oft recount,
A speedy passage one may have to Hell;
To this the monsters fled and made account
Within this cave safe from the noise to dwell;
Which seen, Astolfo from his beast alighted
And ceased the blowing that them so affrighted.

And for he did with heed the cave's mouth mark,
He nearer doth approach unto the same,
And with a listening ear he then doth hark
If any sound from thence unto him came;
The entrance looked all like a dungeon dark
With smoke that seemed to come from smothered flame.—
But more of this hereafter I will treat,
For now this book begins to be too great.

1. Leonardo da Vinci and Giovanni Bellini.
2. Michelangelo.
3. What painter Harington intends by "Flores" is not evident; in his commentary he mentions "Sebastian" at this point, and the Italian reads "Bastiano," probably in reference to Sebastiano del Piombo, without mentioning the Flemings.
4. See Canto XXXII, note 19. The account of early Frankish kings in the next eight stanzas is hardly historical.

5. Pepin, Charlemagne, Stephen II, Alfonso, and Desiderius were all historical figures of the second half of the eighth century.

6. Pepin, the son of Charlemagne, died in 810 after failing to capture the Venetian islands.

7. Hugh of Arles became King of Italy in 926; in 945 he compounded with the Berengars; the power of his son Lothar II did not long survive Hugh's death in 948.

8. Charles of Anjou, King of Sicily 1266-1285.

9. Harington, who writes "the good" in 1591, later changes it to "evil," losing the irony of Ariosto's reference to Urban IV.

10. The well-known Sicilian Vespers of 1282; Charles died later.

11. Gian Galeazzo Visconti, Duke of Milan 1395-1402.

12. In 1391 Jean, Earl of Armignac, died at the siege of Alessandria on the Tanaro River; Froissart says he died of a palsy, not of wounds.

13. Alfonso V of Aragon and his son Ferdinando I, fifteenth-century Spanish rulers of the Kingdom of Naples.

14. Charles VIII invaded Italy in September, 1494, and entered Naples in the following February.

15. The giant Typhoeus was supposed to have been buried under Etna, but Ariosto apparently refers to Vesuvius, near Ischia.

16. Inico d'Avalo, Marquis of Vasto.

17. The Faro, or Lighthouse, of Messina.

18. Alfonso d'Avalo, Marquis of Vasto.

19. Zeus, grandson of Uranus otherwise known as Caelus.

20. Ludovico Sforza, Duke of Milan 1494-1499.

21. Ferdinando II, King of Naples 1495-1496.

22. Francesco d'Avalo, Marquis of Pescara.

23. Louis XII occupied Milan in 1498.

24. Gonsalvo Ferrante.

25. In other words, Louis XII brought the Papal power to Bologna.

26. The battle of Agnadello (1509).

27. Chiassi.

28. The battle of Ravenna (1512), won with the aid of Alfonso, Duke of Ferrara.

29. At the battle of Marignano in 1515 Francis I defeated the Papal and Imperial forces.

30. Francesco II, Duke of Milan 1521-1535.

31. Federico Gonzaga, son of the Marquis of Mantua.

32. Venice.

33. Francesco d'Avalo, Marquis of Pescara, and Alfonso d'Avalo, Marquis of Vasto.

34. The battle of Bicocca (1522), won with the aid of Prospero Colonna, an important military commander.

35. Fortune.

36. Francis I, who suffered his worst defeat at Pavia (1525).

37. The sack of Rome by the soldiers of Charles V in 1527.

38. Clement VII.

39. Odet de Foix, Vicomte de Lautrec.

40. Filippino Doria.

41. Bradamant.

42. Gradasso and Renaldo.

43. A sword which was once Orlando's, now in the possession of Gradasso.

44. Gradasso's armor, according to the *Orlando Innamorato,* had once been Samson's.

45. Archbishop Turpin, Ariosto's reputed source.

46. A Christian magician.

47. He had visited France once before, as recounted in the *Orlando Innamorato.*

48. He is killed by Orlando in Canto XLII.

49. Portugal was joined to the Crown of Spain in 1580; naturally this is not mentioned by Ariosto.

50. Cadiz: the course which Astolfo follows thereafter is not altogether clear, but in general his flight was eastward along the north coast of Africa.

51. Cyrenaicans.

52. The founder of Cyrene.

53. The temple of Jupiter Ammon in Libya.

54. On the other side of the Nile, as the Italian explains.

55. A legendary Christian king of Ethiopia, so humble that he signed himself only John the Priest (Prester).

56. Harington adds the oath to Saint George, a neat touch since Astolfo is an English prince.

The Thirty-fourth Canto

O FOUL Harpias, greedy, hunger-starved,
   Whom wrath divine for just revenge hath sent
To blinded Italy, that hath deserved
For sins both old and late so to be shent:
The sustenance that should for food have served,
For widows poor and orphans innocent,
These filthy monsters do consume and waste it,
Oft at one meal, before the owners taste it.

He doubtless guilty is of grievous sin
That first set open that long-closèd cave[1]
From which all filth and greediness came in
To Italy and it infected have;
Then ended good, then did bad days begin,
And discord foul so far off all peace drave
That now in wars, in poverty and pain
It long hath tarried and shall long remain,

Until she can her slothful sons awake
From drowsy sleep, that now themselves forget,
And say to them, "For shame, example take;
Let others' valiant deeds your courage whet.
Why should not you the like acts undertake
As in time past did Calai and Zet[2]
That erst like aid did Phineas bring
As did Astolfo th'Ethiopian king?"

Who having driv'n away these monsters fell
From blind Senapo's board, as erst I told,
And chasèd them so far until they fell
Into the cave most fearful to behold,
That fearful cave that was the mouth of Hell,
To harken at the same he waxèd bold
And heard most woeful mourning, plaints, and cries
Such as from Hell were likely to arise.

Astolfo minds into the place to enter
And visit those that have forgone this light
And pierce the earth e'en to the middle center
To see if aught may there be worth the sight,
For why he thought, "What need I fear to venture
That have this horn with which I can affright
Foul Satan, Cerberus with triple chaps,
And safely keep myself from all mishaps?"

He ties his flying beast fast by the reins
With mind to Hell itself to bid defiance;
His horn fast tied about his neck remains,
In which much more than sword he puts affiance;
But at his very entrance he complains
Of that same smoke that bred him much annoyance,
That savored strong of brimstone and of pitch;
Yet still Astolfo goeth thorough stitch.

But still the further that he forward goes,
He feels the smoke more noisome and more thick
That in himself he gan now to suppose
If further he should wade, he should be sick;
When lo, a shadow seemèd to disclose
Itself to him of somewhat that was quick,
And to his thinking hither waved and thither
Much like a carcass hangèd long in weather.

The English duke, that had desire to know
If so he saw a body or a vision,
Strake with his sword thereat so fierce a blow
As would indeed thereof have made division
If it had been as it did seem in show;
But when he saw his sword made no incision,
He guessèd that it was, by that blow's giving,
A passèd spirit, not a body living.

Then heard he how thus woefully it said,
"O you that to these lower parts descend,
Bring us no hurt though you can bring no aid,
And be not so to those whom none can friend."
The duke amazed both hands and footsteps stayed
And said unto the ghost, "So God thee send
Some speedy ease of this thy painful smart
As thou wilt deign to tell me who thou art;

"And if to work your good lay in my lot
Above or here, I should be glad to do it."
"Ah," said the ghost, "my plague with such a knot
Is tied as mortal strength cannot undo it;
Yet your request deny you will I not;
Because you have so great a mind unto it,
I will declare to you my stock and name
And eke the cause why to this place I came.

"My name is Lydia, born of princely birth
And bred in pomp and solaces delightful,
Though now in place excluded from all mirth
I lie condemned by God's high doom and rightful
Because, while I did live above on earth,
Unto my love I showed myself so spiteful;
And many more be here for like offences,
As He that all doth rule their plague dispenses.

"Here lies that fair but cruel Anaxaritee
Whose corpse a stone divine revenge did make;
Her ghost in smoke that no light aye shall clarify
Doth most severe but most just penance take
Because she could without all sense of charity
Behold her lover[3] hanging for her sake;
Here Daphne lies that now repents her shunning
Of Phoebus whom she scaped with overrunning.[4]

"Too tedious it would be for me to tell
The sev'ral names of every female spirit
That for reward of their hard hearts in Hell
Appointed are such portions to inherit.
Yet far more are the men that there do dwell
For like offence, who for their evil merit
Are placèd much more low though somewhat nigh them,
Where fume doth smother them and flame doth fry them.

"And reason good, for sith our sex is weak,
The greater sin it is us to deceive,
As Theseus and Jason[5] well can speak
And he[6] that Latin did of rule bereave,
With him[7] on whom fair Absalom did wreak
The wrong that ravished Thamar did receive,
With diverse that of t'one and t'other gender
Refused or left their loves for causes slender.

"But that I may particularly touch
The cause that brought me to this endless pain,
My beauty while I lived and pride was such
As none or few did to the like attain;
And both of them in me excelled so much
'Twas hard to say which greater was of twain;
But this I know full well, my proud mind grew
Out of conceit of my well-pleasing hue.

"It happened that a valiant knight of Thrace,
In state and living of the better sort
And hearing praise of my praiseworthy face
Confirmèd oft by more than one report,
He purposed and performed it in short space
Unto my father's kingdom to resort
That he might sue to me and only serve me
In hope by his great value to deserve me.

"In gallant sort when he to Lydia[8] came
And saw with eye what he had heard with ear,
He calleth scant report and niggard fame
That did to him so barren tidings bear;
And ravished with my look, he straight doth frame
Himself to wait in court and tarry there
And showed such worth and usèd such behavior
As justly might deserve my father's favor.

"Exceeding was his service and desert
If to a grateful prince it had been done;
So perfectly he had of war the art
That for my sire by his conduct he won
All Caria and of Cilicia part;
And after these exploits he then begun,
For recompence of these his merits rife,
To pray my father I might be his wife.

"My father him repulsed with answer sour
Because to match me higher was his will,
Not to a private knight, whose chiefest dower
Was virtue, of whose worth he could not skill;
His greedy thoughts did nought but gain devour,
And covetise, the branch and root of ill,
Made him no more regard his virtuous suit
Than doth an ass the sound of sweetest lute.

"Alcestè (so was named the worthy knight)
Took this so foul repulse in great disdain,
Proceeding thence from whence he ought of right
Expect great recompence for his great pain;
Wherefore he parted thence in great despite
And vowed revenge, nor was his vow in vain;
Unto th'Armenian king he thence doth go,
My father's emulous and ancient foe.

"Him, ready to accept each light occasion,
He soon persuades, without all intermission,
To make upon my father fierce invasion
And make him chief lieutenant by commission;
And having won him thereto by persuasion,
They thus agreed of spoils to make partition,
As namely all the towns he won should be
The king's, and for himself he asked but me.

"This league thus made, what woes my sire he wrought
I know not how in speeches to express;
Four royal armies quickly came to nought,
Dispersed or dead in half a year and less;
In fine, Alcestè by his value brought
My father and his friends to such distress
They took them to a fort with such small treasure
As in so Scarb'row warning[9] they had leisure.

"When here a while he us beseigèd had,
To such despair he then my father drave
To yield me up he would have been full glad,
To be his wife, yea e'en to be his slave;
Nor would my sire have thought the bargain bad
If half the realm with me for dower he gave,
So sore he feared ere long to leese it all
And die in woeful bands a captive thrall.

"Wherefore in season to prevent the worst,
Me that had been the cause of all this ill
He minds to offer to Alcestè first
To win thereby his favor and good will;
I went, for why none other do I trust,
With mind herein my sire's mind to fulfill
And offer mine own self at his devotion,
With half the realm if he accept the motion.

"Alcestè hearing I came him to look,
Against me forth he comes all pale and trembling;
Not like a conqueror was then his look,
But rather a captivèd man resembling;
Which when I found, my first plot I forsook,
For well I saw that this was not dissembling;
With low'ring look I held my peace a while;
Then fit for his estate I framed my style.

"I waxèd bold the more I see him faint,
And first I cursèd this unlucky love,
And of his cruelty I made complaint,
Which harmed my friends, and chief that he would prove
Against my will to have me by constraint;
I further did most sharply him reprove
That he so parted with the first denial
And never sought to make new friendly trial.

"I told him that his manners were too fierce,
That though my father his just suit denied
Because perhaps his nature is perverse
And would not at the first attempt be plied,
He should not, though, all his good deeds reverse,
But rather ought with constancy have tried
By patient suff'ring and by painful serving
To come unto reward of well deserving.

"And if my father would not have been won,
I would, I said, his favor have procured
And would have prayed him to make him his son
If I had found his love to me had dured;
Or else in secret I would that have done
By which of me he should have been assured;
But sith he needs would try another mean,
I told him plain, my love was altered clean.

"And though I now came in this humble sort
To yield my body as the price of peace
Because my father whom he held so short
Entreated me to sue for his release,
Yet did I vow to mar his hopèd sport;
And if to offer force he would not cease,
I sware that rather I myself would kill
Than grant such joys constrained against my will.

"These words and such as these to him I spake,
Finding my power was over him so great,
Wherewith I did him as repentant make
As ere was saint in hermit's desert seat;
He fell down at my feet and prayed me take
His naked dagger and did me entreat
To stab him with the same into his heart,
To take just vengeance of his lewd desert.

"Now when I saw him at this pass, I thought
To follow this great conquest to his end;
And straight a little hope to him I brought
Of favor if his error he would mend,
And if my father's freedom might be wrought
And state restored, and he continue friend
And not attempt hereafter to constrain me,
But with his serviceable love to gain me.

"He promisèd hereof he would not miss
And back unto my sire me safe did send,
Nor once presumèd he my mouth to kiss;
Think you how he unto my yoke did bend.
I think that love played well his part in this
And needed not for him more arrows spend;
Hence straight unto th'Armenian king he went,
Whose all the winnings should be by consent.

"And in the mildest manner that he could,
He prayeth him to grant his good assent
That my poor sire might Lydia quiet hold,
And he would with Armenia be content;
The king Alcestè sharply then controlled,
And in plain terms he told he never meant
To cease that bloody war at any hand
While that my father had a foot of land.

" 'What if,' said he, 'Alcestè's wav'ring brain
Is turned with woman's words? His damage be it.
Shall I therefore lose all a whole year's gain
At his request? I never will agree it.'
Again Alcestè prays him and again,
But all in vain; he sees it will not be yet.
And last he waxèd angry and did swear
That he should do it or for love or fear.

"Thus wrath engendered many a bitter word,
And bitter words did breed more bloody blows.
Alcestè in that fury drew his sword,
And straight the guard on each side him enclose;
But he among them so himself bestirred
He slew the king, and by the help of those
Of Thrace and of Cilicia in his pay
Th'Armenians all he put to flight that day.

"And then his happy victory pursuing,
First he my father's friends did all enlarge,
And next the realm, within one month ensuing,
He gat again without my father's charge;
And for the better shunning and eschewing
Of all unkindness, with amends most large,
For recompence of all harms he had done
He gave him all the spoils that he had won.

"Yea, fully to content him to his asking,
In all the countries that did near confine
He raised such sums of coin by cursèd tasking
As made them grieve and greatly to repine.
The while my hate in love's fair visor masking,
In outward show I seemed him to incline;
Yet secretly I studied to annoy him
And many ways devisèd to destroy him.

"Instead of triumph, by a privy train
At his return to kill him we intended,
But from such fact fear forced us to refrain
Because we found he was so strongly friended;
I seemèd of his coming glad and fain
And promised, when our troubles all were ended,
That I his faithful yoke-fellow would be,
In woe or weal to take such part as he.

"Wherefore I prayed him first that for my sake
He would subdue some of our private foes,
And he each hard exploit doth undertake,
And now alone and then with few he goes,
And safe returns; yet oft I did him make
To fight with cruel giants and with those
That passed his strength, oft with some monstrous beast
Or dragon fell that did our realm molest.

"Don Herc'les never by his cruel aunt
Nor by the hard Euristeus[10] was so wrought
In Lerna, Thrace, in Nemea Eremaunt,
Numid, Etolia, Tebrus where he fought,
Nor Spain, nor nowhere else, as I might vaunt
With mild persuasion but with murd'ring thought
I made my lover still to put in ure,
In hope hereby his ruin to procure.

"But as the palm, the more the top is pressed,
The thicker do the underbranches grow,
E'en so, the more his virtue was oppressed
By hard attempts, the brighter it did show;
Which when I found, forthwith I thought it best
Another way to work his overthrow,
A way by which indeed I wrought the feat
Which yet I shame and sorrow to repeat.

"Against all such as bare him best affection
I secretly did still his mind incense
And ever one and one by my direction
I made him wrong, till all were driv'n from thence;
So was his heart and soul in my subjection,
So had my beauty blinded all his sense,
Had I but winked or up my finger held,
He had not cared whom he had hurt or killed.

"Now when I thus had foiled my father's foes
And by Alcestè had Alcestè won
And made him for my sake foresake all those
That for his sake no high attempt would shun,
I then began myself plain to disclose
And let him know what wise thread he had spun;
With bitter spiteful words I all to-rated him
And told him plain that in my heart I hated him,

"And that I wished his life and days were ended
And would have killed him if I could for shame,
Save then I should of all men be condemnèd
Because his high deserts were of such fame;
Yet him and them I utterly contemnèd
And loathed to see his face or hear his name,
And sware I would wish him thenceforth no better
Nor hear his message nor receive his letter.

"At this my cruel usage and ungrate
He took such grief that in a while he died;
Now for this sin, He that all sin did hate
Condemns me here in this smoke to be tied,
Where I in vain repent myself too late
That I his suit so causelessly denied,
For which in smoke eternal I must dwell
Sith no redemption can be had from Hell."

Here Lydia this her woeful tale doth end
And faded thence; now when her speech did cease,
The duke a farther passage did intend,
But the tormenting smoke did so increase
That backward he was forced his steps to bend,
For vital sprites already did decrease;
Wherefore the smoke to shun and life to save
He clambered to the top of that same cave.

And lest those woman-facèd monsters fell
Might after come from out that loathsome ledge,
He digged up stones and great trees down did fell,
His sword sufficing both for axe and sledge;
He hewed and brake and labored it so well
That gainst the cave he made a thick, strong hedge,
So stopped with stones and many a ragged rafter
As kept th'Harpias in a great while after.

But now the duke, both with his present toil
That did with dirt and dust him all to-dash
And with the smoke that erst did him so soil
As black as soot, was driv'n to seek some plash
Where he himself might of his clothes despoil
And both his raiment and his armor wash,
For why the smoke without and eke within
Did taint his clothes, his armor, and his skin.

Soon after he a crystal stream espying,
From foot to head he washed himself therein;[11]
Then up he gets him on his courser flying,
And of the air he more and more doth win,
Affecting Heav'n, all earthly thoughts defying;
As fishes cut the liquid stream with fin,
So cutteth he the air and doth not stop
Till he was come unto that mountain's top.

This hill nigh touched the circle of the moon;
The top was all a fruitful pleasant field
And light at night as ours is here at noon,
The sweetest place that ever man beheld
(There would I dwell if God gave me my boon);
The soil thereof most fragrant flowers did yield
Like rubies, gold, pearls, sapphires, topaz stones,
Chrysolites, diamonds, jacinths for the nones.

The trees that there did grow were ever green;
The fruits that thereon grew were never fading;
The sundry-colored birds did sit between
And sing most sweet, the fruitful boughs them shading;
The rivers clear as crystal to be seen,
The fragrant smell the sense and soul invading,
With air so temperate and so delightsome
As all the place beside was clear and lightsome.

Amid the plain a palace passing fair
There stood, above conceit of mortal men,
Built of great height into the clearest air,
And was in circuit twenty mile and ten;
To this fair place the duke did straight repair,
And viewing all that goodly country then,
He thought this world comparèd with that palace
A dunghill vile or prison void of solace.

But whenas nearer to the place he came,
He was amazèd at the wondrous sight;
The wall was all one precious stone, the same,
And than the carbuncle more sanguine bright.
O workman rare, O most stupendous frame,
What Daedalus of this had oversight?
Peace, ye that wont to praise the wonders sev'n;[12]
Those earthly kings made, this the King of Heav'n.

Now while the duke his eyes with wonder fed,
Behold a fair old man in th'entry stood
Whose gown was white but yet his jacket red;
The t'one as snow, the t'other looked as blood;[13]
His beard was long and white, so was his head;
His count'nance was so grave, his grace so good
A man thereby might at first sight suspect
He was a saint and one of God's elect.

He coming to the duke with cheerful face,
Who now alighted was for rev'rence sake,
"Bold baron," said the saint, "by special grace
That suffered wast this voyage strange to make
And to arrive at this most blessèd place,
Not knowing why thou didst this journey take;
Yet know that not without the will celestial
Thou comest here to Paradise Terrestrial.

"The cause you came a journey of such length
Is here of me to learn what must be done
That Charles and Holy Church may now at length
Be freed that erst were wellnigh overrun;
Wherefore impute it not to thine own strength
Nor to thy courage nor thy wit, my son,
For neither could thy horn nor wingèd steed
Without God's help stand thee in any stead.

"But at more leisure hereof we will reason,
And more at large I mind with you to speak;
Now with some meat refresh you, as is reason,
Lest fasting long may make your stomach weak;
Our fruits," said he, "be never out of season."
The duke rejoicèd much and marveled eke
Then chief when by his speeches and his coat
He knew 'twas he that the Fourth Gospel wrote,

That holy John whom Christ did hold so dear
That others thought he death should never see,[14]
Though in the Gospel it appears not clear;
But thus He said, "What if it pleasèd Me,
O Peter, that thy fellow tarry here
Until My coming, what is that to thee?"[15]
So though our Saviour not directly spake it,
Yet sure it was so every one did take it.

He here assumèd was in happy hour
Whereas before Enoch the patriarch was
And where the prophet bides of mighty power
That in the fiery coach did thither pass;[16]
These three in that so happy sacred bower
In high felicity their days did pass,
There in such sort to stay they are allowed
Till Christ return upon the burning cloud.[17]

These saints him welcome to that sacred seat,
And to a stately lodging him they brought,
And for his horse likewise ordainèd meat;
And then the duke himself by them was taught
The dainty fruits of Paradise to eat,
So delicate in taste as sure he thought
Our first two parents were to be excused
That for such fruit obedience they refused.

Now when the duke had nature satisfied
With meat and drink and with his due repose
(For there were lodgings fair and all beside
That needful for man's use man can suppose),
He gets up early in the morningtide,
What time with us alow the sun arose;
But ere that he from out his lodging moved,
Came that disciple whom our Saviour loved.

And by the hand the duke abroad he led
And said some things to him I may not name;
But in the end, "I think, my son," he said,
"Although that you from France so lately came,
You little know how those in France have sped;
There your Orlando quite is out of frame,
For God his sin most sharply now rewardeth
Who most doth punish whom He most regardeth.

"Know that the champion your Orlando, whom
God so great strength and so great courage gave
And so rare grace that from his mother's womb
By force of steel his skin no hurt might have,
To th'end that he might fight for his own home
And those that hold the Christian faith to save,
As Samson erst enabled was to stand
Against Philistines for the Hebrew land:

"This your Orlando hath been so ungrate,
For so great grace received, unto his Maker,
That when his country was in weakest state
And needed succor most, he did forsake her
For love (O woeful love that breeds God's hate)
To woo a pagan wench[18] with mind to take her;
And to such sin this love did him entice
He would have killed his kinsman[19] once or twice.

"For this same cause doth mighty God permit
Him mad to run with belly bare and breast
And so to daze his reason and his wit
He knows not others and himself knows least;
So in times past our Lord did deem it fit
To turn the King of Babel[20] to a beast,
In which estate he sev'n whole years did pass
And like an ox did feed on hay and grass.

"But for the paladin's offence is not
So great as was the King of Babel's crime,
The mighty Lord of mercy doth allot
Unto his punishment a shorter time;
Twelve weeks in all he must remain a sot;
And for this cause you suffered were to climb
To this high place, that here you may be taught
How to his wits Orlando may be brought.

"Here you shall learn to work the feat, I warrant,
But yet before you can be fully sped
Of this your great but not forethought-on errand,
You must with me a more strange way be led
Up to the planet that of all stars errant
Is nearest us;[21] when she comes overhead,
Then will I bring you where the med'cine lies
That you must have to make Orlando wise."

Thus all that day they spent in divers talk
With solace great, as never wanteth there;
But when the sun began this earth to balk
And pass into the t'other hemisphere,
Then they prepared to fetch a further walk,
And straight the fiery chariot that did bear
Elias when he up to Heav'n was carried
Was ready in a trice and for them tarried.

Four horses fierce, as red as flaming fire,
Th'apostle doth unto the chariot set,
Which when he framèd had to his desire,
Astolfo in the car by him he set;
Then up they went, and still ascending higher
Above the fiery region they did get
Whose nature so th'apostle then did turn
That though they went through fire, they did not burn;

I say, although the fire were wondrous hot,
Yet in their passage they no heat did feel,
So that it burned them nor offends them not.
Thence to the moon he guides the running wheel;
The moon was like a glass all void of spot
Or like a piece of purely burnished steel
And looked, although to us it seems so small,
Wellnigh as big as earth and sea and all.

Here had Astolfo cause of double wonder:
One, that that region seemeth there so wide
That unto us that are so far asunder
Seems but a little circle, and beside,
That to behold the ground that him lay under
A man had need to have been sharply eyed
And bend his brows and mark e'en all they might,
It seemed so small, now chiefly wanting light.

'Twere infinite to tell what wondrous things
He saw that passèd ours not few degrees,
What towns, what hills, what rivers, and what springs,
What dales, what palaces, what goodly trees;
But to be short, at last his guide him brings
Unto a goodly valley where he sees
A mighty mass of things strangely confused,
Things that on earth were lost or were abused:

A storehouse strange that what on earth is lost
By fault, by time, by fortune there is found
And like a merchandise is there engrossed
In stranger sort than I can well expound;
Nor speak I sole of wealth or things of cost
In which blind fortune's power doth most abound,
But e'en of things quite out of fortune's power
Which willfully we waste each day and hour.

The precious time that fools misspend in play,
The vain attempts that never take effect,
The vows that sinners make and never pay,
The counsels wise that careless men neglect,
The fond desires that lead us oft astray,
The praises that with pride the heart infect,
And all we lose with folly and misspending
May there be found unto this place ascending.

Now as Astolfo by those regions passed,
He askèd many questions of his guide;
And as he on t'one side his eye did cast,
A wondrous hill of bladders he espied;
And he was told they had been in time past
The pompous crowns and scepters full of pride
Of monarchs of Assyria and of Greece,
Of which now scantly there is left a piece.

He saw great store of baited hooks with gold,
And those were gifts that foolish men preferred
To give to princes covetous and old
With fondest hope of future vain reward;
Then were there ropes all in sweet garlands rolled,
And those were all false flatteries he heard;
Then heard he crickets' songs like to the verses
The servant in his master's praise rehearses.

There did he see fond loves that men pursue
To look like golden gyves with stones all set;
Then things like eagles' talons he did view,
Those offices that favorites do get;
Then saw he bellows large that much wind blew,
Large promises that lords make and forget
Unto their ganymedes in flower of youth,
But after nought but beggary ensu'th.

He saw great cities seated in fair places
That overthrown quite topsy-turvy stood;
He asked and learned the cause of their defaces
Was treason that doth never turn to good;
He saw foul serpents with fair women's faces,
Of coiners and of thieves the cursèd brood;
He saw fine glasses all in pieces broken,[22]
Of service lost in court a woeful token.

Of mingled broth he saw a mighty mass
That to no use all spilt on ground did lie;
He asked his teacher, and he heard it was
The fruitless alms that men give when they die.
Then by a fair green mountain he did pass
That once smelt sweet, but now it stinks perdie;
This was the gift (be't said without offence)
That Constantine gave Silvester long since.[23]

Of birdlime-rods he saw no little store,
And these, O ladies fair, your beauties be.
I do omit ten thousand things and more
Like unto these that there the duke did see;
For all that here is lost, there evermore
Is kept and thither in a trice doth flee,
Howbeit, more or less, there was no folly,
For still that here with us remaineth wholly.

He saw some of his own lost time and deeds,
But yet he knew them not to be his own;
They seemed to him disguised in so strange weeds
Till his instructor made them better known.
But last the thing which no man thinks he needs,
Yet each man needeth most, to him was shown,
By name man's wit, which here we leese so fast
As that one substance all the other passed.

It seemed to be a body moist and soft
And apt to mount by every exhalation,
And when it hither mounted was aloft,
It there was kept in pots in such a fashion
As we call jars, where oil is kept in oft;
The duke beheld with no small admiration
The jars of wit, amongst which one had writ
Upon the side thereof, "Orlando's wit."

This vessel bigger was than all the rest,
And every vessel had engrav'n with art
His name that erst the wit therein possessed;
There of his own the duke did find a part,
And much he mused, and much himself he blessed
To see some names of men of great desert
That think they have great store of wit and boast it
When here it plain appeared they quite had lost it.

Some lost their wit with love, some with ambition,
Some running to the sea great wealth to get,
Some following lords and men of high condition,
And some in fair jewels rich and costly set;
One hath desire to prove a rare magician,
And some with poetry their wit forget;
Another thinks to be an alchemist
Till all be spent and he his number missed.

Astolfo takes his own before he goes,
For so th'evangelist doth him permit;
He set the vessel's mouth but to his nose,
And to his place he snuffed up all his wit;
Long after wise he lived, as Turpin[24] shows,
Until one fault he after did commit;
By name the love of one fair Northern lass
Sent up his wit into the place it was.[25]

The vessel where Orlando's wit was closed
Astolfo took and thence with him did bear;
It was far heavier than he had supposed,
So great a quantity of wit was there;
But yet ere back their journey they disposed,
The holy prophet brought Astolfo where
A palace seldom seen by mortal man
Was placed, by which a thick dark river ran.

Each room therein was full of diverse fleeces
Of wool, of lint, of silk, or else of cotton;
An agèd woman spun the divers pieces
Whose look and hue did show her old and rotten;
Not much unlike unto that labor this is
By which in summer new-made silk is gotten,
Where from the silkworm his fine garment taking,
They reave him of the clothes of his own making.

For first in one large room a woman span
Threads infinite of divers stuff and hue;
Another doth with all the speed she can
With other stuff the distaves still renew;
The third, in feature like and pale and wan,
Doth sever fair from foul and old from new.
"Now who be these?" the duke demands his guide.
"These be the fatal sisters," he replied,

"The Parcaes that the thread of life do spin
To mortal men; hence death and nature know
When life must end and when it must begin;
Now she that doth divide them and bestow
The coarse from finer and the thick from thin
To that end works that those that finest grow
For ornaments in Paradise may dwell;
The coarse are cursed to be consumed in Hell."

The duke did further in the place behold
That when the threads were spent that had been spun,
Their names in brass, in silver, or in gold
Were wrote and so into great heaps were done,
From which a man that seemèd wondrous old[26]
With whole loads of those names away did run
And turned again as fast the way he went,
Nor ever weary was nor ever spent.

This agèd man did hold his pace so swift
As though to run he only had been born
Or had it giv'n him as a special gift,
And in the lappet of his cloak were borne
The names of men with which he made such shift.—
But now a while I crave to be foreborne,
For in the book ensuing shall be showed
How this old sire his carriage ill bestowed.

1. Ludovico Sforza?

2. Calais and Zetes, the sons of Boreas, who freed their brother-in-law Phineus from the Harpies.

3. Iphis.

4. Daphne eluded Apollo's love by being changed into a laurel tree when he was about to overtake her.

5. Theseus abandoned Ariadne, Jason Medea.

6. Aeneas, who forsook Dido, succeeded Latinus as king.

7. Amnon in 2 Samuel 13.

8. Her father's kingdom.

9. Such short notice.

10. The aunt of Hercules was Hera, Eurystheus his cousin.

11. Harington allegorizes this: "after a man shall by remorse, and devout consideration, weigh and behold the filthiness of his sin, he must then wash himself with the clear spring water of prayer and repentance; and then and not before, he may mount to Paradise."

12. The Seven Wonders of the ancient world.

13. According to Harington, Saint John signifies the grace of God, the white gown virginity, and the red jacket charity.

14. John the Apostle must, as Ariosto supposes, have gone on living for a long time if he was also John the author of the Fourth Gospel and the Book of Revelation.

15. John 21:22.

16. Elijah.

17. Revelation 14:14.

18. Angelica.

19. Renaldo.

20. Nebuchadnezzar.

21. The moon.

22. Harington explains, "Poor courtiers."

23. The so-called Donation of Constantine, which gave the Papacy temporal power in Italy.

24. See Canto XXXIII, note 45.

25. That is, his wits were lost again. This episode is told in Ariosto's *Cinque Canti,* an abandoned sequel to the *Orlando Furioso.*

26. Representing time.

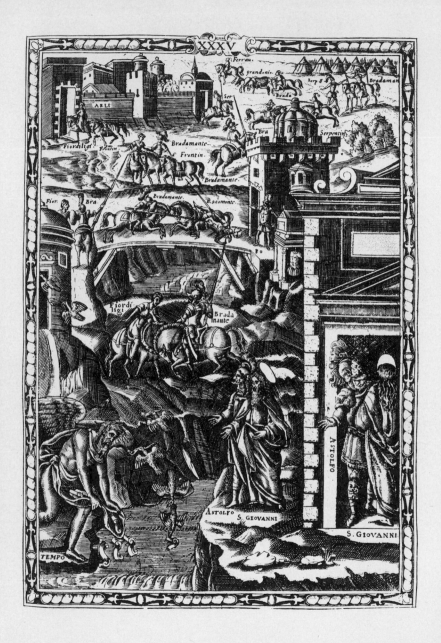

XXXV

ARLI

Ferrau.
grandine.
Brada
Serp S.
Bradaman

Fiordiligi Frontin
Bradamante
Frontin

Bra
Serpentin

Bradamante

Bradamante
Rasimante

Fior. Bra

Fo

Fiordi
ligi
Brada
mante

ASTOLFO S. GIOVANNI

ASTOLFO

S. GIOVANNI

TEMPO

The Thirty-fifth Canto

Fair mistress,[1] who for me to Heav'n shall fly
  To bring again from thence my wand'ring wit,
Which I still lose since from that piercing eye
The dart came forth that first my heart did hit?
Nor of my loss at all complain would I
Might I but keep that which remaineth yet;
But if it still decrease, within short space
I doubt I shall be in Orlando's case.

Yet well I wot where to recover mine;
Though not in Paradise or Cynthia's sphere,[2]
Yet doubtless in a place no less divine,
In that sweet face of yours, in that fair hair,
That ruby lip, in those two starlike eyne,
There is my wit; I know it wanders there;
And with these lips, if you would give me leave,
I there would search; I thence it would receive.

But to return unto that English prince
Whom, if you do remember, with Saint John
By ugly stream I left a little since
The fatal sister spinners looking on,
Who sometime do prolong and sometime mince
Our thread of life: I say he saw anon,
Among a million more, one passing fleece
More fine than that that Jason brought to Greece.

So shone the thread that from that fleece out came
No gold nor orient pearl could look so bright;
Astolfo much desired to know his name
And time of birth that to that thread had right;
Straightways this answer unto him doth frame
He that the dark *Apocalypse* did write,
"The number of his name shall noted be
When twenty shall be ta'en from M and D.[3]

"And as the fleece which here so fair doth show
In finest substance passeth all the rest,
So shall the person that the same doth owe
Make that same age in which he liveth blessed;
For all the gifts that nature can bestow
Or with which study can a man invest
Shall pourèd be on him with large proportion,
Assignèd from above to be his portion.

"There stands," said he, "near to the banks of Po
A village now of small or none account[4]
Whose moorish seat the stream doth overflow;
But in that time that I to you recount,
Unto a city of such state shall grow
As all the neighbor towns it shall surmount,
Nor sole in walls and buildings fine and stately,
But in good arts of old found out or lately.

"Nor think you this preferment to proceed
By peradventure or as 'twere by chance,
But e'en as a thing by God Himself decreed
For one man's sake his native soil t'advance:
As still we see those that good fruit will breed
Do graft the stock and prune and pick the branch,
Or as the goldsmith polisheth the metal
In which he means a gem of price to settle.

"For ne'er shall soul that shall to earth descend
With mortal garment be more comely clad;
Never did God a soul from hence down send
That more choice gifts nor more rare virtues had
Than this, which unto him He doth intend
That shall his country and his friends make glad;
Hippolyto of Est his name shall be
To whom the heav'ns such favors do decree.

"For all those virtues great that wonted are
To set forth diverse diversely divided
Shall joinèd be in this same man most rare
Unto such place by Heav'n's appointment guided;
Maintained shall studies be by his great care,
All quarrels cease, and broils shall be decided;
Whose virtues all if I to tell prolong,
Orlando should expect his wit too long."

Thus much the follower of Jesus spake
The while Astolfo those same webs doth view
From whence our lives end and beginning take;
One spun, one cut, the third doth stuff renew.
Then came they to the foul and loathsome lake,
Dark, deep, and miry, of a deadly hue,
Where was the agèd man that never stinted
To carry bundles of the names inprinted.

This was the man whom, as I told before,
Both use and nature so swift-paced had made
He never rested but ran evermore,
And with his running he did use this trade:
A heap of names within his cloak he bore
And in the river did them all unlade;
Or plain to speak, away he cast them all
Into this stream, which Lethe we do call.

This prodigal old wretch no sooner came
Unto this cursèd river's barren bank,
But desp'rately, without all fear of blame
Or caring to deserve reward or thank,
He hurled therein full many a precious name,
Where millions soon into the bottom sank;
And scant in every thousand one was found
That was not in the gulf quite lost and drowned.

Yet all about great store of birds there flew,
As vultures, carrion crows, and chatt'ring pies
And many more of sundry kinds and hue
That made lewd harmony with their loud cries;
These, when the careless wretch the treasure threw
Into that stream, did all they could devise,
What with their talons some, and some with beak,
To save those names, but find themselves too weak.

For ever as they sought themselves to raise
To bear away those names of great renown,
The weight of them so heavy downward weighs
They in the stream were driv'n to cast them down;
Only two swans sustained so great a praise;
In spite of him that sought them all to drown,
These two do still take up whose names they list
And bear them safe away and never missed.

Sometime all under that foul lake they dived
And took up some that were with water covered,
And those that seemed condemnèd they reprieved,
And often as about the bank they hovered,
They caught them ere they to the stream arrived;
Then went they with the names they had recovered
Up to a hill that stood the water nigh
On which a stately church was built on high.

This place is sacred to immortal fame,
And evermore a nymph stands at the gate
And took the names wherewith the two swans came,
Whether they early come or whether late;
Then all about the church she hanged the same
Before the sacred image in such rate
As they might then well be assured forever,
Spite of that wretch in safety to persever.

Astolfo had a great desire to know
The mysteries most high and hidden sense
Of that old man that still ran to and fro
And precious things so lewdly did dispense,
And of the birds and of the nymph also
That from the swans took names and bare them thence,
And therefore askèd what they signified,
To whom the man of God thuswise replied:

"Know first," said he, "there cannot wag a straw
Below on earth but that the sign is here,
And each small act doth correspondence draw
Although in other show it doth appear;
That agèd man that running erst you saw,
And never baits nor resteth all the year,
To work the like effects above is bound
As time doth work below upon the ground.

"When here the fatal thread of life is spun,
Then doth below the life of man decline;
There fame and here their names in metal done
Would make them both immortal and divine,
Save here this agèd sire that so doth run
And there below time doth thereat repine;
He here flings all their names into a puddle;
Time there doth all in dark oblivion huddle.

"And e'en as here rav'ns, vultures, pies, and crows
And such like birds endeavor all they may
To save those names that worthiest they suppose,
But wanting strength, the names still downward sway,
So there promoters, ruffians, bawds, and those
That can the parasites and jesters play,
That by great lords are oft more made of than
The true and plain and virtuous-minded men.

"And these, forsooth, good fellows call you must
Because they learn like ass and pork to be;
But when their lords be laid full low in dust,
Their line of life cut off by sisters three,
Yea oft by their own surfeiting and lust,
Then these same goodly squires of base degree
In their vile mouths their names bear up and down
A while and after in oblivion drown.

"But as the swans that here still flying are
With written names unto the sacred port,
So there historians learned and poets rare
Preserve them in clear fame and good report.
O happy princes whose foresight and care
Can win the love of writers in such sort
As Caesar did, so as you need not dread
The lake of Lethe after ye be dead.

"But surely God their reason so doth blind
And takes from them all sense of wit and skill
That when their rooms on earth they have resigned,
Death both their bodies and their fames might kill,
Where at the least some fame would stay behind
(Admit in part their manners were but ill);
Had they but wit to get some grace with Cirrha,[5]
Their fame should sweeter smell than nard or myrrha.

"Perhaps Aeneas was not so devout,
Nor Hector nor Achilles were so brave,
But thousands have as honest been and stout
And worthy by desert more praise to have;
But those fair lands and castles out of doubt
That their successors unto writers gave
Made them so famous over foreign lands,
Canonized by the poets' sacred hands.

"Augustus Caesar was not such a saint
As Virgil maketh him by his description;
His love of learning scuseth that complaint
That men might justly make of his proscription;
Nor had the shame that Nero's name doth taint,
Confirmed now by a thousand years' prescription,
Been as it is if he had had the wit
To have been frank to such as poems writ.

"Blind Homer writ how Agamemnon fought
And won at last great Troy that long resisted,
And how Penelope, though greatly sought
By many suitors, yet in faith persisted;
Yet sure, for aught you know, he might have taught
The contrary to this if he had listed:
That Troy prevailed, that Greeks were conquered clean,
And that Penelope was but a quean.

"On t'other side we see Queen Dido's name,
That worthy was indeed to be commended,
Is subject now to slander and to shame
Because that she by Virgil is not friended.
But on this point I now more tedious am
Than I was ware or than I had intended;
For I love writers well and would not wrong them,
And I myself do count myself among them.

"I wrate a volume of my Master's praise
For which to me He hath not been ungrate,
But to this height of honor me doth raise
Where, as you see, I live in happy state;
I pity those that in these later days
Do write, when bounty hath shut up her gate
Where day and night in vain good writers knock
And for their labors oft have but a mock.

"So as indeed this reason is the chief
That wits decay, because they want their hire;
For where no succor is nor no relief,
The very beasts will from such place retire."
Thus said the saint, and as it were with grief
Of such offence, his eyes did flame like fire;
But turning to the duke, with sober laughter
He pacified himself a little after.

But here I leave Astolfo safe and sound
With holy John, for forthwith leap must I
As far as from the moon unto the ground;
My wings would fail if I still soared so high.
Now come I unto her that had the wound,
That ever-smarting wound of jealousy;
I told she had, when last of her I spoke,
Unhorsed three kings with Goldielance's stroke,

And how she lay all at a castle sad,
Although in vain she sought her grief to smother,
How at that place she perfect knowledge had
That Agramant was foilèd by her brother
And that to fly to Arly he was glad
With good Rogero and with many other;
This made her unto Provence then to haste
Because she heard that Charles pursued him fast.

Now unto Provence onward as she went,
A comely damsel in her way she viewed
Who though she looked like one that did lament,
Yet could not grief her comely grace exclude;
This dame had traveled long with this intent,
To find some knight that from the pagan rude
Fierce Rodomont, that pris'ner held her lover,
By force of arms again might him recover.

Now when the comfortless Dame Bradamant
Had met a dame as comfortless as she,
Such sympathy she felt of grief that scant
She kept in tears so sad a sight to see;
She asked her what misfortune or what want
Of her sad plight unworthy cause might be.
Fair Fiordeliege, that for a knight did hold her,
The circumstance of all the matter told her.

And in most rueful sort she did recount
Both of the tomb and bridge the woeful story,
And how the cruel pagan Rodomont
Had taken him for whom she was so sorry;[6]
Not that he could in value him surmount
That for his value had obtained much glory,
But that the pagan not to strength did trust
But to a bridge and vantages unjust.

"Wherefore, most noble-minded knight," said she,
"If such you be as by your speech I guess,
Help my dear spouse from bondage vile to free
And plague the pagan that doth him oppress;
Or if you cannot so, yet counsel me
Where I may find some aid for my distress,
Some knight so stout of heart and strong of hand
As may this cruel Saracen withstand.

"So shall you do a brave and noble deed
That wand'ring knights do think they ought of due;
So might you aid a worthy man indeed
And one in love most faithful and most true;
As for his other praise, it is no need
For me to tell mine own griefs to renew,
Sith well I know they plainly are appearing
To all that have their sense of sight and hearing."

The worthy dame, that thirsted still for praise,
Agrees to take this hard exploit in hand
As one that ready was at all assays
On horse, on foot, by water, or by land;
For either thus she shall her glory raise
If so she shall the pagan's force withstand,
Or die she shall, which danger less doth move her
Because she thinks Rogero doth not love her.

And thus she said, "Most lovely loving dame,
Gladly I shall my utmost forces prove
To succor one that merits so great fame,
Yet of his praises chiefly doth me move
Because you give him such a noble name
That he is true and faithful in his love,
Which sith you speak by trial, I must ween so;
Else I durst swear no man alive had been so."

These last words ending with a scalding sigh,
A sigh that came indeed from grievous thought,
Then on they went till they approachèd nigh
The parlous bridge that Rodomont had wrought;
And straight the watch descried them from on high
And blew a horn, by which the pagan thought
That travelers were come the bridge to pass,
Came out all armèd as his manner was.

But when that he one all in armor saw,
He greets them loud with this lewd salutation:
"Ho, stay, and ere you pass observe this law,
Unto this tomb humbly to make oblation
Of horse and arms, with fear and rev'rent awe;
Else with this spear expect sharp castigation."
She, that before had heard of Is'bel's death[7]
And of this tomb, thus stoutly to him saith:

"Ah, damnèd wretch, why should the innocent
Endure the penance of thy grievous guilt?
Thyself shouldst die or suffer punishment
That killedst her, if please her ghost thou wilt;
Her soul, upon my soul, would be content
If by my hand thy guilty blood were spilt,
More than with all the armors, men, and horses
That thou dost win with thy unlawful forces.

"And so much more it will accepted be
To her if thou by my right hand mayst die
Because I am a woman as was she
And only come on thee my force to try.
But let us first upon these points agree:
That if you hap to vanquish me, then I
Shall suffer at your hands so and no more
Than other prisoners have done before;

"But if I vanquish you, as sure I trust,
Then I will have the spoil of all the rest
And make your horse and arms a gift more just
Upon the tomb of her forever blessed;
And then withal to me you promise must
That all your pris'ners straight shall be released."
When thus the dame her mind had signified,
Thus the fierce Turk mildly to her replied:

"Fair dame, you seem to me to speak but reason,
And thereto I my frank assent afford;
But true it is that I for fear of treason
My pris'ners all have sent from hence aboard
So as I cannot free them at this season;
But firmly here to you I pass my word,
If you foil me, of which there is small jeopardy,
I will send word to set them all at liberty.

"But if I conquer you, as sure I shall,
For so it is most likely and most meet,
I will not hang your armor on the wall
Nor send you hence a pris'ner in my fleet;
I will remit to you my conquest all
For that fair face's sake and look so sweet;
Suffice it that this courtesy may move thee,
When now thou seemst to hate me, then to love me.

"Be not, fair dame, in your own strength beguiled;
I offer not such grace to every stranger,
For I am strong." At this the damsel smiled,
But such a smile as showed not mirth but anger;
And whether courage had all fear exiled
Or that despair made her to doubt no danger,
She spurred her horse nor other answer made him,
But with her spear in rest she doth invade him.

This so did move the cruel Rodomont
Upon his horse he doth himself advance,
Not making doubt but that he would dismount
Out of her seat the noble dame of France;
But he was quite deceived of his account;
No sooner was he touched with Goldielance
But e'en as if of strength he had been reaved,
Quite from the saddle backward he was heaved.

But yet the dame herself in danger was
To fall into the stream so swift and fleet,
By means the bridge so narrow was to pass
That hardly two at once thereon could meet;
But Rabican, whose swiftness did surpass
All four-foot beasts, did firmly keep his feet
Although so strait and narrow was the bridge
He was constrained to run upon the ridge.

Now when the pagan lay thus overthrown,
She turned to him, and sporting thus she spake,
"Now, sir," said she, "I hope it may be known
Of us two which the worser cause did take."
But he, like one whose wits were not his own,
He either could or would not answer make;
But still he stood looking on ground and musing,
Neither his foil denying nor excusing.

And having walked some half a dozen paces,
He suddenly cast all his armor off
And hurls it gainst the stones and it defaces
That scant he left unbroke one piece thereof,
Determining after such foul disgraces
To hide himself and go a great way off;
But ere he went, he granted full commission
To free his pris'ners without intermission.

So thence he went, and what of him became
Or what he did no notice clear I have,
But only this, that e'en for very shame
He long lived close within a secret cave,
The while his arms by that victorious dame
Were hanged up at the tomb for triumph brave
The t'other arms and furnitures among
That erst to pagan princes did belong.[8]

But for all those that were from Christians won,
She laid them up and did in safety set,
Among the which was Monodantè's son[9]
And Olivero and stout Sansonet,
Who late before with ill success did run
So that the pagan did their armor get
And them themselves as pris'ners did convey
Unto Algierie, far from thence away.

Among the rest that had their armor lost
Was Sacrapant, the fierce Circassian prince
Who fought for Frontlet[10] to his pain and cost
And with the pagan fought but little since;
But being foiled, he quite forsook that coast
Where men of such disgrace might him convince,
And with great shame; but what could shame him boot?
He came on horseback and went thence on foot.

Wherefore, ashamed in such sort to return,
He minds to follow that his former quest
Of her whose love long since his heart did burn,
Although her love he never yet possessed;
For still her froward mind did ever spurn
Against his earnest and most just request.
Of her return he late had heard the news,
I know not how, but now he her pursues.

And let him her pursue, for I proceed
Of noble Bradamantè's acts to tell,
Who having done this brave and worthy deed
To free the passage where so many fell,
She wrate it so as everyone might read
How all the circumstance thereof befell;
Which having done, then she demands to know
Which way Dame Fiordeliege did mind to go,

Who straight her purpose unto her unfolding,
Told her to pass the sea by ship she meant
At Arly, lest the Turk, his word not holding,
Might keep her spouse too long in prison pent.
"Then shall you," saith the dame, "be more beholding
To me, for sure," said she, " 'tis mine intent
Unto that town to guard you in your passage
So you will do for me but one embassage,

"And that withal you me this grace afford,
To give Rogero this same horse[11] from me
And say an unknown champion sends him word
To challenge him, that all the world may see
He hath been false of promise and of word,
Of which our combat shall the trial be;
And tell him plainly there is no denial,
But that by challenge I will make this trial.

"This say, and say no more; and if he ask
My name, then tell him plain you may not tell,
The while mine arms shall serve me for a mask;
This I desire, do this, and so farewell."
"This is," said Fiordeliege, "an easy task
From you that have of me deserved so well
As binds me both to this that you demand me
And to whatever else you would command me."

This said, she takes the bridle in her hand
And with her leads Frontino on the way
Until they both came to the salt-sea land
That next unto the town of Arly lay;
But Fiordeliege goes to the town by land,
And Bradamant doth in the suburbs stay
To th'end she may convenient respite give her
To him the horse and message to deliver;

Who when the bridge and gate she quite had passed,
She prayeth one of those that kept the ward
To bring her to Rogero in great haste
And through the town of court'sy her to guard;
This done, she to Rogero came at last
And did her message with most due regard
And gave Frontino and then went her way,
Nor would she once to hear his answer stay.

Rogero standeth still, all in a muse,
The messenger and message so beguile him;
He wonders who it is that both doth use
Such courtesy and yet withal revile him;
He thinks the party doth him much abuse
With foulest blot of breach of word to file him;
And of all others least of all he thought
That Bradamant of him the combat sought.

To think it Rodomont he was inclined,
But yet it could not sink into his reach
Why of a sudden he should be so kind
And wherein he could blame his promise breach;
And save with him he cannot call to mind
With whom he had of friendship any breach:
The while the lady with a stately scorn
In token of defiance blew her horn.

Straightways the news to Agramant doth fly
That one without did challenge some within,
And Serpentine that then by chance was by
Asked leave to fight with surèd hope to win
And swears the knight should yield or else should die;
And then the people flocked both thick and thin
And stood upon the walls with young and old
Between these two the combat to behold.

Out Serpentino came in brave array,
And bravely with his spear in rest he ran,
But at the first encounter down he lay;
The horse runs leer away without the man.
But noble Bradamant the horse doth stay
And back restore; then finely as she can
She prays him to King Agramant to speak
To send a stronger knight sith he was weak.

The mighty kings of Afric and of Spain[12]
That from the wall the courteous act did view
From praising of the same could not refrain,
Though none of them thereof the author knew;
Now Serpentino back returned again,
And to his prince he told his message true,
How that same champion did desire to fight
With some more stout and more renownèd knight.

And then Grandonio fierce of Volaterne,
The proudest knight that Spain long time had bred,
Obtained next place and with a visage stern
And threat'ning voice thus to the damsel said,
"Your court'sy small reward for you shall earn,
For either here in fight you must be dead,
Or at the least I will you pris'ner bring
Unto Marsilio, of great Spain the king."

"Well," answered she, "keep these your threats in store;
Your villainy my court'sy shall not let
But that I'll friendly monish you before
That back again unto your king you get,
Ere that your fall may make your body sore;
And say that I desired to have met
A man indeed of courage and of worth,
And not yourself nor him that last came forth."

This her reply so mild and yet so bitter
The pagan with more fury did enflame;
With spear than speech he thought an answer fitter,
And toward her in full career he came,
Intending sure some deadly blow to hit her;
But she that was accustomed to this game
Bare well his blow, and with her Goldielance
She taught him how the somersault to dance.

But yet his horse that loose about did run,
She brought him back, and thus to him she said,
"Lo, sir, you had been better to have done
My message when I court'ously you prayed;
Yet here I will release my pris'ner won
So you will tell your king that I have stayed
To combat with a man in fight well-seen
And not with novices of skill so green."

The lookers-on, that sure thought nothing less
Than that a virgin so could guide a spear,
With murmurings their wonder great express,
Still aiming with surmises who it were;
Some Brandimart and some Renaldo guess
Or others whom the Turks had cause to fear,
But most they would Orlando have suspected
Save they had heard his senses were distracted.

Next stout Ferraw desired to have the place,
Not that he hoped the conquest to have won
But that these knights may have the less disgrace,
"If I," quoth he, "shall do as they have done."
A strong, swift horse he takes and sure of pace,
Well-made to bear the shock and free to run,
The choicest of an hundred that he kept,
And thus all armed upon the beast he leapt.

Against the female champion forth he goes,
And first they interchangeably salute.
"Please it you," said the lady, "to disclose
Your name to me? That shall be all my suit."
He that what longs to civil manners knows
To satisfy her therein was not mute.
"And I refuse you not," then said the t'other,
"Although I rather would have had another."

"Whom?" quoth Ferraw. "Rogero," she replied;
And scarce she fully could bring forth his name
But that a blush with rosy color dyed
Her lovely cheeks with secret, honest shame;
Further she addeth, "him whose value tried
And so much praised was cause I hither came;
None else I seek, nor for none else care I;
Only his manhood I desire to try."

(She spake the words in plain and simple sense
Which some perhaps will subtly wrest awry.)
"Well," said Ferraw, "yet now ere I go hence,
Let me with you have leave one course to try
To see if I can make no more defence
Than those whom last you made on earth to lie;
If I fall as did they, then I will send
That gentle knight that may our error mend."

Her beaver open was while they conferred,
At which when her the Spaniard well had viewed
And marked her beauty worthy of regard,
He was already more than half subdued;
He thought an angel of the heav'nly guard
Could not with greater beauty be endued;
Against her spear what fence can he devise
That is already conquered with her eyes?

Now took they field and ran with all their force,
And now Ferraw is from his saddle borne;
The damsel doth of court'sy stay his horse;
The Spaniard lyeth like a man forlorn,
But back he must unto the king perforce,
Nor true to do his message doth he scorn;
He tells Rogero plain before them all
How this same knight only for him doth call.

Rogero, who it is yet little knowing,
In haste to make him ready doth begin,
A settled hope of conquest plainly showing,
Willing to fight, with mind assured to win;
As for their foils and their foul overthrowing
That went before, he weighed them not a pin.—
But how they met, how kindly him she servèd
Unto the book ensuing is reservèd.

1. Alessandra Benucci.
2. The moon.
3. Harington obscures what Ariosto means, that Ippolito was born in
1480.
4. Ferrara.
5. Town on the slopes of Parnassus, devoted to Apollo.
6. Brandimart, husband of Fiordeliege.
7. In Canto XXIX the drunken Rodomont had unintentionally be-
headed Isabella; as a mark of his repentance he exacted offerings at her
tomb.
8. Rogero slays Rodomont in the last canto of the poem.
9. Brandimart.
10. Frontino, Rogero's horse, which Rodomont had appropriated and
Sacrapant had been unable to win from him in Canto XXVII.
11. Frontino.
12. Agramant and Marsilio.

The Thirty-sixth Canto

stanzas 10-83 of the Italian

THE valiant men did study in time past
   With clemency their honors to increase
And hate no longer than the fight did last;
With victory revenge did ever cease.
So Bradamant, of whom I told you last,
The pris'ners she had ta'en did still release
And stayed their horses when themselves were down
And sent them back again into the town,

And prayed them but her challenge to deliver
Unto Rogero and to call him out
Who meant with spear in rest her answer give her
Unto her challenge that she sent so stout.
Now when the other knights were all together
In presence of the kings, they cast a doubt
Who this should be, and then they ask Ferraw
That talked with her and her bare visage saw.

"Sure," said Ferraw, "it is not t'one nor t'other
Of those on whom before your thoughts were set;
I took it first it was Renaldo's brother
Who is in years a very youth as yet;
But now I rather judge it is another,
For so much force is not in Richardet;
I think it is his sister by her usage
Who I have heard is like him much in visage.

XXXVI

"She hath ere this of value had great fame
Renaldo and the paladins among;
I must confess I found it to my shame
Her than her brothers to be far more strong."
Rogero, when he heard them her to name,
Was guilty straight that he had done her wrong
And blushed in countenance with bashful grace,
And oft his heart shot blood into his face.

Yea fear invaded him, not fear of danger,
For force he fearèd not of any wight,
Of Turk nor Christian, countryman nor stranger;
The very cause of this his doleful plight
Was love, for love fears nothing more than anger;
He doubts lest she conceived not of him right;
Thus waving thoughts his mind do both ways carry
If so he better were to go or tarry.

The while Marfisa, that was present there
And ever had a forward will to joust,
Could now no longer from the same forbear
Though seeing some before her lie on dust;
For all their falls did breed in her no fear,
So much in her great value did she trust;
Wherefore lest good Rogero might prevent her,
First she rides forth and in the lists doth enter,

And mounted on her horse came swiftly running
Unto the place where Bradamant did stay
With panting heart to wait Rogero's coming;
With mind to take him pris'ner if she may
She thinks how she might guide her staff with cunning
As with her stroke do him least hurt she may.
Thus cometh out Marfisa, nothing fearing,
Upon her lofty crest the phoenix bearing,

Or that thereby to boast her strength she meant,
Of her rare strength of which she took some pride,
Or else thereby to note her chaste intent
She had, a warlike virgin still to bide.
But Bradamant, who first to meet her went
And not to be Rogero now espied,
Did ask her name, and by her name she knew
That this was she that made her love untrue;

Or to say better, whom she did surmise
To be the sole withholder of her dear,
Her whom she hates, gainst whom her blood doth rise;
And minding now to make her buy it dear,
With fury great and rage at her she flies;
And that she may make all suspicions clear,
With couchèd spear she fiercely runneth on her
And means to kill her or to die upon her.

Marfisa was constrainèd with the stroke
To kiss the ground as those before her had,
Which to such rage her courage did provoke
That with disdain she seemed as one half mad;
Nor knowing how so great a foil to cloak,
She draws her sword with an intention bad;
But Bradamant cry'th out with lofty heart,
"What dost thou, traitor? Thou my pris'ner art.

"And though I usèd court'sy to the rest,
To use it unto thee I am not tied
Whose mind, as I have heard, is e'en a nest
Wherein is bred all villainy and pride."
Look how great waters rage and do not rest
Whenas the winds do strive against the tide,
So raged Marfisa rather more than less
And for mere spite could not a word express,

But hurls about her blade with all her force,
Not caring what she strikes nor where nor how,
Upon the horseman or upon the horse;
Her rage in her no reason did allow;
And Bradamant as void of all remorse,
With mind to break that that refused to bow,
Ran at her with the spear that would not miss
And made her once again the ground to kiss.

But once again upon her feet she getteth,
And with her sword revengement she intends;
Each fall she hath her fury sharper whetteth;
Yet still she falls and can have no amends;
Nor Goldielance his wonted force forgetteth,
For all it touches to the ground it sends;
Had not the spear been as it was, enchanted,
It could not so Marfisa's force have daunted.

Some of our men were hither come the while,
I mean some of the Christian host that lay
Encampèd near the town within a mile
So as the walls of Arly see they may;
And thinking, for her sex did them beguile,
Some knight of theirs maintained so great a fray,
They hither came with will and with delight
To see so fierce and well-maintained a fight;

Whom whenas Agramant from far espied
And thinks they came to bring their knight assistance,
He thought it best in wisdom to provide,
If they should offer force, to make resistance;
Wherefore he pointed some that of their side
May stand from that same place a little distance;
Of this last crew Rogero was the first,
With whom the damsel so to fight did thirst.

And seeing now how fierce the combat grow'th
Betwixt these two to whom he wished none ill,
Although in sundry kinds he favored both,
For t'one was love, the t'other bare good will,
To suffer them to fight he was full loath,
Although for honor's sake he must be still;
Else sure he could have found it in his heart
To step between them and the fray to part.

But they that with him from the city came
And saw the Christian champion was so strong
Stept in betwixt her and the t'other dame
And so withdrew Marfisa them among;
Which act the other Christians did enflame
So that with mind to venge so foul a wrong
They stepped in too; thus both sides cried alarm,
And soon the skirmish waxèd fresh and warm.

Such as before were armèd out do run;
They that unarmèd were their armor take;
And some run out on foot, on horseback some;
Each to his standard doth himself betake;
The diverse sound of trumpet and of drum,
That doth the horsemen, this the footmen wake.
But Bradamant is malcontent and wrath
To think Marfisa thus escapèd hath.

Then looked she wishly all about the place
To find out him that causèd all her care;
At last she knew him, though not by his face
Yet by the argent eagle that he bare;
And viewing well his person and good grace,
His goodly stature and his feature rare,
She raged to think another should possess it,·
And in these secret words she doth express it:

"Shall any other then that sweet lip kiss,
And I in love thereof still mourn and pine?
Shall any other then possess my bliss?
Shalt thou another's be if none of mine?
No, certes, rather than to suffer this
Thou by my hand shalt die, or I by thine;
If in this life we shall be joinèd never,
Death only be the mean to join us ever.

"Although that thou shouldst fortune me to kill,
Thy death by right should pacify my spirit,
For laws appoint who guiltless blood do spill
Shall for reward the doom of death inherit;
Yet still I shall sustain the greater ill,
For I should guiltless die, but thou by merit;
I, killing thee, kill one that hates me merely;
Thou, killing me, killst one that loves thee dearly.

"Why shouldst not thou, my head, be strong and bold
That by thy stroke his hard heart may be riven
Who unto me sharp wounds and manifold
In time of love's sweet peace and truce hath given
And doth e'en now with stony heart behold
The woeful state to which poor I am driven?
Heart, now be stout to take thy just revenge;
Let this one death thy thousand deaths avenge."

With that, at him she runs, but first aloud
"Defend thyself, Rogero false," she said,
"And think not thou shalt scape with spoils so proud
Of heart subduèd of a silly maid."
Rogero, who to her himself had vowed
And to offend her greatly was afraid,
Held up his gauntlet unto her in token
That he with her desired to have spoken.

He would her wrath with kind words have appeasèd
And showed her how the cause he brake his day
Was that with grievous wounds he lay diseasèd,
Which forcèd him against his will to stay;
But at this time she was so sore displeasèd
She would not harken what he had to say,
But with her spear in rest on him she runneth
Who such unkind encounter greatly shunneth.

But when he saw she was so rash and heady
And that her choler now so great did grow
That she was in her full career already,
He puts his spear in rest, at least for show,
And forward sets; but when she was e'en ready
Him to have giv'n a sharp disgraceful blow,
Or that it were that she e'en then recanted
Or that her heart to harm him courage wanted,

She bare her lance aloft quite o'er his crest;
And so of purpose that same course she missed,
Yet so as by the manner might be guessed
She could have hit him surer had she list;
And wrath and rage still boiling in her breast,
To bend her force gainst him she did desist,
But in that mood no little harm she works
Unto the other soldiers of the Turks.

In little time she with her gilded lance
Had caused three hundred men on ground to lie,
So that the conquest to the part of France
Was thought to have been gainèd sole thereby;
Rogero seeks her out, and last by chance
He speaks to her and saith, "My dear, I die
But I may talk with you. What have I done,
Alas, that you my conference should shun?"

As when the southern wind with lukewarm blast
Doth breathe on hills where winter long hath dwelt,
Resolves the rocks of ice that hung so fast,
And all the newmade mounts of snow doth melt:
So with this gentle prayer, though spoke in haste,
The damsel such an inward motion felt
That suddenly her hardened heart did soften,
As unto womenkind it chanceth often.

Yet answer made she none, but held her peace;
She only turnèd Rabican aside,
And hasting to get out of that same press,
She beckoned him that after her he ride;
Thus went she thence, with mind inclined to peace,
Unto a valley where on either side
A grove of cypress so e'en set was seen
As if they all of one self stamp had been.

Amid this grove a goodly sepulture
Was built which these fair cypress trees did shade,
Of porphyry and marble white and pure
And fair engrav'n to show why it was made;
But of the tomb she took no care nor cure,
But there expected in the open glade
Until Rogero, having made good haste,
Approached the wood and damsel at the last.

But of Marfisa now I must you tell,
Who having got by this her horse again,
Her lofty heart with rancor great did swell
To be revenged of this foul-suffered stain;
And seeing where she went, as it befell,
And how Rogero followed her amain,
She little thinketh that it is for love
But rather that they may the combat prove;

Wherefore to follow them she thinks it best,
So as she came almost as soon as they.
But what a tedious and unwelcome guest
She seemed to both one soon conjecture may;
Much sure it did the Dordon dame[1] molest
Who sole to her Rogero's faults did lay;
She deemed that to come thither nothing moved her
But that Rogero in ill sort had loved her.

And "false" Rogero she again doth name;
"And was it not enough, false man," said she,
"That of thy falsehood I should hear by fame,
But that I with these eyes the same should see!
But sith I find thou dost thy actions frame
To drive me with unkindnesses from thee,
I am content to die; but ere I die yet,
She that did cause it dearly shall aby it."

Thus as a viper angry and malicious,
With mind indeed to do ber best to kill
Her that was come in manner so suspicious
(Though she came more for wrath than for good will),[2]
With gilded lance she gives a blow pernicious
That quite unhorsèd her for all her skill;
Backward Marfisa fell and in the dirt
Her beaver stuck, but had no further hurt.

Duke Ammon's daughter, that resolves to die
Or kill her foe, so much herself forgetteth
That thinking to despatch her by and by
Before her head out of the mire she getteth,
The golden lance she will no farther try
But throws it down, as wrath her courage whetteth;
And to perform the feat her sword she draws
Therewith of fear to cut away the cause.

But ere she came so near, Marfisa met her
Like one with rage, with spite and scorn half mad
To think that now again she sped no better
And that a while before she sped so bad,
So that Rogero could by no means let her
From fighting, which to stop great will he had;
But both of them with choler were so blinded
They fought like bedlam folk and desp'rate-minded.

They came unto the half-sword at the first,
And with their rage forgetting rules of skill,
Their overmuch desire to do their worst
Was only cause that they could do none ill;
Their hearts were ready for despite to burst,
And either, purposing to die or kill,
Did leave her sword aside, in mind supposing
With stab to kill each other at the closing.

Rogero sunders them and both entreateth
To pacify themselves, but all in vain;
Then of their daggers he them both defeateth
And by persuasions moved them both again;
Sometime he speaketh fair, sometime he threateth
Except they will at his request abstain;
But these viragoes will not tho desist;
Though weapons want, they fight with feet and fist.

He steps between again, and back he draws
Now one and then the t'other by the sleeves
And makes them both against their wills to pause,
At which Marfisa not a little grieves;
Herself too greatly wrongèd in the cause
And him to be too partial she believes;
Wherefore his friendship she doth quite disclaim,
And open wars with him she doth proclaim.

And taking up her sword, in terms most vile
She saith he plays the churlish villain's part
And that he greatly doth himself beguile
To think her fight against her will to part;
She swears she will within a little while
Of his own folly make him feel the smart
And that she will henceforth so short him curb
He shall not dare her combat to disturb.

Rogero still bare all her words as words
And sought by speech her to have pacified,
But seeing that it needs must come to swords
And that with blows, not speeches, she replied,
No longer time to talking he affords,
But to his weapon he himself applied;
And being movèd now with rightful anger,
To save himself he oft put her in danger.

But ne'er did spectacle breed more delight
In stately Rome or Athens so well-learnèd
Than Bradamant did take to see this fight
In which she now apparently discernèd
That of their love she had not judgèd right;
Now jealousy and all that it concernèd,
Suspicion, fear, mistrust, and wrath, and frenzy,
Are of the sudden quite put from her fancy.

And taking up her sword, she stands not far
With mind not yet a while the fray to part;
She thinks in him she sees the god of war,
Such grace Rogero used, such skill, such art;
And t'other seemed in that unpleasant jar
Some hellish fury; so she played her part;
Yet true it is that he a while forbare her
Nor did his worst, but did of purpose spare her.

He knew the secret virtue of this blade
Which he had tried in many battles well,
That evermore a way and entrance made,
Whose charm all charmèd arms did far excel;
Wherefore he doth not fiercely her invade
With bloody blows nor fearful thrusts and full,
But flatling still he caused his blows to light
Till once he was of patience put out quite.

For once Marfisa with intention shrewd
Strake with such fury at Rogero's beaver
That with that blow she very plainly showed
That to have killed him she did her endeavor;
Rogero with his argent eagle trowed
From danger of the stroke himself to sever,
But though the shield brake not, gramercy charm,
Yet underneath the shield it stunned his arm.

It happy was Don Hector's shield[3] was there;
Else had she put him into further pain;
Scarce could he now the massy target bear;
Scarce now the silver bird he could sustain.
Now he intends no longer to forbear
But hurleth out a foin with force so main,
In rage with that late blow so fierce and bitter,
Woe unto poor Marfisa had it hit her.

I know not what good angel did her keep;
The thrust missed her, and in a tree it strake
And entered in the same a shaftment deep,
And on the sudden all the hill did quake;
A secret horror on them all did creep;
They see the hill, the trees, and tomb to shake,
Till from that sepulcher a voice proceeding
Spake unto them, all human voice exceeding.

The voice to them with no small terror cried,
"File not your hands and hearts with so great sin;
It is a kind of cruel parricide
To seek to kill and be so near of kin;
Wherefore I charge you lay all hate aside
And mark my speech and all contained therein.
I say you both were gotten of one seed;
One womb you bare; one breast you both did feed.

"My dear Rogero, my Marfisa dear,
Let not the sister seek to kill the brother,
But learn of me some things that touch you near
Which former times in ignorance did smother.
Your sire Rogero hight, who that same year
He gat you of Dame Gallacell, your mother,
Was by your uncles of his life deprivèd,
Who also your destruction thus contrivèd:

"They put your mother in a steerless boat,
Who was as then of you twain great with child,
And in the ocean wide they let her float
There to be starved or drowned in waters wild.
But lo how fortune holp the luckless lot
And ere you yet were born upon you smiled,
For why against all hope or expectation
Your mother made a happy navigation.

"And being safe arrived at Syrtee[4] shore,
There at one burden she brought forth both you,
And then, as if she ought this world no more,
Her blessèd soul to Paradise up flew;
But there by hap (to God be thanks therefor)
Was I at hand, and when the cause I knew,
I did as much, ere I the place did leave,
As such a barren soil would give me leave.

"Your mother then in dust of earth I lapped,
Our ancient mother whereto all must go,
And in my cloak your little selves I wrapped
To seek some means to nourish you, when lo,
A lioness that late had whelped there happed
To come in sight while I went to and fro;
Her did I make to leave her proper whelps
And give you suck then wanting other helps.

"Ten months and ten in forests wild and moorish
The lion's tits you usèd were to suck;
I after learned with wild flesh you to nourish,
Such as I could, of bears or stag and buck;
But when you now began in strength to flourish,
One day when I was lack by evil luck,
A band of fierce Arabians coming thither
Would have conveyed you both from thence together.

"But thou, Rogero, when thou sawst them coming,
Didst save thyself from that mishap by flight;
But thou, Marfisa, not so swiftly running,
Wert ta'en and quickly carried out of sight;
To fetch thee back again I wanted cunning,
For which I sorrowed many day and night;
But as the loss of t'one did make me sad,
So of the other greater care I had.

"Ah, my Rogero, thou thyself canst tell
If thine Atlanta loved thee while he lived.
I saw the stars some evil haps foretell
That thou shouldst have, which me no little grieved;
Yet I endeavored still, as thou knowst well,
That by my means thou mightst have been relieved;
But finding thee still contrary inclined,
For very grief at last I died and pined.

"But here I built this tomb afore I died,
Where I foresaw you two would make this fray;
And being dead, to Charon loud I cried
To suffer in this wood my ghost to stray
Until this sight to me foresignified
Should happen, which was done this present day.
Now shall my soul from hence depart in peace;
Now Bradamant thy jealousy may cease."

Thus said the voice and left them all amazed
With wonder great and strangeness of the case,
And when a while each had on other gazed,
They met in kindest manner and embrace;
Nor Bradamant herself, who erst was crazed
With jealousy, now took it in disgrace
To see her spouse when he most kindly kissed her,
Now well-assurèd that she was his sister.

Thus they agreed at last, and either twin
Do call to mind some acts of childish years,
What they had said and done, where they had been,
Which e'en with tender heart did move their tears;
At last the worthy brother doth begin
To tell Marfisa what great love he bears
To Bradamant whom he to wed intends,
And so at length he made them faithful friends.

Then all parts pacified so well at length,
Marfisa doth entreat her noble brother
To tell to her the story more at length
Of that so strange exiling of her mother,
And if their sire were slain by fraud or strength,
And who it was that wrought the t'one or t'other;
"For sure," said she, "I think I never heard it,
Or childishness did make me not regard it."

Rogero tells her how of Trojan race
From Hector they be lineally descended,
By means Astyanax, of special grace
That scaped Ulysses and the snares intended,
Did leave a child of like years in his place
And from that country to the sea descended
And came to Sicil after travel long
And took Messina and grew very strong.[5]

"His offspring, still increasing in renown,
Calabria ruled in part and thence to Phare[6]
And came at last to dwell in Mars's town;[7]
And many a noble emperor and rare
In stately Rome have worn th' imperial crown
Of such as from this stock descended are,
From Constance and from Constantine accounting
To Pepin and his son, them all surmounting.

"Rogero first and Jambaron of these,
Rovus, Rambaldus, and Rogero[8] again,
Of whom, as Atlant told, saved from the seas
Our mother by the shore brought forth us twain;
Their acts in ancient stories they that please
To look may find them there recorded plain."
Then tells he how there came King Agolant,
With Almont and the sire of Agramant:[9]

How that king's daughter,[10] a most noble maid,
In feats of arms so valorous did prove
That divers paladins she overlaid,
And then with that Rogero fell in love,
And of her father's anger not afraid
Did match in Christian state, as did behoove;
How after this one Beltram[11] sought by treason
Incestuous love of her without all reason.

"And for that cause his brothers and his sire
And his own native soil he did betray
And open Risa[12] at his foes' desire;
Which being ta'en and seized on as a prey,
Fierce Agolant and his, inflamed with ire,
Took Gallacell our mother where she lay
Six months with child and put her in a boat,
And in the ocean wide they let her float."

Marfisa all this while with gladsome cheer
Unto her new-known brother's tale attended
And in her mind rejoicèd much to hear
That of so noble house she was descended,
From which Mongrana came, as doth appear,
And that of Clarimont so much commended,
Which houses both long in great fame had flourishèd
For divers noble persons they had nourishèd.

But when of Agramant she heard him say,
How both his grandsire, uncle,[13] and some other
Consented had their father to betray
And in so cruel sort to use their mother,
She could not suffer any longer stay,
But breaking off his tale said, "Noble brother,
With your good favor, you have too much wrong
To leave your father unrevenged so long.

"If not in Almont nor Trayano's blood
You can avenge this ill sith they be gone,
Yet ought you to avenge it on their brood;
Live you and let you Agramant alone?
This blot, except it quickly be withstood,
Will shame you ever if it once be known
That he that did this wrong not only liveth
But that to you he entertainment giveth.

"But for my part," said she, "by Christ I vow
(Whom as my father did, so serve I will)
That I will not leave arms till I know how
To venge my father's and my mother's ill;
And much I shall lament and do e'en now
If in that pagan camp you tarry still
Or ever should be seen therein hereafter,
Except it were to work their harm and slaughter."

Oh how did Bradamant at this rejoice,
Advising him to follow that direction
And to give ear unto his sister's voice,
To leave so vile a place and base subjection
And cleave to Charles as to the better choice
Who gladly would receive him in protection,
Of which, she said, one sure sign she did gather:
She heard him often so extoll his father.

Rogero answers thus with great regard:
"My dear, to have done this at first I ought,
But then indeed the truth I had not heard
Whereby I might my duty have been taught;
Now sith that Agramant hath me preferred,
If his destruction should by me be sought
That am his servant and a daily waiter,
The world might justly deem I were a traitor.

"But this my meaning was, and so it is,
To find some means I may with honor part;
Which when I have, then sure I will not miss
To come and to requite your great desert;
And that," quoth he, "I had performed ere this
Save that a cause of which I felt the smart
Enforced my stay, the wounds the Tartar[14] gave me
So as my friends had much to do to save me:

"As she[15] knows well that holp me at my need
And every day did sit by my bed's side."
Thus much he said, but they that took good heed
To all he said in earnest sort replied,
Howbeit at the last it was agreed
That he so long with Agramant should bide
Till he some honorable cause might find
To leave his master and to change his mind.

"Well," quoth Marfisa, "if he needs will go,
Then let him go, but I will you assure
That shortly I will use the matter so
He shall not long with Agramant endure."
This said she unto Bradamant, but tho
She told not how she would the same procure.
Thus for that time Rogero brake this parley
And turned his horse to turn again to Arly.

[In Cantos XLIV, XLV, and XLVI, not published until 1532, Ariosto brings the love of Bradamant and Rogero to a complicated denouement: her ambitious parents seek to marry her to Leon (Leo), the son and heir of the Emperor of Constantinople; Rogero, determined to kill his rival, goes to the East in disguise, is captured and released by Leon, and agrees to take his place in single combat with Bradamant, who has made Charlemagne agree that she can marry only a man who overcomes her in battle; Rogero, acting for Leon, demonstrates his superiority to her and thus wins her for his rival; but when the full truth is revealed, Leon magnanimously gives Bradamant to Rogero, and the couple are at last united in marriage.]

1. Bradamant.
2. More for wrath against Bradamant than for good will to Rogero.
3. Rogero had inherited his armor from his ancestor Hector.
4. Syrtis, a gulf on the North African coast.
5. The *Orlando Innamorato* had already given this unorthodox account of Astyanax, which Harington finds incredible.

6. The Faro, or Lighthouse, of Messina.

7. Rome.

8. Rogero II, the father of Rogero and Marfisa in the poem.

9. Trayano (Troiano), a son of Agolant.

10. Gallacella, the daughter of Agolant.

11. Brother of Rogero II and uncle of Rogero and Marfisa in the poem.

12. Apparently a town in Calabria.

13. Agolant and Almont, respectively; the Italian includes Trayano with them.

14. Mandricardo.

15. Marfisa.

The Thirty-ninth Canto

stanzas 45-61 of the Italian

[A large Christian force under Astolfo is engaged in besieging
Biserta in North Africa when the camp is thrown into confusion
by the appearance of a madman among them.]

ASTOLFO eke whenas he did behold him
  And saw how madly he about did range
And no man durst him meet nor none could hold him,
He wondered greatly at the sight so strange,
And by the marks that erst Saint John had told him
He knew it was the man; but such a change
There was in all his shape from top to toe
He rather seemed a beast more than a man in show.

Astolfo straight did call unto the rest
And said, "My lords, this man that you had viewed
Orlando is." At this themselves they blessed,
And everyone his woeful pickle rued.
"Well," said the duke,[1] "to help our friend is best
And not to wail; and therefore to conclude,
Come join your force to mine, and let us take him,
And I do hope ere long I'll sober make him."

To this they soon assent, and Brandimart
With Sansonet and Olivero jolly
And Dudon closed him round on every part;
But he, as full of strength as fool of folly,
At Dudon strake, and save the blow in part
Was broke by Oliver and fell not wholly
On Dudon, sure I think that staff accursed
His shield, his headpiece, head, and all had burst.

343

His shield it brake and thundered on his skull
That noble Dudon therewithal fell back,
But Sansonet strake with his sword so full
That of the staff three yards he made him lack;
Now Brandimart thinks backward him to pull
And leaps behind, a pick-pack on his back,
And holds his arms; the duke doth then devise
To hold his legs and Oliver his thighs.

Orlando shakes himself and with a spring
Ten paces off the English duke he cast,
But Brandimart from him he could not fling
That was behind him and did hold him fast;
But yet with Oliver he was to bring,
For with his fist he smote him as he passed
That down he fell and hardly scapèd killing,
From mouth, nose, eyes the blood apace distilling.

Of headpiece strong he never had more need,
For sure he could not have escapèd death
Except it had a good one been indeed.
This while Astolfo now had taken breath
And Dudon, both who late for want of heed
Were by Orlando tumbled on the heath,
With Sansonet, that pared his staff so well,
All these at once upon Orlando fell.

Good Dudon, that endeavors him to cast,
With Brandimart about his shoulders hangs;
Astolfo and the rest his arms hold fast;
He seeks to loose himself with sudden pangs.
Whoso has seen a bull with mastiffs chased
That in his ears have fixed their cruel fangs,
How he doth run and roar and with him bears
The eager dogs that still hold fast his ears:

Let him imagine that Orlando now
In such sort drew the warriors on the plain;
But Oliver, that had the broken brow,
Again on foot recovered up again,
Did cast within his mind a reason how
To do with ease that they did seek with pain;
He doth bethink a way that will not miss
To do the feat, and his device was this:

Full many a hawser and full many a cord
With sliding knots all knit he doth provide,
And to the legs and arms of this mad lord
He made them on the sudden to be tied,
And then their ends on each side by accord
They all of them amongst themselves divide;
Thus were those princes fain to do unto him
As smiths do to an ox when they do shoe him.

Then fell they on him when he lay on ground,
And then they bind him sure, both hand and foot;
Orlando when he felt himself thus bound
Doth strive in vain, for striving will not boot.
Astolfo, that doth mean to make him sound
And saw his skin look black as any soot,
Requested them unto the shore to bear him,
Which soon was done, for now they need not fear him.

Then sev'n times was he washèd in the place
And sev'n times dippèd over ears and head
To get the scurf from off his skin and face
Which with his naked going had been bred;
Then with some herbs the duke gat in this space
He made them stop his mouth, for why he said,
For certain secret reasons that he knows,
He must not fetch his breath but at his nose.

Then kneeling down as if he asked some boon
Of God or some great saint, that pot he brought
Which he had carried from beyond the moon,
The jar in which Orlando's wit was caught,
And closed it to his nostrils; and eftsoon
He drawing breath, this miracle was wrought:
The jar was void and emptied every whit,
And he restored unto his perfect wit.

As one that in some dream or fearful vision
Hath dreamt of monstrous beasts and ugly fiends
Is troubled, when he wakes, with superstition
And feareth what such ugly sight intends
And lying wake thinks of that apparition
And long time after in that fancy spends:
So now Orlando lay, not little musing
At this his present state and uncouth using.

He holds his peace, but lifting up his eyes
He sees his ancient friends King Brandimart
And Oliver and him that made him wise,
All whom he knew and lovèd from his heart;
He thinks, but cannot with himself devise
How he should come to play so mad a part;
He wonders he is nak'd and that he feels
Such store of cords about his hands and heels.

At last he said, as erst Sileno said
To those that took him napping in the cave,
"*Solvite me*,"[2] with countenance so staid
And with a cheer so sober and so grave
That they unloosèd him as he them prayed
And suffered him his liberty to have
And clothèd him and comforted his sadness
That he conceivèd of his former madness.

Thus being to his former wits restored,
He was likewise delivered clean from love;
The lady whom he erst so much adored
And did esteem all earthly joys above
Now he despised, yea rather quite abhorred;
Now only he applies his wits to prove
That fame and former glory to recover
Which he had lost the while he was a lover.

[With Orlando restored to his wits, the Christian army easily captures Biserta; and the war with the Saracens is won when Agramant, Gradasso, and Brandimart have been slain in personal combat on the island of Lampedusa.]

1. Astolfo.
2. "Untie me": two of his pupils had tied down the drunken Silenus (Virgil, *Eclogues*, 6.24).

Glossary

This list includes only the meanings of unusual words and the unusual meanings of common words in the preceding text.

aboard: abroad
aby: pay for
aglet: metal tag on clothes
agnusdei: (1) figure of lamb bearing cross, (2) sacred host used in the mass
aloof: at a distance
amount: mount
an if, and if: if
apay: satisfy
apply: ply
argent: silver
assign: appoint
assure: engage
astony: stun, amaze
aye: ever

bait: stop, halt
balena: whale
balk: pass by
bases: skirt worn with armor
bate: depression
beaver: lower part of helmet
behoove: require, be necessary
bewray: betray
bill: kind of weapon
boot: help
bounce: knock
brack: bracken
bring: deal (?)
by and by: soon, at once

caitiff: wretch
carcanet: necklace
cast: conjecture

caul: netted cap
certes: certainly
chap: jaw
clepe: name
clown: peasant
control: check
convince: convict
cony: rabbit
corpse, corse: body (living or dead)
could: knew
couth: known, knew
covetise: avarice
curat: breastplate
cure: heed
cursed: shrewish, malignant
cypress: fine cloth from Cyprus

dittany: healing plant
dore: fool
doubtless: fearless

eke: also
ensue: follow (transitive)
errant star: planet
erst: first
eschew: avoid
exclude: banish
expect: wait
eyne: eyes

fain: inclined, eager
file: defile
fleece: wool or other material prepared for the distaff

349

foin: thrust
former: front
for why: because, wherefore
frank: generous
fro: from
froward: perverse
furniture: horse furnishings

ganymede: boy who is the object of pederastic love
gin: snare
gipsen: gypsy
girse: saddle girth
glose: pretense
go: walk
gorget: wimple
gramercy: thanks to
griffith: griffin (fabulous beast)
guerdon: reward
guilty: conscious of guilt
gyve: shackle

half-sword: close quarters
hard edge: close conflict
harnish: harness
harquebus: portable gun
hight: is named, was named, named
honesty: chastity
horse loaf: loaf made of food for horses
host: put up

in fine: in the end, briefly

kirtle: gown, skirt
knave: servant, rascal
knock: clash, collide

lack: missing
leer: (1) learning, (2) unburdened
leese: lose
let: prevent, obstacle
level: aim
list: wish
lore: rein
lust: wish

mage: magician
make: mate
matachina: masked dancer
mere: pure
merely: altogether
mickle: great, much
mince: cut
mo: more (plural)
moldwarp: mole
moorish: swampy

name: repute
narre: nearer
natheless: notwithstanding
ne: nor
nephew: grandson

ought: owed
overthwart: adverse
owe: own

pard: leopard
parlous: perilous
pass: care
patch: booby, fool
perdie: certainly
pick-pack, a: like a bundle borne on the shoulders

piece: person
posy: brief motto
pouldron: shoulder armor
prest: quick
prevent: forestall
price: prize
primer: chief
prize: price
purposes: riddles

quadrons: four columns at the corners of a building
quean: strumpet
quick: alive

rate: style, manner
rather: sooner
ray: array
reduce: bring back
region: air, sky

sample: example
scale: ladder
scorse: exchange
seld: seldom
self: same
shaftment: handbreadth
shagbot: sackbut (obsolete musical instrument)
shend: blame
shiver: splinter
shrewd: malignant
shroud: lop
silly: simple
sith: since
skill: know
skull: headpiece
smaragd: emerald
soft: leisurely

somedeal: somewhat
sound: swoon, swooned
sowdan: soldan
start: withdraw
state: man of rank
stories: histories
strange: foreign
Swizzers: Swiss

targe: shield
task: tax
thick: thicket
tho: then
thornpool: thirlepoll, whale
thorough stitch: considerable distance
thwarts: obstructions
to-dash: thoroughly splash
t'one: one
to-rate: thoroughly berate
t'other: other
travail: toil
troth: truth
trow: think

ure: use

warly: warlike
weeds: clothes
ween: think
where: whether
whilom: once
wight: man
win: defeat
wink: sleep
wishly: wistly, intently
wood: mad
wot: know

yerk: kick